D1458515

PORTRAIT OF DEVON

Portrait of
DEVON

by

D. ST. LEGER-GORDON

ILLUSTRATED AND WITH MAP

LONDON
ROBERT HALE & COMPANY

© *D. St. Leger-Gordon* 1963, 1968, *and* 1970

First edition March 1963
Reprinted February 1965
Second edition April 1968
Third edition October 1970
Reprinted May 1973

ISBN 0 7091 1858 9

Robert Hale & Company
63 Old Brompton Road
London S.W.7

PRINTED IN GREAT BRITAIN BY
LOWE AND BRYDONE (PRINTERS) LTD., THETFORD, NORFOLK

CONTENTS

BIBLIOGRAPHY 8

INTRODUCTION 9

I DEVON B.C. 13

II EXETER 19
  1. In History; 2. The Royal City; 3. Exeter Today

III THE GOLDEN DAYS 30
  1. Tudor Sea Saga; 2. Plymouth

IV FROM ROSE TO ORANGE 37

V WATER, WATER EVERYWHERE 43
  1. River and Marsh; 2. Fishing

VI ROADWAYS 60
  1. For Hoof and Tyre; 2. Iron Ways

VII HEDGEROWS AND WOODLANDS 70

VIII AGRICULTURE 82
  1. Crops and Stock; 2. Rabbits

IX DARTMOOR 99
  1. The National Park; 2. Forest and Fire;
  3. Commons and Commoners

X WILD DARTMOOR 112
  1. Spirit of the Moor; 2. A Touch of Mystery

XI WOOL AND ITS LEGACY 120

XII TIN 127

XIII FROM COPPER TO CLAY 135

XIV THE STATELY HOMES OF DEVON 142

XV   SOME LITERARY FIGURES   150

XVI   WILD LIFE OF DEVON   161
       1. How the Buzzard made History; 2. Birds
       of the Moor; 3. Moorland Music

XVII   FROM FEATHER TO FUR   179
       1. Deer and Fox; 2. After Myxomatosis

       Index   188

ACKNOWLEDGEMENTS

The illustrations numbered 1 and 10 are reproduced from photographs by Sport and General; 2 by Eagle Photos; 6 and 12 by Mr. Roy J. Westlake; 8, 13, 14, 15, 17, 18, 21 by Mr. J. A. Brimble, A.R.P.S.; 16 by Mrs. N. W. Kieffer.

The remaining eleven are reproduced from photographs by Mr. Reece Winstone, A.R.P.S.

ILLUSTRATIONS

1   Devon's north coast looking towards Hartland *facing page* 16
2   Spinster's Rock, near Drewsteignton   17
3   West front of Exeter Cathedral   32
4   The Guildhall, Exeter   33
5   Statue of Sir Francis Drake on Plymouth Hoe   48
6   Burrator Reservoir near Yelverton   49
7   Shipping at Appledore on the Taw–Torridge estuary   64
8   Hexworthy Bridge on the West Dart   *between pages*
9   Dartmouth Castle guards the river at the end of   64 *and* 65
      its journey
10 The famous Bideford Bridge before repair   *facing page* 65
11 Cold East Cross with its modern signpost   80
12 The old oak tree at Meavy   81
13 Network of hedgerows round Widecombe-in-the-Moor   96
14 A typical South Hams landscape   97
15 The Erme valley. Sharp Tor in the background   112
16 Dartmoor ponies sheltering at Sharp Tor   113
17 Harford Bridge, relic of pack-horse days   128
18 Haytor, most frequented of Dartmoor rock-piles   129
19 Bowerman's Nose   144
20 Buckfast Abbey, cradle of the woollen industry   145
21 Dartmoor's wool-bearers, mainly Scotch sheep   160
22 The mouth of the Teign, from which clay is exported   161
23 Statue of Charles Kingsley at Bideford   176
24 A deer-haunted Exmoor coombe   177

BIBLIOGRAPHY

Transactions of the Devonshire Association
Victoria History of Devon
Place Names of Devon Gower, Mawe & Stenton
Memorials of the City of Exeter Izacke
A Short History of the Worshipful Company of Weavers, Fullers and Shearers of the City of Exeter Beatrix Cresswell
Devon W. G. Hoskins
Two Thousand Years in Exeter W. G. Hoskins
Medieval Exeter
Land Utilisation Survey: Devonshire
From Trackway to Turnpike Gilbert Sheldon
Guide to Dartmoor, Part V William Crossing
Devonshire D. St. Leger-Gordon
Under Dartmoor Hills D. St. Leger-Gordon
Dartmoor R. Hansford Worth
Dartmoor Harvey & St. Leger-Gordon
History of Devon T. Moore
Church History Fuller
Synopsis Choreographical of Devon Hooker
The Story of Plymouth R. A. J. Walling
Picturesque South Devonshire W. H. K. Wright
The South Hams
Agricultural Statistics 1958–1959

INTRODUCTION

When writing this *Portrait of Devon* to succeed the County Book *Devonshire*, a certain amount of both repetition and contradiction was unavoidable. Historical generalities must be repeated, while in the matter of seeming contradiction, changed circumstances may have completely reversed conditions. Also, we live and learn and research which has no end often sheds new light upon controversial subjects. Modification of opinions once generally held, indeed, is not infrequent.

The aim of this book has been to picture the present rather than the past while following the course of Devonshire's history from ancient to modern times. It does not dwell upon manners and conditions that have passed or upon people of a type which no longer exists. That has been exhaustively done elsewhere.

Again, the scope has been confined to Devonshire alone and to matters of particular Devonshire interest, avoiding those which apply equally to other counties. It is in *distinction* that so much of Devonshire's attraction lies—those special characteristics which all who know this land of deep, dark valleys, rich red earth and many waters, are so anxious to preserve.

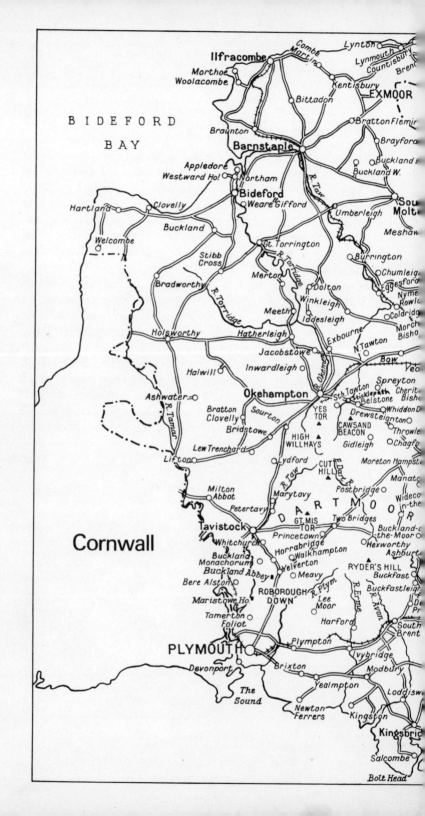

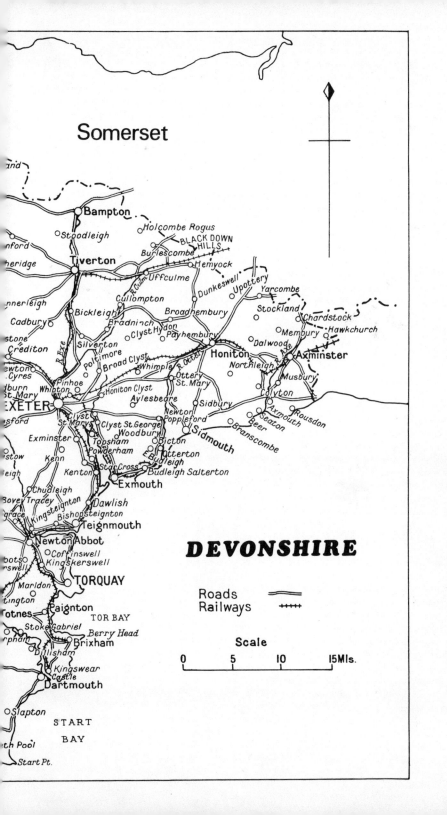

I

DEVON B.C.

PREHISTORY has no positive beginning; it can only be measured by time whose limits recede like the rainbow. The expression "time", indeed, has lost all meaning as science now reckons years by millions. Recorded "history", which should be a true recital of indisputable events, is almost as elastic since research so often involves the discovery of error.

For the portrait of a county it is not necessary to delve into the dark and controversial unknown, any more than one need study the original shape of a stone from which an image has been sculptured. One is concerned rather with the time since it emerged from the primitive background gradually to assume distinctive characteristics. Primitive Devonshire over which the buffalo and the sabre-tooth tiger roamed, now grazed by milch cow and patrolled by domestic cat, was merely part of a vast savage continent bearing little resemblance to the Europe of today. It is a picture of wild country, wild men and wild beasts, and apart from scanty evidence that the earth has preserved, one can only draw upon imagination. Pronouncements are always subject to contradiction or at best the challenge with which Kipling's "Maker of Pictures" or bone-artist was confronted: "How does the picture-man know?" Scientific research has established the identity of many early inhabitants, who they were and in most cases whence they came, each race in its turn occupying the terrain until ousted or liquidated by another and more powerful claimant.

★   ★   ★

Speaking generally, and always allowing for the inevitable exceptions, man for many ages has not been a subterranean race, for obvious reasons. It is easier to build a dwelling than to excavate one of appreciable size and much safer to occupy it. Even if part of a hut roof fell in, the damage to life and limb might not be extensive but should the ceiling of a cave subside, complete obliteration might be anticipated. Also in troubled times a cave might prove a perilous cul-de-sac unless provided with an emergency exit—a principle recognized by many burrowing animals. Most of the caves adapted to human use were natural, and since extensive natural caves are rare, when occupied by man it must have been a case of Mahomet going to the mountain. Devonshire can claim very few caves worthy of mention. The best known are Kent's Cavern near Torquay and others at Brixham, Ashburton, Buckfastleigh and on Cattedown. These are all on the southern slope and while some parts of the Mendip Hills in Somerset are cave-riddled, nothing of a similar character has come to light on Dartmoor.

That Paleolithic man made use of underground quarters when available seems certain, as evidenced by relics found in places such as Kent's Cavern. They have yielded few human bones, however, the remains found being mainly those of beasts including carnivorous species. One of the principal objects of interest to which a visitor's attention is directed in Kent's Cavern is the skull of a sabre-tooth tiger embedded in the rock. Bear and hyena remains have been identified buried among the crude weapons used for their destruction, and one can scarcely imagine that such were cases of joint occupation. If not, who were the real tenants? Did primitive man enter the caverns to hunt the beasts or did the beasts enter to hunt primitive man, for the same reason indeed as a stoat enters a rabbit-burrow? Ill-equipped as they were, either for defence or attack, it is difficult to imagine how such men fared in competition with the larger and fiercer carnivorae. Such weapons as the Bronze Age brought could not have been very effective even against the wolf—the most formidable beast that survived the prehistoric era, and which must have been singularly destructive among flocks and herds. Kipling's story of the progressive tribesman, who travelled far and eventually gave an eye in exchange for the first steel blade that reached the West Country, was realistic as well as imaginative. It illustrated the advantage of iron over stone and bronze weapons. In any case the most serviceable tools during these early days must have been human hands, theirs being the principal work that survives, no matter what implements were employed. It is probable that the stones used in construction of ancient dwellings, walls or monuments, if shaped at all were shaped by nature, the only labour expended being in their erection and that was notable indeed.

Whether or not the long burial mounds or barrows were raised by strong grimy hands unaided by implements scarcely less primitive, is a secret which Neolithic man kept to himself. A flat stone with energy behind it makes quite a serviceable shovel and for actual digging the potentialities of a strong stick, particularly gorse, are often overlooked. Evidence as to the methods employed is entirely lacking, however, partly because only two dolmens—Spinsters Rock and a dilapidated remnant on Corringdon Ball—have survived in Devon, the latter having been only recently classified as such. A possible third example was discovered by the late R. Hansford Worth on Cuckoo Ball, near Ugborough, but he could make no definite pronouncement as to its identity.

Upon the whole, people of the Stone Age left few footprints upon the sands of Devonshire's saga. Much of the work with which they were once credited is now ascribed to their successors of the Bronze period. Remains of Bronze Age activities are numerous upon the Moorland, partly because such country suited these people and their manner of life; and partly, no doubt, because the Dartmoor wastes have escaped the obliterating effects of cultivation.

The stone circles, the pounds, the "avenues", the kistvaens and the menhirs have been described in every guide book and will doubtless provide matter for controversy as long as archaeologists and antiquarians remain. Excavation of numerous hut dwellings has revealed comparatively little. This is not surprising. Every hut was doubtless ransacked centuries ago for loot rather than interest and in any case it is improbable that occupiers of a tiny hut would have kept indoors more than necessity demanded. It is sometimes argued that the huts must have been inhabited by a pigmy race since, however roofed, they could scarcely have afforded standing room to anyone of ordinary height. It seems more likely, however, that they served mainly for shelter and sleeping quarters, like the low tents which formed the main part of an old-fashioned gipsy encampment. The essential fire would have been outside—indeed with any vestige of realism one cannot imagine it anywhere else. Above all, they were tough people with a standard of living little higher than that of wild creatures.

Only the dogmatic pronounce upon the unknown, and since the gospel of today so frequently becomes the heresy of tomorrow, current theories upon insoluble or controversial problems should not be taken too seriously. The early inhabitants of the hut settlements may have been peaceable or predatory, summer campers or perennial residents, pastoral or miners by occupation. Little more can be said about them To some extent they must have been pastoral since it would have been necessary to keep sufficient herds to supply their domestic needs. If summer campers only, against which supposition the solidity of the hut is sometimes urged, strong building would have been essential to preserve the structures during winter, whether occupied or not. Again the almost invariable proximity of the huts to ancient workings lends strong support to the possibility that they were also tin-streamers. Examples are far too numerous to be dismissed as coincidental. Indeed the juxta-position is virtually the rule, and obviously a common need of water does not provide the reason. With regard to a water-supply most of the hutments could have been much more conveniently placed. Very few were situated actually beside a brook for the simple reason that while water was essential for tin-streaming it was not so essential for domestic purposes. Therefore while the hutments almost without exception were within easy distance of the workings, these workings usually divided them from the water. Actually, little water may have been required. "Milk drawn from the mountain goat" was the drink to which the hunter prisoner of Chillon had been accustomed and it does not seem unreasonable to imagine that Bronze Age men of the hills quenched their thirst from a similar source. Again, water for domestic purposes would scarcely have been required upon the scale now considered indispensable. Turf floors required no scrubbing and there is no reason for supposing that personal ablutions figured largely in the daily toilet. Presumably, if the mistress of a mansion required a skinful of water for any special purpose, she could always fetch it from the nearest brook or spring, even if half a mile away, her time not being too heavily occupied with housework.

Another and more plausible theory to account for the proximity of settlements to surface-mining is that the same terrain suited both purposes. Many tin deposits lay on southern and therefore warmer slopes, but whatever the reason, everything indicates a definite connection between the hut dwellings and industry. Nobody would suggest that all were contemporary. Palpably it could not have been so. The slow pageant of human life on Devonshire hills was spread over ages, and centuries may conceivably have elapsed between one phase of activity and another or even between the settlement of areas situated widely apart. Many circumstances may have led to the birth and growth of a new settlement, like a gold strike in other parts of the world, involving the abandonment of old quarters.

Every possibility considered, the meagre evidence available rather tends to support the theory—for it can be nothing more—that the hut-dwellers were pioneers of the tin industry which later developed upon so large a scale. Their standard of life was probably no more

Devon's north coast looking towards Hartland

savage and primitive than that which prevailed in other parts of the
county nor is there any reason for assuming that they were a race
apart. The ancient trackways provided a crude system of communication, the existence of which presupposes their use. The few possessions
unearthed by investigators indicate that these people moved with the
times, although not upon wheels, and if they traded by barter, tin
might conceivably have been an eminently marketable commodity.
There are no records to indicate the exact period during which
overseas commerce began, so all remains theoretical.

Modern historians quite legitimately insist upon the complete
absence of evidence that any Devonshire metal collected by Iberians
ever reached the early Mediterranean tin-traders. On the other hand,
entire lack of proof to the contrary might be argued with equal
justification. Indeed, the objection applies to any unsubstantiated
theory. There is no proof positive that the hut-dwellers did not move
upon all fours, or that they were not cannibals. The early people of
the hills certainly obtained products from elsewhere. Their flint
arrow-heads were not shaped from local stone, and arrow-heads
necessitated shafts and bows and expeditions to the forests for suitable
wood. Incidentally whatever these arrow-heads procured for Iberians,
they provide food for thought today. Archery in Britain is assumed
to have been a Roman innovation but that merely opens further fields
of controversy.

How the infiltration or invasion of the Celts with their advanced
iron tools and more efficient methods affected life on the uplands is
another matter for speculation. On the Cornish Peninsula, as elsewhere,
one can assume the gradual merging of old conditions with new, and
no cataclysmic change or positive line of demarcation. While Solomon
built his temple which possibly, though not probably, contained
material to which Devonshire contributed, these Celts erected their
fortifications and with their activities the curtain slowly rose upon the
long slow-motion pageant of Devonshire's history.

And so from the dark and remarkably inscrutable past emerged the
Ancient Briton whose early story is almost as obscure as that of his
predecessors. However the hill people originally lived, much suggests
that the Celts were far from being men of peace. They certainly
anticipated strife with their neighbours, if not with other overseas
invaders, and therefore constructed the earthern forts, camps or
"castles", relics of which still figure upon so many West Country hill-
tops. These entrenchments are widely dispersed over the county, and

2

Spinster's Rock, near Drewsteignton

probably commemorate centuries of tribal warfare or conflict with further marauding bands from overseas, until all were required to make common cause against the Roman invasion.

It is particularly difficult to estimate the precise date of earthern mounds or trenches. When once the turf has spread its healing crust over the raw soil, erosion is almost as slow as the levelling of the fabled mountain by a little bird's beak, and a hundred years are literally "but as yesterday". Imagination can trace an irregular chain of forts almost from coast to coast, but spaced too far apart to suggest a little Siegfried Line to oppose invasion from the East. The defences, although always strategically placed, could have been by-passed too easily by a conquering army and lines of advance were not so elongated in ancient as in modern war. Studied in retrospect, the scope of military operations narrows rapidly. In recent war the Russian battle-front advancing on Germany spanned Europe. Borodino was fought within two square miles while a few acres provided Ancient Britons with ample space in which to settle their differences.

The absence of fortifications on High Dartmoor is not surprising. Indeed, their presence would have been merely remarkable since serving no purpose. A rocky mountain top is self-fortified and, in the unlikely event of anybody wanting either to attack or defend, it would prove a tougher proposition than any elaborate system of artificial trenches. Against whom the defences were constructed, whether fair-haired Celts fought dark Iberians, or rival tribes fought one another matters little. However all that may have been, Celt and Iberian gradually mingled eventually to form the community recognized as the Dumnonii or Dammonians which occupied the South-Western Peninsula with the still undefined Devonshire as its central area.

II

EXETER

1. In History

WHILE the national evolution of Britain slowly progressed, the area which represents the Devonshire of today pursued its own affairs upon the "whatsoever King may reign" principle. When the Romans took over, however, they were not content to let the *status quo* continue indefinitely and Celtic defences proved quite inadequate to prevent the capture of Exeter, then the entrenched settlement known as Caerwisc, or "Camp by the River", renamed Isca Damnoniorum. Below rolled the tranquil Exe, beyond which the conquerors constructed no further fortifications, having presumably already encountered trouble enough without seeking more further westwards. Also, Exeter has ever been the heart and nerve centre of all that Devonshire involved and probably even at this early date, with its fall, armed resistance to the formidable invaders ceased.

When comparative peace had been restored, the Romans reconstructed Exeter and its fortifications according to their own improved standards, remnants of their work having survived the ensuing nine centuries. They doubtless proceeded to administer as much of the county as came under their direct control with the efficiency which characterized their methods, and Devonshire became *Brittania Prima*. The name seems a trifle misleading in view of the county's remote situation from the seat of government. *Brittania Ultima* would have been more appropriate unless *Prima* intimated *Britannia* first and Devonshire afterwards, upon the "all were for the state" principle. As time went on and civilizing influences progressed, missionaries of religion followed conquest by arms and when the Romans finally evacuated England, the descendants of savage Iberian and Celt had developed, if only superficially, into a Christian community.

Of those who resisted the Romans no West-country name has been handed down to posterity. Damnonia apparently lacked a Boadicea or any leader of either sex outstanding enough to get into the news. That is characteristic. Every history book dealing with the period records that Exeter fell to Vespasian, but few, if any, mention his opposite number, the Celtic chief who defended the fort unsuccessfully. The reason is that all historians of the period were Roman, Britons not having acquired the art of writing. Not long ago when discussing the war of the Spanish Succession with an Austrian professor, I remarked that I had been unable to discover much about the part played by Prince Eugene, English accounts being mainly concerned with Marlborough's achievements. His answer was that he had suffered from a corresponding difficulty, since Austrian history dealt largely with Eugene but made little mention of Marlborough.

Exeter can scarcely have been a "residential" city in Roman times but rather a garrison community bringing its own population, after the manner in which social life always follows the army. To this, local British aristocracy could contribute little, for lack of the qualifying social standards. Luxury-loving people create their own luxurious conditions and post-war excavations suggest that the Romans, after four hundred years of occupation, left a very different Exeter and a very different Damnonia from that originally penetrated by Vespasian's legions.

It is not necessary to trace Damnonian fortunes under the petty dynasties of which King Constantine was the best-known, or more correctly perhaps, the least-unknown personality. It was a featureless period, devoid of epoch-making incident, and provided no outstanding historical or even legendary figure of primarily Devonian setting.

The Saxon conquest of Damnonia was no spectacular *coup d'état*. Unlike the Roman and subsequently the Norman invasion, it was not a national affair carried out systematically by a well-organized army. The first English came as bands of adventurers seeking not so much warfare for war's sake, as a land upon which to settle and thereafter to live at peace. Pioneers of agriculture, the Saxons came figuratively with sword in one hand, spade in the other; sword to clear the way, spade to cultivate the ground so gained. By slow stages they dug themselves in—and those stages were slow indeed. Thinly populated as the country must have been, the Britons, aided by the savage terrain, put up a long resistance. After a victory at Pensylwood in 658 had enabled the Saxons to overrun Somerset as far as the present Devonshire border, more than a quarter of a century elapsed before they penetrated to Exeter. Even then, the Damnonian King Geraint, probably the original of Tennyson's fictitious husband of Enid, continued to rule over the western half of the county until 710. Then he was finally defeated by the Saxon Ine, King of West Sussex, presumably also losing as much of Damnonia as he had managed to annex. After that date there is no record of a Damnonian State.

How the first kingdom of Wessex, including Devonshire, evolved from the liquidation of the Geraint régime is a long story. Alfred gained one of his most notable victories over the Danes at Northam, and since Danish raiders also penetrated to Exeter more than once, it would seem that Devonshire attracted its quota of outside visitors even in those remote days.

In so far as history relates, no Roman Emperor had considered a trip to Exeter worth his while. It was too long and uncomfortable a journey to be undertaken unless urgently necessary. Remote outposts of Empire or Kingdom saw little of their reigning sovereign before the days of faster travel. Edward the Elder and his son Athelstan had incorporated the western province into the country as a whole but Devonians knew little about kings of national status until William the Conqueror brought their first impression of absolute monarchy to Exeter in person.

Later, when styled Queen of the West, Exeter became very much of a royal city ranking as fourth in the land, being inhabited at frequent intervals by Saxon kings such as Alfred and later by his descendants Edward the Elder, Athelstan and Edgar. After the petty kings of Wessex had acquired the status of national monarchs, Devonshire was more intimately connected with the background of early English kings than is generally recognized. It was upon Elfreda, Countess of Devon, that Edgar the Peaceful—but not the scrupulous—looked with distinct favour. This led to a hunting party on Dartmoor where the Saxon king, like David, King of Israel, under similar circumstances, contrived to remove the obstacle to his passion. So, aided by further manoeuvre on the part of Elfreda, came Ethelred worse than "Unready", and through his ineptitude, the period of Danish rule. To Exeter also fell the privilege—although not necessarily regarded as such—of selection to provide part of the revenue essential to maintain Emma, Ethelred's Queen, in appropriate dignity. And Emma, "Paramount Lady" of Exeter, presented the realm with the doubtful blessing of Edward the Confessor. All considered, therefore, Devonshire's influence upon the line of Saxon succession was scarcely fortunate. It came to a tragic end in Harold, whose associations with the county, through the great Earl Godwin and Gytha his mother, were sufficiently strong to establish a definite connection between Devonshire and the Hero-King.

It is unlikely that Exeter ever saw the ill-fated Harold in the royal state, but a call from William I was not long delayed. Probably owing to its strong Saxon sympathies and associations, he personally led an expedition against the city in 1068. Exeter did well to defy the victor of Hastings for as long as eighteen days and it was fortunate perhaps, from the defenders' point of view, that they could withstand him no longer, since William had a drastic way of dealing with trouble-makers. As it was, Exeter opposed him stoutly enough to win his respect without arousing his wrath, and the inhabitants were treated more leniently than might have been expected.

In any case the destruction of so important a city was the last thing to be desired by so realistic a ruler as William I. Both in Saxon and early Norman days, the place provided a useful base for the tentative penetration into Cornwall. Control of the Exe was also desirable in view of possible trouble from the Danes, as the mighty fleet of Sweyn still menaced the English coast.

As the Romans had done before him, William also strengthened and renovated Exeter's defences, for which precaution his grandson Stephen must have felt no gratitude, since it enabled the city to withstand his efforts for three months, nearly seventy years later. When competition for the throne arose between Stephen and Maud, partly owing to pressure from interested and powerful sources, Exeter had declared for petticoat government—a principle regarded with disfavour by Norman eyes. It had become a matter of defending a lost cause even before the king's forces reached the gates. In spite of friction within as well as strife without, resistance continued until brought to an end not by assault but by the failure of the water-supply—an ironical circumstance in this county of many waters. The citizens, who had endured the siege more or less under protest, surrendered willingly enough. The garrison made its own terms, while Stephen upon recognition of his sovereignty exacted no crushing penalties.

2. The Royal City

After Saxon times Devonshire provided no more wives or mothers of kings, although Exeter, as became a royal city, continued its contribution to their maintenance, having indeed no option in the matter. The reigning monarch being overlord, his Queen automatically acquired the title "Lady Paramount of Exeter", and to her, by custom if not by statute, was allotted the greater share of the dues exacted by the crown. This, judged by modern standards, was not a vast amount but "no increase" had been one of the conditions accepted by William I upon the surrender of the city, and his successors had honoured the guarantee. Standards were rising even in those days, however, and since Henry III could demand no more in the way of income, he decided upon a capital levy, suggesting that every Exonian who owned any property should transfer one thirtieth of it to his sovereign liege. This was probably due to the "increasing prosperity" of Exeter, the King considering himself entitled to a larger share than William's clemency allowed. Whether the claim was made on behalf of himself or his Queen was a point that Exonians must have regarded as immaterial.

With Plymouth still a "mene place" and Devonshire as a whole scheduled a Royal Forest, Exeter had no commercial rivals. It seems probable that her potentialities as a port were never regarded very seriously. Dover and Southampton were so much nearer London, and therefore more conveniently placed for shipments to France. The Devonshire coast was mainly used by people who desired an unopposed landing or embarkation, as the case might be. The Exe was mostly useful for Exeter and local commerce, and when the Countess Isabel of Redvers monopolized control of the river shipping, her activities were regarded with indifference by Westminster, being of little national importance. Later, when the infinitely superior facilities of Plymouth had become recognized, Exeter in effect abandoned all further attempts to establish a first-class port and thereafter pursued the role of a prosperous inland centre of trade and industry.

Differ as they might about their own affairs, however, Exonians were never allowed to secede from the royal city status and all that it implied, nor was it in this case by any means a matter of "whatsoever king shall reign". The conditions demanded loyalty, and the Lord or Lady Paramount remained so to the end. Possibly other considerations carried additional weight. Unless his outlook has altered more than appearances suggest, the economically minded Devonian would have been ill-disposed to see a monarch, for whom he had provided financially, dethroned by anybody. Further, another king or his lady might incline to a more advanced standard of living, and demand higher contributions. Anyhow, whether from motives of loyalty, expediency or innate conservatism, Devonshire—upon general principle—mainly favoured the *status quo*, and when the Wars of the Roses

broke out with a Lancastrian upon the throne backed by the strong
Courtenay influence, Exeter's support for the existing régime followed
as a matter of course.

To Exeter's credit it must be recorded and emphasized that royal
"appeals" for funds, when urgently needed, had always been met, if
not necessarily with unbounded enthusiasm, at least with a good grace.
It had become a case of the willing horse with consequent additions to
its burden, and already Henry VI had made substantial requests for
expenses incurred in the French wars. The modern Devonian varies his
charges for service rendered according to the social status of the
person served. He calls it "honouring" the individual so selected—
a recognition of his rank—and to be "honoured" upon the same
principle had always been Exeter's proud fate. Therefore when Henry,
complete with Lady Paramount, paid his state visit, the magnificence
and pageantry of his reception left nothing to be desired. With the
Lancastrian star bright in the ascendant and the King enthroned in the
improved local palace, who could then "his direful doom foretell"?
Nothing seemed less probable and after a week of entertainment upon
truly regal lines, Henry left with the flower of Devonian chivalry
"battled at his side" to stamp out the smouldering remnants of Yorkist
resistance.

While Exeter worked to replenish depleted coffers, Henry marched
to the field of St. Albans and his subsequent extinction, leaving his
redoubtable Queen Margaret, Lady Paramount in character as well as
title, to reap the advantages of the city's loyalty. This remained
unshaken through all the vicissitudes of ensuing years, as long as
Margaret upheld the struggle. Exeter possessed a sufficient sense of
realism, however, to accept an apparent *fait accompli* in the establishment of the new régime after the appalling disaster at Towton.
Therefore, when Edward IV in the arrogance of irresistable might
advanced upon the city, the gates opened wide to receive him as
monarch and lord. It was the policy that common sense and
expediency necessitated. The star of Lancaster, once so bright, had
set in blood seemingly for ever; Margaret had fled overseas, and
Edward not only received a great ovation but also a substantial
contribution to his exchequer to the amount of 100 nobles, an exceedingly useful sum in those days.

Queen Margaret was far from being finished, however, nor the
tribulation of Devonshire on her behalf. In national as well as in
private affairs the unexpected often happens, although in this case the

turn of events did not lack precedent. Edward IV had gained the throne mainly because his cause was championed by the stout Earl of Warwick but the Warwicks, or their representatives in all walks of life, have been liable to set a high value upon their services. The demands upon gratitude may be excessive and the over-strained cord breaks. There are no enemies more bitter than estranged friends, so when Edward and Warwick differed, the alliance was changed to deadly hostility. Unlike many monarchs or politicians before and since, the King was not sufficiently strong to kick down the ladder by which he had climbed. Warwick seized power, and while Edward fled to Burgundy Henry VI was nominally restored.

So Queen Margaret again became Lady Paramount, and her son, Prince Edward, the Seigneur of Exeter, with the city a centre of Lancastrian activity. And thus matters remained during the final fluctuations of the struggle between Margaret and Edward IV which ended at Tewkesbury in the death of her son, the young seigneur, and 3,000 Devonians, including the Earl of Devon, the fourth successive holder of the title to lose his life when fighting for the Red Rose.

After Barnet and Tewkesbury, Devonshire's share in national affairs became less active, although remaining always a centre of Lancastrian intrigue. With the principal figures either dead or overseas, however, the county no longer constituted a source of danger to the now firmly seated Edward, and the city was spared the embarrassment of yet another royal visit for several years. The next occurred when minor disturbances inevitably brought Richard III to the gates. This "call" seems to have been largely a contest of diplomacy. Exeter had little love for the sinister monarch, conspirators against whom were leaving the city by one gate while he entered by another, as the shrewd Richard must at least have guessed. It served his purpose best, however, to accept assurances of loyalty, particularly since they were backed by a peace token of 200 nobles, silence with regard to awkward questions being golden from his point of view.

Soon after came Bosworth Field, and with the final blending of the Roses, an end to the troubles suffered by Devonshire through so often supporting the losing side. The county's share in the long struggle had not been a happy one, although in the main, creditable. To be split frequently by conflicting factions and influences was as inevitable then as now, and at times Exeter in particular might have been accused of keeping a foot in both camps. Temporary allegiance to the House of York, however, was always rendered under duress, there being no alternative. It was the price of survival. Despotic kings ruled by right of might, as modern legislators by right of election. None the less, while placating the ruling monarch, even to the extent of "greasing his palm" with lucre, there was always an underground movement in favour of the dynasty regarded as rightful. Justly styled the "ever faithful" as well as the royal city, Exeter then, as at all times, remained ready to take up arms at a moment's notice in support of the sovereign whom she regarded as her own, and never abandoned the cause while any hope remained.

Devonshire's loyalty was put to further tests when Henry VII, firmly established on the throne, began to exact further contributions in money and men, ostensibly to help the Duke of Burgundy in resisting French aggression. Exeter was again "honoured" by a liberal demand, which as usual was met without recorded protest, but a more formidable trial came when the Yorkists for the last time put up another candidate for the throne. Whether Perkin Warbeck was the genuine son of Edward IV or a mere impostor mattered little to Lancastrian Exeter. In any case he was an aspirant to be resisted upon grounds both loyal and confident. So when Warbeck arrived with his heterogeneous force—at the western gate this time—demanding admission, he was met by uncompromising refusal. Yet another siege ensued. Undisciplined though his troops were, their attack proved formidable and very nearly successful. A force hastily mustered by the surrounding gentry relieved the city however, and Exeter again stood high in the royal favour. In proof of this, Henry, who had hurried westwards to crush the insurrection which actually crumbled without a pitched battle, paid Exeter the inevitable "state" visit. The object of this one was to express his royal gratitude for services rendered, which he did by the gift of a sword, still preserved in the Guildhall. History records no offers of compensation for damage incurred in defence of the city, but possibly Henry's appreciation was adequately demonstrated by his omission to exact contributions for the royal exchequer, such abstention not being customary with the first of the Tudors. However that may have been, after being entertained with the usual regal magnificence, Henry of Richmond eventually withdrew in state and in departing, all unwittingly ended a long epoch.

During the ensuing century and a half, Exeter saw nothing of the five sovereigns who each in turn occupied the throne throughout the period. The interests of Henry VIII were mainly directed elsewhere.

Devonshire offered no potential brides, and the dissolution of the monasteries was a national measure not affecting any one county more than another.

Diametrically opposite in this respect was the so-called "Prayer Book Rebellion", the next event which shattered the peace after half a century of freedom from "war and rage", The issues involved in this case were in no sense local. The disturbance might have arisen anywhere and the "accident" that it occurred in Devonshire was the county's misfortune rather than fault. That the flag of insurrection should have been raised in the remote little village of Sampford Courtenay, within the ancient Barony of Okehampton, lent a touch of irony to the situation. Henry VIII had considered it advisable to terminate the Courtenay influence in Western Devon by beheading the last representative of that particular line and this proved unfortunate as well as ironical. Under the restraining power of the Courtenays, a revolt of any kind would scarcely have been possible.

"Rebellion" was perhaps a somewhat misleading term for an affair which rather took the form of disorganized riots, beginning as a demonstration against the new form of Church service, with no ulterior political or national objective. Its original ring-leaders had no more idea of overthrowing the established régime than the Cornishmen who traditionally marched to the tune of "Shall Trelawny Die?". To the Protectorate it came as an embarrassment at a difficult moment rather than an actual danger, although the situation was not without grave possibilities. These became apparent when the trouble, once started, spread like a fire irresponsibly lit and the peaceful end originally sought became lost in the means, as usually happens. The rabble of undisciplined countrymen which set out from Sampford Courtenay had been joined by numerous influential sympathizers, some no doubt with axes of their own to grind. The plundering of Exeter, rather than Prayer Book reform, had become the main objective, at any rate for the time being. So when Lord Russell, dispatched by Lord Somerset to "pacify the insurgents", arrived, he found the city beset, and a situation quite beyond the ability of peaceful measures to control. The final issue, of course, was never in doubt. By standing firm in the cause of law and order, and bearing the brunt of the affray, Exeter—true to tradition—had again proved herself an invaluable pillar of the Crown. Confronted by Lord Russell's army, the rioters quickly disintegrated and the disturbance ended with the execution of several hapless ring-leaders, who must have wondered how they brought themselves to so

sorry a pass, or their lives in the quiet Sampford Countenay countryside to such tragic and unnecessary termination.

3. Exeter Today

While figuring so largely in history as the fortified city whose gates
so often "rolled back the tide of war", Exeter since early times was the
western centre of civil administration, culture, religion and justice.
Within my own day, the city was also regarded with respect among
primitive Devonians on the eastern side of the county as containing
the nearest prison—Princetown being too remote to be visualized.
The declaration that if some poultry-thief, poacher or other male-
factor could be caught he would "go to Exeter" meant that he would be
handed over to the law, with a gaol sentence as the probable consequence. The prison was indeed expressly pointed out to me upon first
visiting the city when an eight-year-old boy, as the inevitable destination of evil-doers. That, however, is merely incidental, a passing
example of Exeter's hold upon Devonian imagination.

Here since early Saxon times stood the Abbey, since replaced by
the present Cathedral, and with the Cathedral was its Bishop, the
principal religious figure of the West. It was characteristic that when
Edward the Confessor appointed the famous Leofric to the See of
Crediton, the sage prelate petitioned the Pope to order his transfer to
Exeter, as more compatable with his dignity and more conducive to
his personal safety. The munificence and pageantry with which he was
finally installed by the Confessor left nothing to be desired, creating,
indeed, a standard which must have proved difficult to maintain upon
subsequent ceremonial occasions.

Another, although in this case terrible tribute was paid to Exeter's
ecclesiastical status nearly 900 years later when, allegedly as a reprisal
for the bombing of Cologne Cathedral, much of the city was devastated
during two raids by the Luftwaffe. This was regarded as an act of
wanton vandalism. None the less, the selection of Exeter to be devastated as a reprisal for Cologne was a grim recognition of outstanding distinction. Interesting too was the attitude of an injured German
pilot, the crashing of whose machine had brought him as a patient
into the city hospital. Formerly a student at the University College,
as it then was, he seemed genuinely concerned about the possible fate
of historic buildings, and questioned the officiating surgeon as to which
structures, if any, had escaped the bombs dropped by his countrymen.

It was an ironical situation which to the surgeon must have been particularly exasperating. However, the terse answer "Find out"— although a natural reaction enough—cannot have struck the injured enemy as very imaginative, to "find out" being the obvious purpose of his questions.

With Plymouth, the Royal City shared the brunt of the blitz, although in Exeter the loss of life was mercifully not so great, the total being less than a hundred, while in Plymouth more than a thousand died as the result of one raid. Most of Exeter's historic buildings, such as the Cathedral, the Guildhall and the Castle escaped destruction although the Cathedral suffered a certain amount of damage. The main devastation occurred on the eastern side of the city, so that now the visitor is confronted with two Exeters, the old and the new. The complaint of those who loved the old is that too much sacrifice was made, and is still continuing, in favour of modern ideas, modern standards of architecture and modern traffic. Upon the architecture no comment is needed, since its style may be taken for granted, conforming to the pattern of the day. One can only say that the reshaping of the devastated areas has been carried out with imagination and taste, and that pleasing effects have replaced much that was dingy and sordid.

At the time of writing, relics of the blitz are still visible even among the innovations, and in a city so full of ancient features a stranger none too deeply versed in antiquarian lore might find difficulty in distinguishing the ruins of time from wreckage wrought by Hitler's bombers. Exeter's long history has been of periodical war ravage and repair, so possibly the task of antiquarians in a remote future will be to identify the traces left by each in turn. The architecture which the Second World War necessitated should be easily recognizable unless the old entirely disappears in course of time.

I have followed the theme of Exeter's importance too far into modern times, however, and the next chapter must return to Tudor days where the historical threads were dropped after the Prayer Book Rebellion.

III

THE GOLDEN DAYS

1. Tudor Sea Saga

EVEN as Devonshire provided the last Saxon king, so she very nearly supplied England with at least one more Tudor. Henry VIII thought fit to execute his relative and former favourite the Earl of Devon, whom he had recently created Marquis of Exeter as a special token of regal esteem. His sole apparent motive was jealousy of a personality infinitely more brilliant then his own, and Tudor jealousy was a thing to avoid like death itself—the usual consequence. The despotic king further extended his animosity to Henry Courtenay's twelve-year-old son, whom he deprived of all hereditary rights and imprisoned in the Tower. Helpless, but like Napoleon's son in similar case, regarded as a potential source of danger, he remained in close captivity for the ensuing fifteen years, until at last released by Queen Mary who for personal reasons had decided to have a look at him. The result of the inspection was highly favourable, eventually leading to the gracious suggestion that Courtenay, in compensation for his injuries, should share her throne and with luck ensure the male succession so much desired. Naturally Courtenay was not averse to so flattering a prospect, particularly since "bloody Mary" did not lack personal attraction. Unfortunately for himself, however, although perhaps fortunately for England, before the step became irrevocable he discovered that the charms of the Princess Elizabeth excelled those of her elder sister. A request that he might be allowed to transfer his affections to her possible successor was a policy which did not commend itself to Mary at all. Besides, Queens resent their favours being unappreciated even more, if possible, than ordinary women. Courtenay went back to the Tower, Elizabeth was placed under supervision elsewhere and the offended Mary placed her scorned hand in that of the King of Spain.

The latter unpopular gesture provoked agitation on behalf of Elizabeth and Courtenay, which found strong support in Devonshire. Under such a union, loyalty to the Crown could be combined with loyalty to the great house with whose fortunes those of the county had for so long been inseparable. There followed revolts from which Elizabeth promptly dissociated herself. She had formed a poor opinion of Courtenay, whom she regarded as shallow and a mere travesty of his brilliant father. A throne shared with such a partner in no way appealed to her cool brain. Even had the revolts on her behalf proved successful, it seems doubtful that she would have been persuaded to present the Tudor line with an heir of Devonshire blood. None the less, it was curious that Henry's vindictiveness so nearly restored the house of Courtenay to a position of even greater privilege and power, and so nearly provided Exeter with yet another claim to her title of Royal City.

As it happened, the Virgin Queen never set stately foot upon Devonshire soil—unless indeed any adhered to Raleigh's cloak when it enjoyed that distinction. The fact that neither historic Exeter nor the noblest Devonian mansion can display a bed in which she slept seems an almost incredible break with tradition. None the less her influence upon the county's fortunes and story far surpassed that exercised by any other sovereign before or since. This influence had no marked effect upon industrial development, although during her reign the wool trade prospered with its many beneficial consequences. Those were conditions which Elizabeth accepted while taking a line of her own.

During a precarious girlhood, her main protection against an all-powerful sister's animosity and jealousy had lain in her popularity with the Fleet. Destined to be styled the "Restorer of Naval Power and Sovereign of the Northern Seas", she laid the foundations for that title while still in her teens. In the character of "Madame Elizabeth" she had been regarded as the sailor's Princess, and when coming to power, it was to the Fleet that she turned in the framing of her policy. For the benefit, directly and indirectly, of her royal predecessors Devonshire had produced tin, silver, lead and wool. The woollen industry still boomed to enrich all concerned with it but Elizabeth saw brighter possibilities in minerals which the county could not directly provide, but which Devonshire men could procure by search elsewhere. She envisaged the "wealth of seas", which meant sea-borne treasure, and this required seamen to collect it. For these Elizabeth turned as a matter of course to Devonshire, the cradle of England's navy and the main starting point of maritime adventure. Indeed, she is reputed to have said that all her best men, her bravest admirals, her most skilful generals and her wisest councillors came out of Devonshire. And from Devonshire certainly the sea-dogs came, Raleigh, Gilbert, Drake and Grenville,

Hawkins, Frobisher, Davis and others—names which have since become almost legendary, including many who already had little to learn concerning maritime adventure, but were glad enough to have their acts of bare-faced piracy legitimized. The only trouble was that when the Queen commissioned or connived at an expedition, the lion's share of the spoil went, not into the sea-lion's den but into the royal coffers. Beyond a shadow of doubt a tough old captain, like the modern tax-evader, declared no more of his potential "income" than stern necessity demanded. It is needlesss to add that such necessity was stern indeed with the headsman's axe, kept ever keen, for defaulters. Again the "ratings" of those days had serviceable pockets, and trousers that rolled up conveniently. All considered, therefore, maritime expeditions were profitable for everybody concerned and consequently popular, at least in England generally. The queenly smile or frown depended upon the outcome of an adventure, for Elizabeth, like most strong characters, had little use for failure. Raleigh's final fall from grace was mainly due to his return with empty ships after a voyage from which substantial revenue had been expected. Other countries, particularly Spain, not unnaturally took a poor view of Devonshire seamen and their methods for balancing England's Budget.

To be a sailor princess in the literal sense might well have been Elizabeth's role but apart from her formal state visit to the *Golden Hind*, there is no record of her ever leaving the shore. When she boarded the *Golden Hind* at Deptford, she made naval history. Until then a buccaneer and sea adventurer, Drake had just set up a maritime record, having been the first Englishman to sail his ship around the world. For Elizabeth the choice had lain between diplomacy and expediency, or in other words whether it was more advisable to run the risk of offending the Spanish King, or to secure the services of an obviously accomplished mariner who might prove a tower of strength should war with Spain materialize. Whether to ignore Drake or to honour him was the question and the far-sighted Queen decided upon the latter course. It had been, like others, a fateful question upon which the trend of history hung as by a thread. Later Charles I was faced with a similar problem when uncertain whether to allow Cromwell and Hampden to emigrate before the Civil War, both being potentially dangerous men but most valuable citizens none the less. It was characteristic that the cool Tudor made the right choice, the impetuous Stuart the wrong. Had Elizabeth turned a cold shoulder upon Drake—and that shoulder could be very cold indeed—he would probably have

West front of Exeter Cathedral

ended his days as a mere pirate. Instead he was knighted on board his own ship, and the adventurer become one of Britain's greatest admirals who did more perhaps directly to save the country at a time of utmost need than any other. Had Charles I in his turn possessed similar acumen, there would have been no Cromwell and no Ironsides to turn the tide in many a vital battle, and Prince Rupert would have charged rough-shod to victory almost before the Civil War had begun.

As the war-clouds darkened over Spain, Elizabeth turned her attention more and more to nautical matters and the source of naval protection. This meant to Devonshire, whence came the ships and the men who sailed them. To Drake, therefore, was entrusted the charge of meeting the Armada and breaking its power—if he could.

That Devon ships and Devon men bore the brunt of the Spanish attack when at last it materialized is historical and needs no further elaborating here. It was largely an incident of geography, since the Armada first came within fighting range off the South-Western sea-board. It might almost be described as Devonshire's war, Plymouth providing as many ships as London—actually seven—while Barnstable contributed another three. Indeed the fate of the Armada was virtually decided before it had journeyed far up the Channel. The real fighting strength of England's fleet was drawn from the maritime county. The Devonshire ports also provided their ships and crews without charge to the royal exchequer, for which the Queen expressed her gratitude in her famous letter to the people of Exeter, "her ever faithful city".

As defender of England's shores, Drake obtained his halo of glory, but after the Armada his triumphs over the Spaniards ended. As the war continued he set forth upon his two final and unsuccessful expeditions, to die at last on board his ship in Nombre de Dios Bay, with his disappointed heart in Plymouth, if the sea song commemorating his end is really based upon his dying sentiments. His was the rover's spirit, and sea adventure his true vocation. "Next to my own shippe I do most love that old shippe in Exon—a tavern in St. Martin's Lane," he is alleged to have said of the old inn near the Cathedral Close but his "own shippe" came first.

Yet the spirit of Drake dominates Plymouth today, even as that of Sir Richard Grenville pervades the atmosphere of Bideford and Barnstaple Bay. Nobody could imagine Plymouth anything but a naval town steeped in historical romance. Standing now in the crowded pleasure-grounds of the Hoe or of Devonport and looking seawards over the mighty Sound, one scarcely notices the holiday-makers or the

3

The Guildhall, Exeter

amenities created for their amusement. The numerous sailing or motor boats again seem out of place. In imagination's eye, still afloat upon the blue waters of the Sound are sea-craft of a very different character— Drake's fleet which fought the Spaniards, wooden frigates which sailed with Nelson, and the great ironclads of our own time. In Victorian and Edwardian days, Plymouth remained more or less the head-quarters of the great Home Fleet with battle ships and cruisers afloat on the wide Hamoaze, a harbour which was capable of containing the entire British Navy even in the days of its supreme magnificence, when the three-power standard still prevailed and England was mistress of the seas indeed. And still the warships cross Plymouth Sound and steam in state up the Hamoaze but they are mainly aircraft carriers, destroyers and the occasional cruiser. Gone are the great battleships which will soon have become as much a feature of the past as the wooden navy. The last of her kind to float on the tidal waters of the Tamar and Tavy was the grand old *Vanguard*, ironically misnamed in one respect, since her final sailing marked the end rather than the beginning of a long sea epoch. Conspicuous among all other naval vessels she lay for long off Devonport, as though reluctant to leave the haunted scene, home of Britain's former maritime glory. Drake's drum should certainly have beaten a farewell tattoo when the *Vanguard* crossed the Sound and passed his island for the last time, but only his statue witnessed her departure, and that may see changes far more spectacular before the story of Plymouth and Devonshire's sea saga has ended.

2. Plymouth

"Plymouth is beautiful,"—was Queen Victoria's pronouncement and such appears to be the opinion of a recent correspondent to the *Western Morning News*. The modern city, however, could scarcely differ more from that so praised by the "great little" Queen-Empress a century ago. Plymouth—in many respects regarded as Exeter's rival—was not, even before her devastation, an ancient city. She only evolved in medieval times from an insignificant fishing settlement, and mainly owed her subsequent importance to the decreasing value of Exeter as a port. Plymouth, indeed, grew as Exeter declined, inheriting much that the Queen of the West was obliged to surrender but always lacking Exeter's historic background. Much depends, however, upon the definition of "historic" since everything that happens makes history. Plymouth never acquired Exeter's royal status or tradition, being too "modern" for any connection with Roman, Saxon, or even Norman kings, actually supporting the Parlimentary cause in the Civil War. On the other hand, while in medieval times the Queen held the title of "Lady Paramount of Exeter", in later Hanoverian days the Prince of Wales was traditionally styled "The Lord High Steward of Plymouth", wands of office being bestowed upon any heir apparent when first visiting the city.

It may be, therefore, correct to say that Plymouth, originally known as "Sutton", has no ancient history, with emphasis on the adjective. Apparently her value as a port was first fully appreciated by Edward I, subsequently becoming the naval base for many expeditions. Why so remote an embarkation point was chosen, with the obvious difficulties of transporting armaments overland, is not always apparent. Dartmouth was considerably nearer and, one might think, would have been quite as suitable. The port of Plymouth or Sutton, of course, then meant the mouth of the Plym, the harbour now comprising Cattewater and Sutton Pool. There were no docking facilities on the Hamoaze in those days, and it is curious that the finest harbour on Devon's coastline was the last to be developed. The Black Prince inaugurated the Saltash Ferry, the story of which has now ended, but Devonport dockyard owed its construction to the long-sighted William of Orange, who possibly held views as to its ultimate advantages in his life-long struggle with France.

Devonport, originally known as "Dock" —just as a new mining settlement might be called "Pit"—until its claim to the title of Devonshire's port became indisputable, developed rapidly, combining in course of time with Plymouth and Sutton to form the United City of Plymouth today. Each town still retained a measure of indentity, not without inevitable rivalries and jealousies. At one time a complaint arose that Devonport was monopolizing too big a share of the common water-supply. Devonport reacted by making arrangements to provide for herself, to which Plymouth, possibly contemplating the loss of water-rate, objected even more strongly—but such is usually the result under joint ownership. Despite minor differences there arose a fine united city, the main base for naval operations since medieval times, but not subjected to the ravages of civil war to the same extent as Exeter, or to attack by invaders other than pirates.

For Plymouth the Wars of the Roses were remote affairs. Her only experience of "battle's rage", with armies, not navies, as combatants, came when she was besieged by the Royalist troops under Prince Maurice. The Plymouth of Stuart days was a very different place from that of which the Normans had never heard, and about which neither Yorkist nor Lancastrians unduly bothered. But the Plymouth which stood at the outbreak of the Second World War had achieved an importance regarded by the German High Command as eminently detrimental to its interests. So most of Victorian Plymouth and Devonport, with subsequent additions, was devastated, and few who visit the new city for the first time—and indeed many of the younger residents —realize that there was ever any other.

As might have been expected both in Devonport and Plymouth the destruction was greatest in the neighbourhood of the dockyard and the sea-board. There, for years, rows of skeleton buildings awaited final demolition, while nearer the city centre, as though specially spared, the block which contained the publishing offices of the *Western Morning News* stood almost alone amongst surrounding desolation. Replanning and rebuilding presented a prodigious problem, resulting in notable achievement. To those who knew the pre-war city the effect is bewildering and to those familiar with the post-war waste, incredible. The new Plymouth might be summarized in three adjectives— splendid, spacious, imposing. In place of the congestion of earlier days, and later ruinous desolation, there are vistas of wide walks, green verges and flower-beds, approaches to the sea-front upon which the shades of Drake and his captains might lose themselves from sheer inability to recognize their surroundings. The Nissen huts, in which the great commercial stores made valiant efforts to carry on business after the blitz, have been replaced by huge establishments, compared with which the former premises were insignificant, and with buildings such as St. Andrew's Church and the Guildhall restored in a manner to retain their original character, Plymouth has not so much been "restored" as arisen in new shape. To get a realistic impression of the change one should study air photographs of the city before and after the transformation. The wide spaces now displayed suggest the inevitable question—what has become of the many thousands who inhabited the old, vanished city with its winding streets and forest of chimneys? The answer is spread over the surrounding country where new building estates house Plymouth's increasing population, numbering approximately a quarter of a million people. The atmosphere of the new city as compared with the old is beside the point, the architecture being inevitably that of the period. Such applies, however, to all war-ravaged cities where changed character testifies to the part they bore in the national suffering.

IV

FROM ROSE TO ORANGE

With the passing of the great Elizabeth, Devonshire's share in national events became less prominent for a while. There was nothing in the change of dynasty for the "ever faithful city" to oppose, nor did the execution of Sir Walter Raleigh arouse demonstrative protest in his native county. James I was not a regal personality, anxious to display himself in all parts of his kingdom. As long as he received any dues that might be payable and to which he attached supreme importance, he saw little point in visiting the Western capital. Also royal magnificence to conform with precedent would be required, and that might prove costly. So James remained where he could live as quietly and economically as the state of royalty permitted, and since peace prevailed in his reign, Devonshire, which meant Exeter, saw nothing of the first Stuart.

Loyalty, like friendship, is tested when need arises and should monarchs require it they usually know when and where to apply the test. So, when James I at last slept with his fathers—metaphorically, since previous Scottish kings had lain north of the border—his son, the ill-fated Charles I, soon found cause to seek both loyalty and friendship, nor did he look in vain to the "Royal City". When war broke out, Exeter as ever was all for the monarchy, with its traditions and associations. At first, however, matters went singularly awry for Exeter. The King had raised his standard at Nottingham, the West being too remote once more to become the centre of operations, and in consequence the main tide of war set northwards. The importance of Exeter as a potential centre of loyalist support in the West had not been overlooked, however, by the Parliamentary leaders. The Earl of Bedford was dispatched not only to establish a Parliamentary régime throughout Devonshire, but also to raise troops in support of the Commonwealth. Exeter was occupied in the name not of the King but of the State. New taxes were levied to further the cause which Devonians, almost to a man, only desired to resist.

With Parliamentary control apparently established, Bedford returned to the main seat of war, leaving his second in command, Lord

Stamford, in charge at Exeter. As far as Devonshire was concerned however, the struggle had barely begun. Awaking at last from the bewilderment caused by the swift and efficient occupation by the Parliamentary troops, all available Royalist forces quickly mobilized until most of the county was in arms. Stamford was quite unable to meet the situation with the limited army at his command. After numerous engagements, he retired within the fortifications of Exeter as so many had done before him, and prepared for the inevitable siege. He had already strengthened the defences which had not been renovated since the Prayer Book Rebellion. He went farther by clearing all near approaches to the city from trees and houses which might give cover to an attacking force. The attacks were resolute none the less, but the fortifications could not be carried by storm and Royalist Exeter found herself in the ironical position of being defended by Roundheads against her will, while besieged by Royalist and fellow Devonians with whom the vast majority of the inhabitants were really in whole-hearted sympathy.

The control of the West, so essential to both sides, now hung upon the struggle for Exeter, and the Earl of Warwick, supported by a fleet, was sent to raise the siege. An attempt to advance up the Exe ended in fiasco, however, while a Royalist army under Prince Maurice approached the city from the east. Stamford was faced with no other course than surrender and Devonshire became again a solid stronghold of Royalist support.

A proof of this was soon forthcoming. With London and the southern ports in Commonwealth hands, the King had been obliged to make Oxford his headquarters and there he held temporary court. To the Queen Henrietta Maria this seemed uncomfortably near Westminster Hall and its undesirable new occupants. She preferred some safer birthplace for her anticipated royal baby. That the choice should fall upon the "ever faithful city", the refuge of all queens and princesses in distress, was inevitable and so in 1544 Exeter again had the honour of affording shelter to the Queen and Lady Paramount. She was accommodated with appropriate munificence at the town house of the Earl of Bedford and there in due course was born the ill-fated Henrietta of Exeter, destined to play so tragic a part in European history.

The Queen's stay in the faithful city was short however. The loss of Exeter still rankled in Parliamentary minds, and before Princess Henrietta was many weeks old, news arrived that an army under the

Earl of Essex was advancing against the capital. The presence of the Queen, whose capture would prove a strong trump card in political bargaining, made Exeter an even greater prize, but Henrietta Maria was in no way disposed to play into Parliamentary hands. She left Exeter more hurriedly than she had left Oxford, accompanied by the city's blessing, which also took financial shape. This was a gift of £300, Exeter's customary manner of paying more than verbal tribute to a member of the reigning house. She embarked at Falmouth for the Continent, never to return. The little Princess was left in Exeter under the charge of the "Governor and Citizens". She was of no political importance owing to her sex and could therefore be abandoned with safety.

The King meanwhile had not been insensible to the situation with all its potentialities and while Essex, having captured Tiverton, was planning his assault on Exeter, the approach of the royal army under Charles himself with the Prince of Wales, gave the Parliamentary general other food for thought. He retreated westwards, keeping respectfully wide of Exeter which Charles entered in triumph to greet his new daughter but not his Queen. So Exeter for the first time saw a Stuart King, and in his son the city's titular lord, and did not fail to make the most of the occasion. The King was installed in the house recently vacated by the fugitive Queen and now promoted to the dignity of a palace. It was, at any rate, the best that the city could provide, and since the Exonian purse had always been the Royal purse even beyond reasonable limits, it contrived with almost incredible elasticity to raise another £500 for the King and £200 for the titular lord. They were even provided with an additional substantial sum for the shoeing of their horses, but whether the City Fathers were prudent enough to ensure that the horses were actually shod or that the money had gone to the blacksmiths before paying up, is a point not recorded. However, upon the strength of such support—at least underfoot— King Charles took very active steps against the Earl of Essex who still hovered uncomfortably near his western flank. Having driven the Parliamentary general to a safe distance, he returned to Exeter for a final council of war and a further appeal to his ever-loyal Devonians.

Exeter had already done her utmost in the matter of loose cash, but no sacrifice was ever too great in the Royal cause, whether Saxon, Lancastrian or Stuart. Commerce was at its lowest ebb owing to the war, but everyone from the landed gentry to the modest tradesmen gave of their best, and put their marketable possessions into the pool. A large additional sum was raised for the further conduct of the war, and with as many more men as could be mustered to his standard, Charles I at last quitted his western "Palace" and marched away to Naseby and his doom.

For Devonshire and Exeter the rest was tribulation, maintaining a hopeless struggle to its bitter end, long after the capture of the King had reduced the greater part of the country to peace, however unwillingly. The last pitched battle of any consequence was fought at Torrington, and with the ultimate capture of the city by Fairfax, the story of Exeter's last siege ended. The safety of the little Princess Henrietta was secured under the terms of surrender and nowhere was the Commonwealth régime more reluctantly accepted than in the ever faithful city.

That the county should have produced General Monk, born at Merton in 1608—the man mainly responsible for the restoration of the monarchy—and that Exeter headed the list of petitioners was again only characteristic. The Merry Monarch's gratitude when he secured his throne was not extravagantly expressed. He only paid one visit to the "faithful city" when returning from Plymouth and upon that occasion his main idea was to get away as quickly as possible, forestalling preparations made for his ceremonial exit by departing surreptitiously at crack of dawn.

The long face of James II never looked from a coach window at a wildly cheering Exeter crowd. None the less, the popularity of the Stuarts was kept alive by the captivating Duke of Monmouth who, on his "vote-catching" tour of the West, did not neglect the city which might have proved more than useful to him. The question as to how far westwards Monmouth had acquired any real popularity was never put to the test after his landing at Lyme Regis. That a contingent of Devonshire militia under orders from Exeter should have been the first to oppose him at Axminster was merely another geographical accident, and a mere gesture never followed up. At the moment it was the only course open to the county authorities acting for the Crown. Had Monmouth attempted to win the support of Exeter and Devonshire before advancing immediately into Somerset, his story might have been very different. Actually Exeter was more likely to give him a favourable reception than Taunton, with chances of far more valuable support from the numerous county magnates for whom the son of Charles II would have a strong appeal whether his claim to the throne was legitimate or otherwise. What would have been the outcome, one wonders, had a Devonshire rather than a Somerset force, under very different leadership, marched to Bristol? What again in such a case, would have been the reactions of the Royal Cavalry led by Devonshire-born Churchill, later the great Marlborough, who decided the issue at Sedgemoor? As things happened, however, a mere handful of raw Devonians, collected from the Axminster district, marched with Monmouth, and all that Exeter saw of the unfortunate venture was the execution of that hapless few when Judge Jeffreys held the last of his "Bloody Assizes" in the Western counties.

The "Queen of the West" had one final part to play in the destiny of British monarchs. In the case of Monmouth, no chance had arisen again to shape national history since he, with fatal Stuart tendency to act unwisely, had placed all his eggs in the Somerset basket and lost the lot. When Dutch William landed in the county, with Exeter barring his line of advance, the position was very different. Exeter had no love for the mean-spirited James but the King was the King, even though he had never considered it worth his while to make himself pleasant in the West. Had he ever done so, one course only could have been adopted by the Royal City, and that, war to the knife in support of the reigning Stuart monarch and the Lady Paramount. In any case the dour Prince William with his grim military reputation had little to commend him as a successor to the gracious Stuarts of kindly memory, yet his supporters were gathering round; the Russells, the Seymours, the Courtenays, names great in Devonshire tradition. As William approached, the ranks of his army swelling with former Stuart supporters, it remained for Exeter either to block his way and so probably wreck the enterprise, or to open wide her gates and facilities, in which event final success was assured.

The civil authorities, mainly composed of old Stuart die-hards, under the influence of the Mayor, yielded to pressure most reluctantly. But William had come by invitation of England's nobility and the lords of Devon were on his side. Also his wife was the King's daughter and would be Lady Paramount. The Mayor was constrained to yield, but with a very bad grace. The city gates opened but at the last possible moment, as though the hinges needed oil. So Exeter, metaphorically, placed the crown upon the head of William III.

His entry, according to the official broadside issued at the time, was the most magnificent ever witnessed even by the Royal City, the scene of so much former pageantry. Its description rather suggests a circus procession, as William mounted upon a superb white charger rode in, escorted by a heterogeneous procession comprising troops of all colours and descriptions drawn from his overseas possessions. The shrewd soldier prince was by no means unaware of his initial lukewarm reception—a circumstance which he mentioned in his address to the city on the following morning: "I expected you sooner," he remarked to the many who had failed to meet him on the way. It was their services that he required, however, whether willingly or grudgingly given. With the West now solidly committed to William's cause, his further march on London was a mere triumphant procession. Indeed, nobody else dreamed of opposing him. Since even Exeter had accepted his credentials, his claims to the throne were clearly indisputable, and as the discomfited James fled to the Continent bewailing the faithlessness of all mortal men, he must have wondered whether the illustrious Elizabeth had really displayed so much perspicacity when she bestowed the motto *semper fidelis* upon the "fortress above the water".

So ended Devonshire's part in the shaping of dynasties, or in any further efforts to break or support the royal succession. And there ended too, in effect if not in name, all intimate connection between the Royal City and the Crown. No succeeding king nor queen found occasion to seek protection in the "ever faithful" West, and as peace from civil war settled over the country, the strategic or military value of Devonshire and its capital gradually declined. So, steeped in tradition and romance, with a long historical background, Exeter became a commercial city, an agricultural centre. The Exe has gone "rolling along" for many centuries since its waters floated Alfred's first three ships. It still rolls by, and although Norman William might open his eyes at the Exeter which he would find today, traces remain not only of his régime, but even of the Roman occupation. Modern Exeter will still be "historic Exeter" while any part of her remains.

The passing centuries, however, witnessed no change less anticipated than the proposed transformation of the Exe, where it touches the city, into a stretch of water designed for pleasure boating. The area upon which abandoned warehouses now stand will be converted into an entertainment centre as different in character from its present appearance as can well be imagined. The present fine Exe Bridge, being now considered inadequate, is to be replaced by a bridge upon either side, but the innovations will pay some acknowledgement to the past, as this modern recreational centre will be known as "Isca," a tribute to early Roman history.

V

WATER, WATER EVERYWHERE

1. River and Marsh

THE day is predicted when the last drop of fresh water will have been drained from this planet. The theories upon which so dry a conclusion is based need not be analysed here. In any case, however acute the general water shortage may become, Devonshire's supply should be among the last to fail since Dyfnaint, the land of deep, dark valleys, is also the source of many springs. Although lacking any natural lake even comparable with the Surrey "ponds" or the northern tarns, Devonshire has more rivers and streams than any other English county. By curious chance while several run into Devon from all its neighbours, none run out until reaching the sea. Most notable, perhaps, of that list is the gently flowing Tamar which Cornwall might more justly claim, not only owing to its source but because along virtually its entire western bank it washes Cornish soil. Only half of the river may be claimed, however, by either Devon or Cornwall under the new boundary adjustment of 1966. Indeed the Tamar might be regarded as the Tweed of the south, dividing Cornwall not only from its nearest neighbour but from the rest of the world. In other parts of the country, county boundaries are crossed without notice or concern. One might cross the Thames, for example, many times without even thinking that one was passing from Surrey into Middlesex or from Oxford into Berkshire. But nobody can cross the Tamar towards Cornwall without realizing that he is passing from one land to that other for which every touring motorist appears to head. The wonder is that no toll-gate system was ever instituted until the cost of maintaining the new Tamar Bridge rendered a charge necessary.

The unruffled Tamar cares as little as Galileo for such things, until, joining forces with the exclusively Devonian and wild-born Tavy, she swells to form the glorious Hamoaze, upon whose haunted flood every warship in the British Navy must have floated at some time during its career. It seems inappropriate somehow that Dutch William should have been responsible for building the great dockyard at Devonport,

43

with all its English and eminently Devonian traditions. To dock at Devonport, the farthest western port that the maritime county could reach, was a suitable end to an adventurous voyage, and the upper water of the Hamoaze also provides a last resting place for many ships whose sea-going days are over.

Since early days, crossing the Tamar—both before and after her confluence with the Tavy—has always presented a problem, there being no road-crossing below Gunnislake until the opening of the new bridge. Two ferries plying from Plymouth formerly carried all vehicles across the Hamoaze, but since these are proving unable to cope with the ever-increasing traffic, the great inlet was required to bear yet another burden. But that will be a matter for another chapter. Her head waters impounded to form the Bude reservoir—the only sip that Cornwall demands—the Tamar suffers little from artificial interference before reaching the Saltash viaduct, in which respect she is more fortunate than her sister stream, the Tavy, with whom she seeks the sea.

Rising in wild and desolate country under lone Fur Tor where often even today no sound except the raven's croak may be heard from dawn to dark, the Tavy, like most Dartmoor rivers, has many heads, each of which with equal justice might claim priority. From the outset she seems to be imbued with the one desire to escape from her stern parent hill as quickly as possible. Hastily collecting her tributary waters, the Ammicombe and furious Rattle Brook, she whirls down her grand gorge "in fierce career", like Macaulay's Tiber, and sweeps headlong into the lowland. She is not allowed an uninterrupted course, however, even before approaching civilization; it is a subdued and frustrated Tavy that rolls past Tavistock to gather further support from the Walkham and suffer final indignity at Lopwell Dam under Maristow. Before this final obstruction fretted her course, the Tavy entered upon her last lap, quietly spreading over the long, wide reach between the great woods, as though preparing to meet her more influential sister stream, the Tamar. In old nomenclature the name "Tavy" means the lesser water, the "Tamar", the greater, and such seems always to have been the accepted status. I once heard an eminent Bishop, when addressing an assembly at Maristow—then a home for retired clergy— refer incorrectly to the Tavy rolling by, as the Tamar. He assumed apparently that any big river near the Cornish boundary must be the Tamar, in notoriety, as in other things, the Tavy always taking second place.

The reason why Plymouth originally took her name from the least distinguished of her three rivers was obviously because the shipping of earlier days did not require as spacious a harbour as the great modern ironclads and liners, and the inlet, now known as the Catte-water, with Sutton Pool, served all essential purposes. It was beside the more easterly Plym river-mouth, therefore, that the Plymouth of Drake and Hawkins first came into being. There has always been the picturesque fish-quay on the Barbican and here the lighter craft still ply, either for business or pleasure, this being the nautical harbour of Plymouth—the Hamoaze the naval.

The Plym in itself is a somewhat featureless Dartmoor stream until gathering volume from its principal tributary, the Meavy. Upon the Meavy has fallen the task of providing Plymouth's main fresh water-supply, its early course having been arrested to form the great reservoir at Burrator, the best known perhaps of Dartmoor's five artificial conservations—that is to say if the group at Hennock, not actually on the moor but partly fed by moor water, can strictly be included in the list.

Eastwards from the Plym, by gorge or estuary, one stream after another seeks the sea. This was the terrain, considered the most difficult in England for the purpose, across which Brunel engineered the Great Western Railway from Exeter, which reached Plymouth in 1848. It necessitated the crossing of the Plym, the Yealm, the Erme, the Avon, the Dart and the Teign, negotiating in all, as river-intersected a stretch of coastline as any within the British Isles. The Yealm, the Erme and the Avon are characteristic Dartmoor streams, of which it would be difficult to say that one is more attractive than another. Waters which "in the desert rise", however, have lately acquired an attraction very different from any aesthetic consideration, and the potentialities of the upper Avon have led to the construction of yet another reservoir near Huntingdon Warren, completed about 1960. Whether artificial water reserves beautify or deface the landscape is a matter of opinion but they certainly attract the sightseer, and beyond doubt more people have visited the quiet Avon valley since the reser-voir took shape than were previously aware of its existence. A possible exception might be found in those far-off days when Erme Pound and Ryder's Rings, ancient hut settlements in that once wild region, were populated with residents who did not range so far afield for enter-tainment.

Probably the most famous western river, although lacking the historical background of Exe or Plym, the Dart has acquired a romantic glamour peculiarly her own. Like most rivers always given the feminine pronoun—a privilege denied to "Old Man Mississippi" and Fathers Tiber and Thames—the Dart, as the favoured daughter of the moor, could scarcely be regarded as other than "she". Sharing the birthplace of the Taw high on the great blanket bog, she chose the more attractive course to the southern rather than the cold northern sea. With her, as handmaidens, went all the brooks and runnels between the Tavy and the Teign, joining her train as she hurried seawards, until she carried by far the biggest share of Dartmoor's waters. Her song or "cry" as she sweeps down the gorges is the voice of the moor, and indeed the voice of Devonshire, the county of many waters. Every stream that flows from or touches Dartmoor is native and above all moor-born.

By repute "cruel" and demanding the annual tribute of a human heart, in reality the Dart has never taken excessive toll of life or property, nor is she more subject to devastating floods than any river of corresponding size and flow. That flow is swift and copious until after sweeping past Buckfastleigh, Holne and Totnes, the "Oak-tree river" broadens into the imposing flood, which—rolling past the Royal Naval College, at last reaches the sea, not by way of any muddy estuary but between two rocky castle-crowned headlands which appropriately attend her exit.

Even the boldest of reservoir builders have so far refrained from any attempt to impound Dart waters upon an extensive scale. For this we must be grateful while we may. A river once dammed, with its flow regulated, like a bird which has been ringed or a branded animal, is inevitably deprived of its entirely natural or wild character, since neither river nor animal is any longer quite as nature made it. Of making reservoirs, as of many books, there is apparently no end, and when the increasing demands of Torquay again turned water-wanting eyes towards the moor, it was upon the South Teign, the Dart's near neighbour that the thirsty gaze focused. So the Fernworthy conservation came into being. This did not materially affect the main flow of the Teign, the southern branch being a mere poor relation of the beautiful river which, drawing most of its waters from the northerly sources, rivals even the Dart and the Tavy all along its picturesque course to the lowland. Also the construction of Fernworthy reservoir presented none of the customary complications, involving only the purchase of a "marginal" freehold farm to the inundation of which no objections could be raised upon aesthetic grounds. Admittedly, beauty is in the eye of the beholder, but from my own point of view, Fernworthy reservoir is more pleasing, or at any rate offends fewer sensibilities, than most artificial "lakes"—conventionally to call them that which they are not. It was not offensive from the outset, mainly because a decorative setting had already been provided. To create beauty, water and conifer forest admirably combine, and the Fernworthy plantations, covering the adjoining slopes, had become well established even before the water scheme took shape. Also the wild effect had not been marred by the introduction of rhododendrons which, however ornamental in themselves, are scarcely compatible with Dartmoor scenery. They have been freely planted alongside the Burrator and Hennock waters, and it is curious that while exception is often taken to conifers as foreign to the landscape, the even more alien, because exotic, rhododendron is usually accepted without protest and regarded as ornamental. So of course it is, but none the less its presence around any pool imparts an impression of a private or park lake, rather than of loch or mountain tarn which an upland reservoir should resemble if harmony with its surroundings is desired.

Escorting many tributary streams, including the scarcely less beautiful but definitely minor Bovey, the Teign steers a comparatively quiet course through the green meadows of South Devon, as her journey, so spectacular in its early stages, draws to its end. Much frequented at the many beauty-spots to which she lends the main attraction, the Teign might still be described as a lonely or unsociable river. Excepting Teignmouth no town nor village has been built actually upon her banks, although she skirts many. Chagford gave her a respectful berth, and even her namesake Drewsteignton avoided the precipitous gorge down which the wild river had carved its way. In this they followed the example of the ancient hut-dwellers who also went well up when settling above the point where the Teign now leaves the moor. Perhaps the river had a more formidable reputation in olden times, but however that may be, she is no longer regarded as a stream to be dreaded above others when gathering waters roll. Nor is there anything notable in the final exit when, passing under Shaldon bridge, she meets her destiny in sandy Torbay. Indeed, one might say that the placid end of the Teign amounts to something approaching anti-climax.

One might again stretch fancy to the assumption that most Devonshire rivers preferred to seek a less turbulent home than the wild

Atlantic sea-board could offer. Like the Tamar, the Exe turned southward from a Somersetshire source and after a long run past Dulverton and Bampton along the deer-haunted woodland towards Tiverton, proceeded to cross the creamy heart of Devon—where red cattle· were probably grazing while Fairfax laid siege to Exeter, as cattle of every description are grazing there today.

Somerset-born, but destined to become Devonshire's principal river and to give her name to the Royal City, the Exe caused part of the city considerable trouble during the autumn and winter of 1960, by a tendency no longer to respect its own accepted limits. Possibly this is no new departure and was one of the reasons why the residents in the canny old times built high and dry. None the less the floods exceeded anything within living memory, not only affecting the Exe, but its tributary the usually innocuous Creedy. Excessive rainfall did not entirely account for the phenomenon. There had been wetter seasons in the past and more torrential downpours without anything sensational happening. It was rather a combination of effects, like the spates of mountain streams which do not always work according to expectations. A certain amount of flooding was common enough over the low-lying pastures a few miles up-river but for the Exe to overflow its banks to the same extent around the city was an occurrence without precedent. This happened twice, however, during the autumn of 1960, inundating more than four hundred houses in the built-up area of St. Thomas, extending down-river to the parish of Alphington and to Countess Wear, of Isabel de Fortibus fame. There was no loss of human life although boats instead of motor-buses traversed the main roads evacuating residents, and the damage to property was extensive. Indeed, photographs taken at the time suggested scenes in Venice rather than in Exeter.

When houses have been built upon a level which has since proved to be below the danger line, one may reasonably conclude that the possibility of flood had not been anticipated, nothing of the kind being customary. St. Thomas is an old district, formerly a quiet village outside the city boundaries, with a church the restoration of which dates as far into the past as 1656. All of this justifies the supposition that immunity from Exe caprices had been the rule, since old villages did not stand upon ground liable to be water-logged.

Inconsistent as it may seem, modern drainage and preparation of road surfaces largely contribute to swollen streams. The rough gritty roads of the past at least absorbed a considerable amount of precipita-

tion; now they absorb nothing, and instead of a layer of mud with the occasional puddle, during heavy rain one is walking in water, running or stationary according to the gradient. A macadamized road, like a pavement, is the wettest rather than the driest surface for the human foot to tread, and it is water that the speeding motorist disperses freely over the passerby who cannot get far enough into the hedge. During heavy rain many modern roads become running brooks, and with irrigation systems functioning everywhere to carry surface water to the nearest stream long before it would get there by natural processes, the flow of most rivers is augmented abnormally. Such, of course, are only minor illustrations of the many causes that contribute to the exceptional floodings of recent years. On the other hand, while the draining of bogs and marshes is certainly adding volume to streams, the ever-increasing consumption of water for general purposes should have the opposite effect. Such is mainly stored water, however, and the whole matter is rather a case of derangement.

The Exe collects most mid-Devon rivers, the Yeo, the Clyst, the Creedy, the Kenn and many tributary brooks, before meeting the tide at Topsham and expanding into her wide mouth, flanked by Exmouth and Dawlish Warren. There is no bridge below Countess Weir, the crossing from Topsham being by a ferry which last year got into the news through its failure to provide a boatman, and the consequent inability of a certain boy to get to school.

Dawlish Warren, famous for its golf course and as the happy hunting ground of ornithologists, also comes in for its share of the limelight. The English Channel, abetted by the Exe, has long shown an unkind desire to wash Dawlish Warren off the map of Devonshire, nor could it be claimed—even from the most benevolent view-point—that the sandy promontory with its parasitic caravan and bungalow rash, materially contributes to the beauty of the coastline. Efforts to resist encroachment, however, have so far restrained sea and river from more than substantial nibbling, and many golf balls will be lost and many chilly holidays endured before the Warren disappears, if such is its destiny, like Lyonesse beneath the waves.

One might paraphrase Byron to the extent of inquiring whether the river of gentle Coleridge association shall "pass unheeded here". In any case, no description of Devonshire waters could overlook the stream beside which the young Raleigh sat and dream-gazed into the glistening west where lay so much of his future. Yet the little Otter, also of Somerset extraction, has no particular significance in Devonshire

4

Burrator Reservoir near Yelverton

history, although giving names to more places than the magnificent Dart. Flowing mainly through populous country, the most picturesque part of the Otter's course is run before reaching Devonian soil. Hers is, in the main, a quiet way to the wild-fowl haunted marshes of Budleigh Salterton through which she unostentatiously enters the sea. Eastwards from the Otter, streams seek the Channel at widening intervals, the tiny Sid providing place-names for three parishes merely by the accident of geography.

The Axe comes last of Devonshire's south-bound waters and since the county has a propensity for attracting tourists, like the Tamar from Cornwall and the Exe and Otter from Somerset, so the Axe turned Devonwards to represent Dorset. Of all Devonshire rivers, by birth or adoption, the Axe with its main tributary, the otter-haunted Yarty, runs the least spectacular course. Indeed, for Devonshire its entire lack of feature is remarkable; as compared with the way of every Dartmoor river, no contrast could be more complete. The Axe threads no grand mountainous defiles where great oak-woods climb and hoary crags tower mile after wondrous mile. No ancient "castles" guard her route, suggesting a historic past. On her meadows domestic cattle graze peacefully, and peace is indeed the tone of the Axe, as she follows her desultory way through East Devon.

Unlike exclusive Cornwall, effectually cut off by the Marsland Brook and the Tamar, neither Dorset nor Somerset insisted upon a water barrier to sever any possible hint of connection with Devonshire. Dorset, indeed, asserts a very different character almost immediately the "frontier" has been crossed. Somerset and Devon, on the other hand, rather mingle than divide, and residents along the boundary—when passing to and fro—seldom know if, when, or where they have crossed the border. The name given to the Devon and Somerset Staghounds suggests a common country and topographically Devonshire should have included all Exmoor as characteristic terrain.

As remarked before, the Atlantic sea-board was unpopular with West-country rivers when the question as to choice of career arose, and few went northwards unless the lie of the land gave no option. Among these few is the little Lynn, known mainly for the beauty of its rocky valley until in 1952 it acquired a tragic fame. Before it actually happened, the Lynmouth disaster, if contemplated at all, would have been dismissed as a contingency entirely beyond the capacity of the Lynn, a comparatively insignificant upland stream of little importance, and as a source of danger entirely negligible. Yet after a cloud-burst away in the hills, this disregarded Lynn suddenly sprang into activity, like a dormant volcano, and acquiring unimagined power and volume whirled down the rocky valley, sweeping away every obstacle that barred its onset and claiming the grim toll of thirty human lives. It was a freak flood resembling those of Exeter and should not have been caused, one would have thought by any rain-storm, however torrential. The month being August, it was not even a case of melting snow. The entirely abnormal volume of water was partly attributed at the time to a number of deep grooves, scored down the hill-sides by timber dragged to the bottom of the valley. These may have provided easy channels down which rain water streamed as along pipes, instead of reaching the river by far slower natural pro-cesses. However that may have been, the tragedy occurred, and it should be noted that storms over other parts of the country during the same period took similar freakish forms, although upon a minor scale.

Most notable was one at Belstone. There, a mere runnel from the moor, scarcely even a brook, which a pipe normally carried under a parish road on its way to the river Taw, as suddenly as the Lynn, became a raging torrent. It swept away the road under which it usually passed with ample space to spare, and carved a wide channel through adjoining gardens and a meadow beyond. Here it exposed a number of peat-preserved birch trunks which had lain buried for centuries.

Unnoticed before, the behaviour of the Lynn has since been watched, and recorded over the radio during abnormally rainy periods, but even without all the precautions taken to avoid a repetition of the disaster, recurrence seems improbable.

If the Lynn flowed northwards because obliged, the Taw from a far more distant source on Dartmoor was also impelled in the same direction. Whether sisterly animosity towards the Dart made her turn away from their common birthplace at the outset, is a matter between rivers, but when once started down the long gradient towards the northern "in-country", she had no choice other than to proceed. Prevented from union with the West Okement by the great shoulder of the northern blanket bog, one takes the higher, the other the lower route, and it is the Taw which reaches the "in-country" by way of Belstone and its famous Cleave.

Taw Marsh, once the undisputed home of blackcock and ring-ouzel, had the misfortune to become the happy hunting ground of the water-seeker early in the present century. The immense natural basin, with enclosing heights which converge to a comparatively narrow cleft as the Belstone ridge inclines towards the opposing slope of Cosdon Beacon, seemed ideal for the construction of a reservoir with capacity beyond a water-engineer's wildest dreams. The first attempt to appropriate it was staved off however, the House of Lords returning an emphatic "No:" to a Bill which aimed at acquisition. Even as a stoat was inexorable in pursuit of a rabbit—and still would be if it had the chance—so the hunt for Dartmoor water, regarded as anybody's game, is unrelenting, and once bitten by no means involved being twice shy. Since the Water Board could not get water from above ground, the next best course seemed to get it below, where it came from, tapping the supply at its source. Authority to dig proved more easily obtainable than permission to impound. "Digging", of course, in this connection meant boring, and there was a great deal of imaginative talk, not necessarily among the experts, of a great underground lake beneath the heather-carpeted surface of the marsh. One had somewhat misty ideas as to its formation, whether like milk in the heart of a coconut, pure liquid as the term "lake" suggested, or after the character of a sponge in which an excavator would be unable to swim if unlucky enough to fall through the crust.

Seriously, however, the "lake" theory in the ordinary interpretation of the term may be discounted, since it would presuppose an immense underground pool with solid roof and clear depth of water. None the less, the bed of the marsh is unquestionably the source of innumerable springs swamping the surface and eventually leaking through to the river. Anyhow, the borings struck water—no matter what form it took—and that at a highly opportune moment, during the long drought of 1959 when general shortage prevailed. By a masterpiece of organization on the part of the North Devon Water Board, the newly found supply was distributed by plastic pipe-lines, laid overland, to areas most in need of it, meeting a situation which might otherwise have proved calamitous. This beneficent but sinister-looking improvisation wandered like a huge, black, earth-encircling serpent over the county. One encountered it everywhere, and to the question "Whither wending?", there was often no answer, its objectives being so numerous. Fortunately perhaps for the Water Board, the 1959 drought was followed by eighteen months of exceptionally heavy rainfall, during which period of respite the hastily improvised system was replaced by a permanent and ambitious scheme for supplying many parts of north and central Devon. Stacks of pipes met the eye everywhere, and the air throbbed with all the mechanical sounds which accompany the advance of "progress" through a normally quiet countryside. Crossing the Taw at the foot of the marsh and following its course below the boulder-strewn Belstone ridge, the passage of the pipes proved anything save unopposed. None the less, it was yet another case of irresistible force meeting hitherto immovable obstruction. Even the great granite rocks, upon which crowbar and chisel, manipulated by human brawn, made slow progress, could find no answer to mighty modern excavators and mechanical grabs. Alongside the rapidly shaping bed of the pipe-line, the boulders lay in more tumbled disarray than the original grand upheaval of ancient days had left them, and once clear of the granite, the way of Taw water through channels other than its own was comparatively simple.

All the same, considerable time must elapse before nature can totally efface man-made scars, no matter how skilfully camouflaged. The whole atmosphere of the valley, although restored to tranquility, nevertheless seems subtly changed by alien disturbance. On the western side of the stream heather covers the mounds thrown up by tinners, the "old men" of long ago. Possibly in a remote future, when thirst is quenched by a pill, and hydraulic service as obsolete as horse-power today, signs of the North Devon Water Board's activities will be considered as interesting as relics of tin-streaming have become to the present generation. In the meantime, while using the water, we regret its cost, not only upon rural rates but in the loss of Taw Marsh as an undisturbed beauty-spot.

The latest reservoir project, begun in March 1970, has impounded the headwaters of the West Okement in the deep and beautiful Meldon gorge above Okehampton, after encountering strong opposition from amenity societies. These courageous voices, with Meldon lost, had been obliged immediately to switch to yet another battle front. The thirsty attention of the Water Board was diverted to the Swincombe valley, site of the notorious Fox Tor mires (Sherlock Holmes's Grimpen Mire) where it met with parliamentary defeat.

At present, supplied by countless springs still overloaded after many months of saturation, the Taw flows on along a course too strictly defined to allow the slightest deviation. Although possessing incomparably greater potentialities for disastrous flood than the Lyn, to date she has done no further damage than temporarily to inundate fields, or carve a wide passage through cultivated land during spasmodic spate. She skirts the gardens—often at whirling speed—but at highest flood, as yet with several feet to spare below lawn level. Rolling past old mill-wheels which no longer require her services, and accepting tribute from all wandering waters between Exe and Torridge, she crosses the Plain of Devon, heading for Barnstaple Bay, invitingly spread for the reception of Devonshire's two north-flowing rivers. Never acquiring quite the romantic glamour of the Torridge, from source to mouth the Taw is still a splendid stream, independent because running mainly on her own power, and even on the lowland never entirely losing the wildness of the hills among which she rose and which overlook the greater part of her way. She has been spanned by many picturesque bridges, beginning with the old Gothic arch at Sticklepath which, although carrying the main arterial road to the west, was insufficiently wide within my own memory to admit more than one-way traffic, once indeed traditionally impeding the ample coach of William IV. The last and most important on the list is the famous Long Bridge at Barnstaple which has presented several similar problems.

Seven hundred yards long and with foundations seven hundred years old although rebuilt after two centuries of Taw and tide had "cried havoc" upon the first attempt, the Long Bridge of Barnstaple, like its contemporary across the Torridge at Bideford, has an individuality apart from its structure. It is the central figure in a body, not unlike the Church of England in miniature, possessed of considerable investment and endowment the proceeds of which are devoted, not only to its own upkeep, but to various charitable purposes. But once again, ancient custom has bowed to modern administration. The future welfare of the bridge rests with the Ministry of Transport which assumed responsibility for the essential reconstruction. It had already been adapted three times during its long history, thus the further widening by a few more yards constituted no great departure from tradition. With this object in mind, the innovations were carried out on the upstream side, so leaving the original character of the architecture unchanged when viewed from the seaward approach. In general effect therefore, the Taw may be said to have suffered less than many moorland streams from the demands of progress, and its waters still flow unimpeded to the sea.

From its birthplace shared with the Tamar on the lonely Morwenstowe Marsh, patrolled at night by the Will-o-the-wisp and in the melancholy of an April twilight by the scarcely less ghostly snipe, the Torridge starts uncertainly upon her way. The Marsland Brook having claimed the only easy passage to the Atlantic, the Torridge followed the Tamar's example and turned southwards—a route which at any rate offered a longer life and perhaps a more peaceful end in the English Channel. At Hatherleigh, however, she met the Okement whose forceful impact carried her back in much the same direction from which she had come. At any rate she had little option, for the great upheaval of Dartmoor with its encircling foot-hills towered ahead. While many rivers enter Devonshire, none emerge; by contrast, although many flow from Dartmoor, no river born elsewhere claims passage through her territory. Whether in reality the Okement joined the Torridge, or the Torridge the Okement might be a moot point. In any case, the effect of the marriage seemed to be that the Okement surrendered her name but very definitely took the lead. The Torridge, changing her mind and her way, was pushed along by her more aggressive even if lesser partner. And so, united, they proceed through beautiful, wooded valleys, curiously unlike the grand precipitous "cleaves" down which the head-waters of the Okement escape from Dartmoor, but nevertheless splendid woods of a luxuriant character unknown to the moor. The river passes old Torrington, placed like an eastern fortress city on its commanding ridge, to come at last to Kingsley's Bideford and the final tidal reach under the famous Bideford Bridge, so like that of Barnstaple in some respects, and yet so different.

2. Fishing

So, the north-bound waters of Devonshire make common cause in Barnstaple Bay, the only inlet that pierces the stern coastline, as though to receive them. In Elizabethan days both Barnstaple and Bideford were ports of considerable, if minor importance, as compared with Plymouth. Now neither Taw nor Torridge is navigable for big ships so far inland owing largely to silting, although it is doubtful if they would ever have carried vessels of modern depth. Silting is to some extent a periodical process, channelled passages into all harbours being subject to the effects of abnormal tide or flood.

The most ancient mariners of all still use the water-ways, however, and one of Devonshire's oldest maritime industries continues, when the long salmon run is on, to play a substantial part in local industry and commerce. Once considered illimitable, from all sides now one hears complaints that salmon and sea-trout no longer invade our rivers in countless thousands. Mackerel shoals off the southern coast are mere travesties of those netted long ago. With special reference to Taw and Torridge for the year of 1961, salmon fishers were promised at best a lean season. The harshness of the pill has been somewhat modified by a solitary crumb of comfort found in the theory that periods of plenty or scarcity occur in cycles covering perhaps five years, so that everyone can look forward to bright spots in the future, if he lives long enough. There is always, of course, the suspicion or charge that somebody else is getting more than his fair share, that too many are being netted at the river-mouth, or taken along the coasts generally and even that the much frustrated angler comes off rather too well.

All considered, probably the angler has most cause to complain. Figures convey very little, but a few years ago a personal experience gave me some idea of the lion's share claimed before the rods get a chance. Talking to a net-fishermen near the mouth of the Tavy, under Cotehele, I was invited to look inside a little shed near by. It was about the size of an old-fashioned railway carriage, and piled half full with great glistening salmon, representing that morning's catch. Since I had always been prone to regard the netting of salmon in the same light as netting partridges or snaring deer, I was as much appalled as impressed, and the memory of that shed always comes to mind when the controversy between rod and net breaks out afresh. All depends upon point of view, but it seems probable that apart from natural fluctuations, responsibility for the decline could be evenly distributed. The heavy totals of fish caught by all means in the comparatively recent past definitely suggest the reason why the number is not so great today. In his book on Exeter, Dr. Hoskins remarks that in pre-Roman times, the Exe was probably as full of fish as any British Columbian river at present. This is doubtless true, the reason being that Ancient Britain was about as thinly populated as modern B.C. The principal is world-wide and applies to everything where demand exceeds supply. The extent of that demand may be estimated from the prices now paid for riparian rights. £50 to £60 per yard has recently been realized for single-bank reaches of the river Taw, a fantastic figure, although comprising some of the finest salmon and trout fishing in the country. The actual price recently paid for the rights attached to the Duke of Bedford's estate at Endsleigh on the Tamar was not disclosed. They comprised both banks along a seven and a half mile reach, and when formerly held by Tavistock Abbey, were leased from Calstock Manor for an annual rental of £10. Their present capital value has been estimated at well over £30,000.

Needless to say, the custom of paying tribute to overlords in fishy kind, on the same principle as paying King Edgar with wolves rather than with cash, passed with the days when such dues were demanded or at least paid—not always the same thing. Persumably the payments were made on the staggered system. It seems improbable that the over-lord would have desired, in the language of Jorrocks, "all his wittles at once" and in such a case a rental of eighty salmon, to cite one example, might conceivably have caused more embarrassment than gratification if paid in a lump sum so to speak. The system of fish in lieu of rent passed out of fashion at an early date. It became too much of literally paying the recipient in his own coin, since the lords of land and water claimed riparian rights as they do now, although, in early times, for utility rather than for sport. The period during which the noble and the great first adopted angling as a pastime is difficult to deduce from history. One cannot readily visualize some despotic ruler of the past setting forth to cast a line from an insecure river bank. The retinue required for carrying his kit would certainly have stampeded every fish within vibration distance.

Indeed, in remarkable contrast with its present wide popularity, fishing was never described in early writings as a sport of kings or even of the nobility. Fish-hooks were mentioned in the Old Testament, but originally everything connected with the sport was described under the head of "angling". This was the case when in 1496 Dame Juliana Berners produced the *Book of St. Albans* which contained the first treatise on the subject, while later we find Izaak Walton publishing his *Compleat Angler*. Although by no means actually so, the term rather suggests the camp-stool on the tow-path business, described by Johnson in his *Sportsman's Encyclopedia*, published in 1831, as a favourite diversion of Londoners—adding with delightful but, I think, quite unwitting irony "probably for lack of any other". Scott depicts his Redgauntlet as spearing salmon from the back of a horse which—ruling out the horse —is a form of sport now mainly confined to night poachers with their flares and pitchforks.

One sometimes reads about "spearmen" of the above description transfixing salmon as they leap to clear a weir, but this may be dismissed as unrealistic—or indeed, a practical impossibility. There is nothing more spectacular in the river pageantry than the salmon's "jump", particularly when sunlight catches the great gleaming body as it des-cribes the dramatic loop sometimes with life at stake, since even a salmon cannot fall short on rock unscathed. King of all fresh-water fish though he may be, from a gourmet's point of view he is neither necessarily king of the table nor the angler's favourite. In both respects preference is often declared for the sea-trout or peal, unanimously voted a sporting fish, well worth catching from every point of view. This fine species, more generally known as the salmon peal, has within comparatively recent years become increasingly popular among fly-fishermen. Its size, of course, when compared with the salmon seems insignificant. A friend, who is probably the most experienced fisherman on the Teign and Bovey, tells me that the largest ever landed by him turned the scales at 8 lb. 5 oz. Far bigger peal have been claimed, weighing anything up to 15 lb., but none officially classified as such. These, in the opinion of the most knowledgeable, were really young salmon or grilse—distinctions unmistakable to an expert not always being recognized by the less experienced. Two Dartmoor rivers, the Taw and the Teign are particularly famous for salmon peal and I am confining my remarks mainly to the Teign as a representative stream more directly under my notice in this respect, for neither salmon nor sea-trout penetrate to the higher waters of my nearer neighbour, the Taw.

On the Teign the story of general deterioration over the years is much the same as elsewhere, due largely to the extraction of water to supply various undertakings—although a certain amount of allowance must be made for inevitable exaggeration. In the case of salmon, extensive netting at the river mouth again accounts for the lion's share of the fish, an annual total of 1,000 upon average being certainly somewhat disproportionate to a possible 150 taken by rod. As for peal, a total catch by rod on Teign and Bovey of 1,000 to 1,200 fish would be regarded as a good season, with an individual record by one good fisherman of about 150. On Taw and Dart as larger rivers of corresponding quality, the figures would, of course, be comparatively higher.*

From a purely fishing standpoint, Devonshire streams have perhaps suffered more than many others within the past quarter of a century from the extensive draining of adjoining marsh-land. This applies to Devonshire more than elsewhere since in most counties similar measures for agricultural advancement were adopted earlier. It means, of course, that while more water is actually brought to the rivers, or at any rate sooner than would have been the case by natural processes, much of the advantage derived from spate conditions is lost. Formerly after abnormal rain, such as heavy thunderstorms, fishermen could depend upon two or three days of favourable water. Now the effects of a downpour have passed off within a few hours, as the flood water reaches the river more quickly to be sooner carried away. These, incidentally, are the effects which helped to produce the Lynmouth disaster.

---

* Since the above was written, a sudden decline has taken place in salmon fishing, both by net and rod. Salmon disease in all the main rivers has been partly responsible for the scarcity of fish. In addition catches have been greatly reduced on account of netting in Scandinavian waters, a growing practice that prevents the salmon from reaching the Devon estuaries in their former abundance.

Devon is still, and always must be, the county of many streams and rivers, with the sound of running water providing an auditory background. They at any rate cannot change, although most of the little streams described in the Devonshire County Book, as running picturesquely through old towns and villages have since been covered, in the interests of modern traffic. Things like that, must be, and we can only bow to the inevitable. So leaving the rivers to flow on as best they may, we pass from ancient waterways to thoroughfares of a very different description.

VI

ROADWAYS

1. For Hoof and Tyre

WHILE Devonshire is the county of many outstandingly beautiful water-courses, she is also the county of many roadways which have no pretence to beauty. It has been stated that Devonshire's road problem is greater than that of any other county; also that the actual roads are the worst in England. Such may well be the case, since there are 6,677 miles of roadways with which to cope. They vary in character from the great A30 thoroughfare to the comparatively quiet "sunken" lanes where farm carts once rumbled and which agricultural implements now negotiate with difficulty and frequent execration on the part of their drivers.

The mileage given does not include the most ancient thoroughfares of all, the old and, in some cases, prehistoric tracks across Dartmoor. Many of these have for long been unused because no more required and comparatively few of them are even traceable today. There are no longer tinners to carry their wares from remote hut-settlements and workings to sea-port markets, or as they did in later days to the nearest Stannary town. Funeral processions are no longer obliged to follow the grim "trail of the dead" from the southern moor to Lydford, when burial elsewhere was forbidden. Heather and weather are fast obliterating even the once well-defined paths worn by turf-cutters and whortle-berry-pickers, trodden within easy living memory. So washed out and overgrown have these old tracks in general become, that even modern ramblers, if able to identify them at all, usually find it easier to take their own line from point to point. The cruising helicopter probably gets a better impression of the lines and systems they followed, which is a very different proposition from threading their doubtful course on foot.

Many "in-country" foot-and bridle-paths have also fallen into disuse, partly because so few people walk far nowadays, and indeed could not in modern footwear along paths churned up daily by riding schools. Again, until the recent registration of parochial rights of way, they were liable to be disputed or even blocked by land-occupiers who, not unnaturally, wished to discourage public passage through their property. A typical example is the cross-country track known and mentioned in most guide books as the "Mariner's Way", by means of which sailors were said to walk from coast to coast in former days, to reach either the northern or southern ports. Why they should have wanted to take this lengthy stroll sufficiently often to establish a recognizable route is a question that has never been convincingly explained. The alleged path, stretches of which are shown passing through every parish between Dartmouth and Bideford, seems to have made a special point of taking the most difficult line. One cannot but think that any "mariner" who trod it for choice must have been even more bemused than Coleridge's ancient representative of the profession. The roads in general use, however imperfect, would have provided a course no more devious, besides offering infinitely better chances of help by the way. One is justified in suspecting that the Mariner's Way, like the smugglers' path leading from every beach however unsuitable for smuggling, was a way trodden by fewer sea-boots than any others.

It is, however, the main road system of modern Dartmoor, rather than byways of the past upon which the problem centres today. This problem—like the system—has always been there, or dates as far back into the past as one need look. It has taken various forms all down the centuries, the main trouble being inadequacy. When royal carriages and subsequently stage coaches trundled along the highways, it was bad surfaces which jolted portly kings, or overturned the heavily-loaded public conveyance. Nothing could get along except at snail's pace and all who reached their destination were lucky. Now with surfaces as smooth as glass they get along too fast; competition to complete the journey sooner than anybody else, makes ultimate arrival equally fortunate.

The route by which Norman, Lancastrian or Stuart kings entered Devonshire and approached the Royal City differs little from the high-speed track of today, although to say that the identical roads are used would be somewhat far-fetched. The highway of 1970 with all its reduced gradients, widening, straightening, reinforcing and general remaking, has as much in common with the thoroughfare of 1066 as the old countryman's pocket-knife had with its original after various renovations of blades and handles. In some cases foundations of old Roman roads still support a modern surface upon stones themselves imperishable, planted under the eye of some autocratic centurion whose job it was to enforce proficiency. Roman roads, however, provided merely a skeleton service in more ways than one, implementing the system already in existence. Of course the traffic problem exists in all counties more or less, but is accentuated in Devonshire owing to the character of the roads which, with the exception of the main arterial thoroughfares, twist about as though to hamper rather than facilitate passage along them. Why they steered the devious courses when first constructed is variously explained, but never convincingly. As often as not, like the Duke of York's troops, they seem to ascend hills merely to go down again, when level courses were not only available but more direct. Rectangular turns when breasting a hill may have aided ascent, but they occurred just as frequently on the level—serving no apparent purpose whatsoever. We know that they evolved for the most part, rather than were ever engineered upon a big scale, and that they mainly developed upon a maze of miscellaneous tracks and wheel-paths. What we do not know, however, is why such tracks ever happened to be there, or since all the roads and lanes were more or less made and fenced at various times, why their constructors finally made them where and how they did. However, there doubtless was, as there always is, a reason for everything, although by no means necessarily a good one. The devious course of roadways may often have been due to a short-term policy of expediency. Old foot- and bridle-paths frequently hugged hedgerows leading in approximately the desired direction, to avoid the unnecessary trampling of cultivated crops, and when the necessity for carriage-ways arose it was usually simpler to follow the same lines. There would have been less opposition from landowners who might have objected to more direct routes being taken across their fields, and since the new roads required fencing off—which meant raising banks in those days some such barrier was already provided.

On the other hand many old routes were abandoned, possibly because they mainly served out-lying hamlets or farms and were too tortuous as wheeled traffic increased and quickened. It did not all happen overnight, As new roads were wanted they were made and usually followed the line of least resistance in every sense. There may be, and often is, some interesting local history behind some apparently purposeless twist or divergence. Some truculent landlord may have opposed its course over his property at the gun's point, figuratively or even literally. Similar difficulties often obstruct modern schemes, and in such cases, compromise usually proves the easiest solution. Occasionally too, thoroughfares were diverted to accommodate commercial interests, public or private. In this neighbourhood there are some extensive, although now disused, quarry-workings covering ground over which the road from South Tawton to Spreyton originally passed. This interfered with the excavations, so the owner of the property provided an alternative road, a sort of bypass round the quarries, serving the purpose although more circuitous and undulating. As more roads were wanted more were made by somebody, often causing many that existed to appear superfluous. The greater number of the old lanes only served for providing access to fields, with the occasional wayside cottage built merely because the lane was there, rather than the lane being there to serve the cottage.

Until Tudor times the maintenance of all essential road-services devolved upon the land-owners, then largely represented by the monasteries. Under Elizabeth, however, responsibility was transferred to the parishes, from which gradually evolved the present situation. Devonshire is still mainly entered by the Kings' highway, very literally in the plural, although royal visitors nowadays are more likely to arrive by air than by road. None the less, both the southern and central main roads converge as ever on the Royal City, the long-distance visitors who choose northerly routes when passing through the county not being very numerous. If few highways enter the county from the east, however, still fewer leave from the west, since to get out of Devon on that side, the Tamar must be crossed. South of Gunnislake this can only be done by ferry, and for this reason the opening of the new road-bridge across the Hamoaze in October, 1961, was something in the nature of a "D-day" for countless motorists. Waiting for the ferry had become, as often as not, a matter of hours—which did not suit the "speed king" at all—although apparently more people preferred to wait and pay the toll rather than make the Gunnislake round, which would have been quicker and more economical. This great suspension bridge is an imposing structure, out-towering and entirely eclipsing Brunel's once triumphal arch which, opened by the Prince Consort in 1859, for more than a century has carried the Great Western express trains to the Cornish Riveria. The new road-bridge was designed to replace the Saltash ferry service, and in its early days carried a vast volume of traffic, since any novelty attracts the tourist—and for that matter the general public likewise.

Actually, congestion on Devonshire roads is no new thing. Incredible as it may seem, the same problem arose as long ago as the days of the pack-horse. All roads until the end of the eighteenth century or later, in many places were distinctly perilous. They might be impeded by boulders, fallen timber, bogs, mud and deep pits. Turnings were obscured by thick hedgerow growth and trees—good lurking places for robbers, highwaymen and assassins. When Westcote, the historian, travelled through Devon in 1630, he wrote: "Passing from Chagford, we are travelling to the moor to find Gidleigh where, if we take not great heed, we may soon wander and stray, and so make longer stay in this coarse place than we willingly would." Whether the "coarse place" refers to the moor, Gidleigh or Chagford is not quite clear.

So bad were the "in-country" roads, in fact, that until early in the nineteenth century the Dartmoor tracks were often used in preference for pack-horse "traffic" trading between the north and south coasts. In those days, it was a real hazard, when walking or riding in a narrow lane, to meet a string of laden packhorses in full career, coming down from Dartmoor. There was no stopping them as they came slipping and slithering along on each others' heels. Their bulging loads filled the width of the lane, brushing the overgrown hedges on either bank.

As with motor traffic today, the danger to the general public became officially recognized, and certain safeguards and restrictions were imposed. Pack-horse drivers were obliged to have bells fitted to the harness to give warning of the cavalcade's approach—as cars must have horns in working order today. Then the number of horses in a "string" was limited to six or seven—that being the most that a driver was considered capable of controlling. When a wayfarer, on horseback or on foot, heard the sound of approaching bells, he made tracks for safety—either scrambling up the bank, turning into the nearest gateway, or availing himself of any natural "lay-by" until the whole string had clattered past. On the open moor, of course, it was easier to avoid these hazards and dangers of the narrow lanes. Thus, until the two main tarmac roads were made across Dartmoor in the 1790s, there was still a surprising amount of coming and going along the old moorland ways. Many of the old stone crosses still stand at road junctions, marking where a rough Dartmoor track joined an even rougher in-country road, the tall Marchant's cross near Meavy being one such example. That was a long time ago, and while the pack-horse ambles back to his shadowy pasture, we must return to the roads and roadsters of our own time.

In Devonshire, even as elsewhere, the traffic problem today may be dismissed in one word "insoluble", that is to say as long as motoring

Shipping at Appledore on the Taw—Torridge estuary
Hexworthy Bridge on the West Dart

for its own sake continues to be the main recreation of the "leisured masses". We have become, in true journalistic language, a nation on wheels, without sufficient room in which those wheels can rotate. On every highway and byway there is nerve-racking and often perilous congestion. In every town of importance, parking facilities are utterly inadequate. Every beauty or pleasure resort is crowded to overflowing, not by seekers of beauty, but by people seeking somewhere to go, and usually moving on to pursue the vague quest elsewhere. As for road accidents, little definite abatement can reasonably be expected until more drastic action is taken to prevent them. In Czarist St. Petersburg, before the days of cars indeed but when, as in Victorian London, traffic was a thing to be treated with respect, every vehicle involved in a street accident was automatically forfeit to the Crown. One might suppose that the confiscations reached astronomical numbers, but on the con-trary there were few accidents. Anyone who owned a carriage or even a cab preferred to keep it, and made a point of avoiding collisions. Were forfeiture of car and licence the penalty for misuse of them to-day, even English road-hogs would probably think twice—if capable of responsible thought, which sometimes seems doubtful. Road im-provement schemes designed to promote safety, and perennially in process, cannot do otherwise than have a twofold effect. Widening, straightening bends, and creating dual carriageways here and there certainly relieves congestion, but just as certainly and obviously tends to encourage a further increase of speed which is far too great already.

The idea of attracting either the travelling public or heavy traffic to the railways is unrealistic, particularly in a county like Devonshire through much of which no train has ever passed. The county on the whole is adequately and more conveniently served by roads, excepting perhaps between a few of the largest towns such as Exeter and Ply-mouth. In any case the railway came late, the first train reaching Exeter in 1844.

2. Iron Ways

Fifteen more years elapsed before Plymouth in 1859 was connected by modern means with the modern world according to the standards of the times, while various branch services came into being during the ensuing half-century. Even so, until the present day the lines have been few and far between, and now minor services are gradually disappear-ing. Many branch lines have been closed or are about to close for lack

5

Dartmouth Castle guards the river at the end of its journey

The famous Bideford Bridge before recent repair work

of patronage but all under protest. While nobody used them, everybody seemed to oppose their abolition upon sentimental grounds. The latter attitude is not always easy to follow since few were really old, and most were constructed and discontinued within living memory. No particular associations were attached to any and probably, when first laid, their construction was opposed quite as vigorously.

A typical example was the occasion when the branch railway line from Plymouth to Turnchapel ran its final trip in September, 1961. The life of the line was no more than sixty-four years, and during the preceding decade it had carried no passengers but merely trucks loaded with freight. Yet, for its last journey, a hundred railway enthusiasts crowded into eight vans, eager photographers got to work at every vantage point—even scrambling up the signals—while the embarrassed driver and his fireman were besieged by autograph hunters. The same excuberant pattern was followed with subsequent closures.

One of the most lamented closures was that of the little Princetown line, which meandering across the moor from Yelverton was seldom used within recent years by residents in either place. The main attraction of the line lay in its circuitous route taken to avoid intervening hills, and it was famous as a remarkable engineering achievement. Curiosity satisfied upon this point, however, few people made the trip twice, Princetown being a place made to avoid rather than otherwise. The quaint little train usually steamed to and fro carrying passengers who could have been numbered upon the fingers of one hand. Probably the most profitable trip was its last, the coaches again being packed with people making the journey for the same reason as many funerals are attended when little interest has been shown in the deceased during life.

The story of the Moretonhampstead line, now relegated to the past, was much the same—lamented when closed, neglected when available. Attempts have been made to keep this line alive by private enterprise but grass is growing along the derelict track, parallel with which the motor-buses run as an ironical example of past versus present. The closing of this branch has left the wide expanse of country between the main Southern and Great Western lines without rail service of any description. More recently all passenger trains between Exeter and Okehampton have been replaced by a bus service. The truth is, of course, that in the greater part of Devon, with its widely but thinly distributed population, branch railway lines into remote districts have outlived their original usefulness. The transport which they provided was too slow and inconvenient to meet modern needs. Private cars are now considered indispensable for everyday purposes by country people. It seems to be recognised that each member of a household when old enough should own a car. Indeed many young people have never boarded a train, or even regard such a thing as a means of travel.

Discounting private cars, even in places where rail service is available, as for example between Exeter and any of the main coastal towns, it is the competing motor-buses rather than the trains that are crowded to overflowing. One need not look far for reasons. Buses are cheaper, they can drop passengers wherever desired and they run into towns or villages which trains are obliged to skirt—sometimes widely. At Okehampton, for example, the station is half a mile outside the town, with a stiff hill to negotiate, so the bus is naturally preferred. It is not entirely a case of the road robbing the rail, since the convenient bus tempts many people to make a trip which otherwise they would not even consider. Bus journeys are often made simply because the bus is available. Were it a matter of an inconvenient train journey, most people would think twice before taking the trip. Indeed to a large extent the motor-bus service has created its own demand, rather than supplied a need. That demand, again, will probably lessen as the number of privately owned cars continues to increase. Speaking for the main A30 road here, the Devon General buses which ply to and fro between Exeter and Okehampton—a distance of twenty-three miles— are already running at a loss. Formerly full all the way, they are now practically empty for the greater part of the journey, getting little more than local patronage at each end. How exceedingly local that use is at times, would scarcely be believed. I have actually seen young people stand for half an hour, awaiting a bus to carry them a short quarter of a mile, any question of walking when wheeled transport was available never so much as arising.

Throughout the ever-extending summer holiday season, a constant stream of two-way traffic, commercial and tourist, roars along the highway that was once the quiet village street. Three miles to the westward is a bridge upon which one could stand for a long period of time looking down at the main Southern Railway track, seeing nothing but the comparatively silent way with its empty lines stretching into infinity. It is an anomalous situation. There is the seemingly obsolete and neglected railway, designed for carrying heavy loads and long-distance traffic. But passing over it is the nightmare of the desperately crowded road, designed for the peaceful use of the human race, rather than to provide a speedway along which humanity rushes to destruction. In primitive Eastern countries, still subject to outbreaks of the plague, the native population often prefer to suffer lethal epidemics rather than submit to preventative regulations, and a corresponding outlook seems to prevent any settlement of the road and rail deadlock today. Much of the traffic congestion is caused by immense and heavily loaded vehicles, for the passage of which the narrow roads of Devonshire are manifestly inadequate. It does not seem unreasonable to suggest that such should travel by rail, at least to the station nearest their destination.

Coinciding with the closure of the Okehampton-Bude railway and all its romantic associations, the quaint and in many respects unique little line between Halwill and Hatherleigh passed in 1966 from interesting reality to a picturesque memory. This little railway linked Torrington and Hatherleigh with Okehampton by way of Halwill Junction, where the Bude line also converged. It ran through country scarcely changed since contested by Cavaliers and Roundheads, along a frequently birch-fringed track, curiously suggesting a primitive Canadian railway. One almost expected the engine to be equipped with a cow-catcher—except that it was usually running backwards. Along this antiquated way, backwards and forwards in more senses than one, four trains passed daily, two nominally carrying passengers usually conspicuous by their absence, and two conveying freight—the length of the train indicating whether passenger or freight. One coach as a rule more than sufficed for passengers; seven trucks, the maximum usually being required for freight. The latter consisted of coal, agricultural materials and ball-clay excavated at Petrockstowe to be shipped at Fremington. Indeed, ironically enough, by transporting as much as 20,000 tons of heavy material within a year, this quaint line exemplifies one of the main purposes that the railways might and should serve. The only occasion upon which this Hatherleigh line appeared in the news within recent years was when one of the trains collided with a motor-bus at a quiet level crossing. The accident involved neither casualty nor serious damage, the main interest being wonder how under any conceivable circumstances it could have happened. Figuratively the incident depicted rival interests in violent competition, and both survived, so possibly on a miniature scale creating a major precedent.

It should also be noted that the first Devonshire railways, in their eminently primitive character, were designed exclusively to carry freight, the presumption being that people who desired to go anywhere could and would get there by the same means that they had always employed. The purpose of Sir Thomas Tyrwhitt's horse-drawn trucks along the Princetown line opened in 1823 was to convey coal and agricultural requirements to moorland districts, upon the outward journey, returning loaded with granite for local building, or export from Plymouth. The Haytor line, running or rather crawling and jolting over stone rails, served similar but less ambitious requirements. Also, referring again and for the last time to the Hatherleigh train service, the line was actually the late materialization of a project first mooted in the very early days of rail traffic, its object being to establish a service between Okehampton and Bideford, the nearest port—to facilitate the export and import markets.

In the same way as the old canal and disused wharfs of Exeter are being revitalised into a "marina" so another venture of the same sort has recently provided Morwellham Quay on the Tamar, with a "new look". Evidences of this once thriving little copper-exporting settlement during the early nineteenth century have long lain derelict and forgotten. Now the short canal linking it to the Tavy, its docks, tram-rails, and abandoned machinery has been rescued from a century's oblivion. All has been incorporated into a recreational centre complete with museum, restaurant, car-park and all modern requirements—including a full-time salaried warden.

So, for general utility, the railways may yet fulfil or revert to the original reason for their existence since history is very likely to move in cycles. Also there always remains the unexpected turn of events which figures so largely in public or private problems, and it is more than possible that neither road nor rail will provide the transport of the future. Some years ago, *Punch* published an imaginative drawing of a skyscape, black with aircraft, above a wide empty roadway, along the centre of which an aged countryman trundled a wheelbarrow. Apart from the survival of both barrow and its driver, which is improbable, the caricature might easily prove prophetic.

VII

HEDGEROWS AND WOODLANDS

WHEN Longfellow's lonely Indian listened to "the distant and measured stroke" of the pioneer's axe as it levelled the primeval forest, his emotions can readily be imagined. In a major degree they must have resembled those of more than one old Devonian country-lover when watching the modern bulldozer and chain-saw altering far more rapidly the entire appearance of some once familiar landscape. Speaking of Devonshire generally, the hand of time—wasting or constructive, according to outlook—has fallen heavily upon a county whose main characteristic had been the tenacity with which she clung to old conditions. The effects of both processes are obvious enough, but before attempting to sketch a portrait of change, it might be as well to glance for a moment at conditions as they were within living memory, in order to emphasize that change. All the same, Devonshire landscape is entirely unmistakable; one could not imagine oneself anywhere else unless possibly in a very circumscribed area fringing the south coast, where pine and heather slopes suggest similar stretches in Surrey and Hampshire.

Concerning hedgerows, or rather the great double-banks which are the most distinctive, strangers often inquire, not only how they ever came into existence, but what purpose they ever served. Both questions are reasonable enough and both equally unanswerable. I know banks six or eight feet high with corresponding tops along which an old-fashioned farm cart could easily have been driven, but for wood growth. The price of labour, although low, was relative to general costs, and in the case of the great banks, a barrier of less than half the size would have been preferable since not requiring the same amount of attention and upkeep. In some cases, these broad banks marked definite boundaries between cultivated ground and moor or woodland, but as this was not by any means the rule it clearly does not provide the solution, nor will an answer ever be found—for a very simple reason.

It is a curious thought that while enough hedge-banks could be seen in Devonshire alone to encircle the world more than once, no living man ever saw one made. Many old agricultural workers have repaired banks already in existence, but apart from neat little fences to enclose some new house and garden—a very different proposition—there is no such thing as a new hedgerow bank on the land. Those that exist have always been there as far as mortal men can remember, taken for granted, like the land itself.

Oddly enough, comparatively few big trees were ever grown upon these broad banks, but the wood which they grew often reached a great height, so that from a distance they gave an impression almost of avenues. This was often further enhanced upon rough hill ground where seedlings from the hedgerows remained undisturbed, and in course of time formed a fringe of coppice growth on the leeward side, higher than the hedge itself, some of these seedlings eventually forming fine trees. Indeed, throughout all the wilder parts of the county, that is to say along the Somerset and Dorset boundaries and over all the molinia belt—stretching northwards from Dartmoor to the Atlantic coast, these picturesque, if uneconomic, fences had become not so much features of the landscape as the landscape itself. In the molinia country many will doubtless be seen for some years to come, for, like Rome, they did not arise in a day, and their complete obliteration is not likely to be as speedy as that of the world's greatest cities might conceivably be in this "enlightened" age. "We have read about these things and now we're seeing them," was an exclamation that I once heard from a Canadian tourist when surveying a very commonplace landscape with enthusiastic delight. Enough will doubtless remain to inspire similar sentiments, at least for the near future. All is relative and that which has never been seen cannot be missed.

To all who remember, however, the changes are spectacular. The revolution in the entire agricultural technique began even before the last war brought a brief boom, since when small farmers especially have found it progressively difficult to make a living. The innovations applied to all parts of the country but the effects were particularly noticeable in Devonshire, because involving greater changes. In most of the southern counties the larger fields had already been adapted to the use of modern implements but on the rougher Devonshire farms there was positively no room for them. The fields were too narrow and irregular in shape and by the time even a tractor got under full headway it was brought to a halt by some hedge meeting it at a sharp angle. What with twisting and frequent turning, the ploughing looked more like the work of elephantine pigs, undeterred by rings in their noses, than the tidy, even furrows that the old ploughman loved to see. The farmer began to wonder whether quite so many hedges were necessary. He heard about a strange machine called a bulldozer which levelled hedges, as Minerva's lance laid ranks of heroes low at a stroke. In desperation at last and with great reluctance, the proceeding being costly, he decided to hire one to deal with some extreme case— and that was the thin end of the wedge.

Nothing is done by halves and the removal of every possible hedge-row soon became the fashion. Indeed, the one recognized policy when dealing with a tall hedge was to "rip it out", no matter what purpose it served. It was not all expense since many yielded quantities of fire-wood, and as with a naval man when relinquishing his beard, it seemed to become a case of "shaving the lot". Possibly that might read as a somewhat exaggerated simile. None the less, the policy in many instances has been carried to lengths that entirely alter the character of the countryside. One sees large tracts of land that resemble prairie, or at best the Wiltshire Downs, rather than West-country farms, and one can visualize a future when too few, rather than too many enclosures become the problem.

Another factor which has contributed enormously to the dis-appearance of tall hedgerows and their coppice fringes has been the ever-growing demand for firewood, as cost of other domestic fuel continually mounts. The price of wood, indeed, has also risen sixfold, and in reality it is far from being an economic proposition. All the same, £5 for a ton of logs seems less at the moment when compared with four times the amount for the equivalent weight in coal, even though the wood burns incomparably faster. It also provides inferior heat and proves less satisfactory in the long run, not to mention the labour involved in reducing it to burnable size. Anyhow, the demand often exceeds the supply and the most accessible wood has naturally been the first cut. It is usually easier to get near a hedge for loading purposes with a lorry, than to drive into some swampy tangled spinney, so the line of least resistance was followed. Thus numberless hedges which had not been grubbed up were levelled, in many cases leaving stumps too old to spring afresh, and the fence was maintained by barbed wire.

Coppice growth of every description is fast following the hedges in-to oblivion. Since the one conventional thing to do with a bank was to remove all traces of it, how much stronger was the argument for cutting down a spinney which served no obvious purpose whatever, except the purely ornamental. Also coppice wood, being composed mostly of saplings and "broods" or clusters of poles such as sycamore and alder, can be cut with far less labour than the tops of big trees which have fallen, or been thrown for timber. Therefore, while lorry-loads of green poles are frequently carted away for sale, many tops—although infinitely superior for fuel—often remain, and decay where they lie.

Further encouragement to eliminate coppice land was offered by a benevolent Government Department in the form of a generous subsidy payable upon ground reclaimed for agricultural purposes. This, however, like so many forms of Government aid was subject to abuse. The same benevolent Department, possibly not knowing human, or at any rate Devonian nature, apparently omitted to make the necessary stipulations as to the subsequent use of ground reclaimed at public expense. It was therefore just too easy for the owner of a rough coppice, or "brake" in Devonshire language, to clear the land superficially—the subsidy more than compensating him for the labour involved. Then payment duly received, if he did not consider that cultivation would be profitable, he handed all further responsibility back to nature. Nature, having received no share of the subsidy, merely reclaimed the ground in the literal sense; and speaking for one such area officially "cleared" a few years ago, nobody would believe today that anything of the kind had ever happened. The brake, actually a hazel coppice, looks much the same as it did before "treatment" and certainly the price paid for nominal clearance represents the only profit that it has ever brought to its owner.

Needless to say, one sees examples quite as striking in direct reverse, which was my experience not long ago when revisiting a well-known spot after the lapse of a few years. I was looking for hounds at the time and stopped at a very familiar gate which commanded a wide view over the adjacent country. Formerly it had opened upon a heathery slope separated by a thorn hedge from a birchy brake, known by the picturesque and appropriate name of Faggotty Copse—famous as a favourite haunt of the woodcock and the fox. For the moment I stood bewildered wondering whether memory or eyes or both had deceived me. Heather, thorn fence and birchy copse had disappeared as completely as a picture removed from a screen. I was looking upon a purely pastoral scene, an unbroken expanse of lush grass upon which sheep were grazing with no suggestion that anything as wild as the curlew's call had ever been its prevalent note. The triumph of utility over the aesthetic was complete, and judging from the avidity with which the sheep were munching the fresh green herbage, the conversion—like that of Shakespeare's Oliver—sweetly tasted, at least from their point of view.

The ultimate or probable effect of such "conversions" when predictable—a very significant qualification—will be discussed in another chapter. This is mainly concerned with the wild wood growth of a county which, as in so many respects, differs from almost any other. In Devonshire one seldom sees a compact wood standing among cultivated fields like an orchard—unless indeed within the confines of a park. Over the area from Dartmoor to Exmoor, once covered by the great forest of Donewold, the natural wood growth is now mainly irregular, stretching sometimes for miles along rough hill-sides unclaimed for cultivation and flanking most of the larger streams, in some cases for the greater part of their course. "Brave, beautiful, hanging woods be they, which fall about Dart where she runneth out of the moor," wrote Eden Philpotts through the medium of his inn-keeper story-teller; and although the description would in reality have been very differently worded, it is applicable to the course of almost any Dartmoor river. Tall woods escort the Dart, the Tavy, the Okement and the Taw along their tortuous ways from the great hills to the lowland. They cast their quivering shadows over the minor streams, such as the Walkham and the Bovey, and I once heard a visitor from Scotland describe the raven-haunted gorge of the Teign, where daffodils cloud the oak-covered acclivities like golden snow, as the grandest valley ever seen.

Devonshire's natural woods consist mainly of oak, as the name Dart implies, with birch prevailing in the molinia country. Charles II should certainly have hidden in one, but when making his escape, he apparently overlooked the potentialities of the country always so helpful to royalty when in trouble. Over the Woodbury country there is a considerable sprinkling of Scotch pine to mingle its fragrance with the scent of blossoming heather, but there, as upon Dartmoor, fires too frequently blast the trees, although in any case the Scotch pine can only be regarded as an innovation. It is listed in the *Flora of Devon* as planted or introduced, but perhaps originally indigenous. The tree has become widely distributed by natural means, although more common in the southern half of the county than elsewhere. In an earlier work I described the impressive "clumps" of pines which within living memory surmounted hill-tops, particularly ancient fortifications constituting landmarks visible for many miles. Most of these have disappeared, for the pine is not a long-lived species, and the demand for timber prevailed over the sentiment which had for so long preserved such features. There has been considerable speculation as to why they were ever planted, but tradition affirms that loyalty to the Stuart cause was the main reason. The Stuart dynasty being Scottish, the pine was its recognized symbol and its planting, therefore, a loyal gesture. The theory certainly coincides with the period at which most of the planting was done, and the prevalence of pine clumps in Devonshire is only consistent with the strong adherence to the Stuart cause, so notable among Devonshire land-owners.

Dartmoor's tree is certainly the oak although, upon the high moor it seldom attains any considerable size, owing mainly to altitude. If and when the area was ever more extensively wooded is a question into which one need not enter, since in any case it was at too remote a period to matter very much. There is no reason for supposing that within the calculable past the position differed greatly from that of to-day. Probably always, as now, there was the odd tree or cluster of trees —dwarfed oak, willow, or mountain ash self-sown and too widely scattered to attract much notice, let alone interest. They would doubt-less be much more thickly distributed were it not for the lack of birds to propagate them. The mountain ash, for example, is mainly confined to the vicinity of streams, since the ring-ouzels, the principal planters, seldom go very far from the valleys. Also seedling trees spring up amongst the heather, where their chance of surviving the frequent fires is slight. Now that bracken is replacing heather upon so many slopes, there has also been a notable increase of hawthorns, and if this trend continues many Dartmoor hill-sides will soon acquire a new look. No heather means no fires, and fires have certainly restricted wood growth on the moor side more than any other influence. Two of Dartmoor's three little natural woods owe their survival entirely to the rocks among which they grow and which no blaze can penetrate.

Being so few, these isolated trees become familiar objects to anyone who knows the moorland. During the past fifty years I have watched many grow, and witnessed the decay and fall of as many more—their remains disappearing within a surprisingly short space of time as the herbage covers them, or as the heavier wood sinks into the boggy ground. The latter, indeed, often happens, since the little trees frequently grow on the mounds of old tin workings around which the insidious swamp has crept. I knew a remarkable old holly beside the Taw, just under lonely Steeperton. Its leaves were seared and bleached with age and the bitter mountain wind, but it always produced a wonderful crop of berries, from which a judicious bunch could be picked at Christmas time if the supply was scarce in the lowland. Under such circumstances, one late December afternoon I walked five miles up the wintry way of the Taw, only to find that the holly-tree, like Faggotty Copse on the other occasion, was no longer there. The autumn gales, defied for forty years, had at last torn it from the bog-encircled hillock upon which it had stood, and no trace of it remained excepting a few inches of root protruding from the peaty marsh.

Dartmoor's three little oak coppices have been described so often in guide books and topographical works that old chestnut groves might be a more appropriate term for them. Each trooping alongside the eastern bank of its own wild river, the trees, bearded and hoary with antiquity, suggest ghostly garrisons of ancient fortresses. Piles copse, flanking the romantic but somewhat neglected Erme, has attracted little publicity because seldom listed as a special attraction to the sight-seer. Much the same applies to Blacktor Beare despite its far more spectacular setting of crag and torrent. Surmounted by the mountainous heave of High Willhayes and reaching tentative fingers down to the brink of the once whirling West Okement, Blacktor Beare has been somewhat eclipsed by its imposing surroundings. Lying off the direct route to any special point of interest, it was seldom penetrated except by fishermen until the construction of new waterworks upon the West Okement, not far from the copse itself, robbed the place of its remote atmosphere. The gorge is now visited more than ever before, not because of its stern magnificence, but by Water Board officials, few of whom notice the ancient trees—monuments of antiquity as compared with those of progress.

Wistman's Wood, so termed for courtesy's sake, being probably the smallest as well as the most famous "wood" in England, has captured most of the limelight for various reasons. Situated on the Dart itself in the very heart of the moor, it has naturally come to be regarded as one of Dartmoor's show pieces, and its remarkable character certainly justifies its reputation. Also it was the most remote of its kind, before the road from Moretonhampstead to Tavistock opened so much country until then barely accessible and little known. Now Wistman's Wood can be reached with little difficulty from Two Bridges, and numerous visitors can study the weird little oaks and speculate upon the curious place and its possible history. It doubtless gathers additional attraction from its romantic name, so suggestive of ancient lore and mystery. There is always a danger, however, of attaching too much significance to old place-names, so often bestowed from the sheer necessity of calling a place something. In the case of Wistman's Wood, the mere shape of hoary, bearded trees might have suggested ancient sages or priests. In reality, the name was probably derived from the Celtic *Usig-mean-coed*, "the rocky-wood-beside-the-river". In such a place there must always have been trees of all shapes and ages, from withering remnants to minute seedlings, providing full scope for the imagination—let alone superstition.

Actually, the grotesque shape of the trees in all these little woods is not as much a matter for wonder as is sometimes supposed, being largely due to frequent pollarding in the none so remote past. One can see very similar effects in the growth upon many old hedgerows, where they attract little notice, being taken for granted. They are just old stumps of no value as timber, and little even as firewood, owing to the labour involved in splitting them. There are definite records of wood-cutting in Blacktor Beare a century or so ago, and if this happened in one place it is only reasonable to suppose that it did so elsewhere. Where wood was scarce, fuel must always have been needed by all moor-dwellers from prehistoric times onwards. In old deeds confirming rights to take certain commodities, special exception was made in the case of green oak, the wood of the district. Since there is no reason for supposing that restrictions were observed more scrupulously three hundred years ago than they are today, places such as Wistman's Wood doubtless experienced some rough handling.

As the scarcity of timber developed during and between the two world wars, Dartmoor's lack of natural woodland did not pass un-noticed. There had been a certain amount of experimental planting on the fringes at Princetown and these having proved reasonably success-ful, efforts upon a bigger scale seemed desirable. That the moor with all her wide potentialities was not pulling her weight in this respect, appeared to be the official view, so acquiring as much available land as possible—mostly rough holdings and intakes—the Forestry Commis-sion set itself the target of planting about 5,000 acres. More than half of this has been accomplished over an area extending from Chagford Common almost to Dartmeet, and probably by the time these words are in print much more will have been done. The spruce, which has been so freely planted, definitely is not Dartmoor's tree since it does not take kindly to the heather, or the heather regards it as an unwelcome guest. Indeed, as a new experimental venture in forestry, it has been considered advisable to spray Sitka Spruce plantings with triple super-phosphate from aircraft. The theory is that such treatment promotes the leaf and branch growth to a density which discourages the heather around the roots of the tree.

Many of the trees have made and are still making fine headway. In the neighbourhood of Postbridge, where large plantings stretch south-wards down the East Dart and away to Bellever and Laughtor, a new settlement of forestry workers has come into existence during the past few years. Among residents, upon the whole, the development is regarded with disfavour. It is not so much the actual planting of the ground to which exception has been taken, as the species of trees planted. Close serried ranks of Sitka Spruce and other conifers in orderly array, within square, wire-fenced enclosures, seem scarcely in keeping with the oak coppices fringing Dart, Okement and Erme, or the deeper woods that shadow the reaches of Taw, Tavy and Teign. Many of us have an inherent love of the "green fir forest" of fairy-tale romance when it *is* a forest and the great pines rock and roar in the gale; but decades must pass before regimented artificial-plantings look any-thing but what they are. Meanwhile the natural character of the land-scape has gone. Fernworthy, where the present afforestation programme began a quarter of a century ago, has now acquired a character of its own, as the trees have become individuals assuming dignity and shape. Bellever, too, is losing something of its park-plantation aspect. But while Dartmoor is gradually absorbing these arboreal innovations, a new and far more serious threat has arisen.

Even as every hydraulic engineer, from Drake to his representatives of today, see Dartmoor as a land with "water, water everywhere" while he has "not a drop to drink", so every syndicate interested in forestry appears to regard the open moorland as a fertile plain where conifers, at any rate, would blossom like the rose. When first the Forestry Commission tentatively besought permission to plant their 5,000 acres, the idea had seemed catastrophic, although some people inclined to the view that upon purely aesthetic grounds certain featureless areas might be better afforested than devastated by incessant fires. When it trans-pired, however, that private syndicates were aiming at the acquisition, not of a mere 5,000 but 50,000 acres for planting purposes, the opposi-tion became more or less general. Exmoor indeed, was called upon to provide some 20,000 acres of this formidable total, but since the re-maining three-fifths of the amount would be drawn from Dartmoor's seemingly boundless store, the prospect becomes staggering.

The battle is now joined, and the Dartmoor Preservation Association, ably led by Lady Sylvia Sayer is fighting to save many prehistoric remains threatened with obliteration under the impending land or tree slide. Upon privately owned ground there is no legislation to control planting or felling. The aim of these timber growing syndicates is to obtain and clear natural woodland, replacing the indigenous growth with conifer. It is argued, and justice must admit truly enough, that very little of the wild wood ever reaches timber size. Oak scrub was useful to provide bark for tanning, as in the Teign gorge years ago, but bark has long since ceased to be a marketable commodity. Again, the planting of oaks for profit is a long-term policy. One must look centuries ahead before they attain their full value and it seems scarcely reasonable to expect land-owners, far less prospectors, to stock their woodlands with trees which from their point of view are worthless. So the oak-scrub is felled and uprooted and the conifers go in, although here and there an effort is made to preserve the character of some favourite beauty spot. Here in the upper valley of the Taw, a hanging wood was bought some years ago for felling and replanting. Actually it clothed one flank of the well-known Belstone Cleave, and the prospect of young conifers in serried lines mounting the slopes, where oak and mountain ash had clustered in picturesque disarray since Wesley's days, so disturbed the residents that funds were raised to repurchase the wood and preserve it for posterity. The reactions of posterity, however, like its taste and standards, are unpredictable. Incompatability with surrounding tradition is no safeguard against conifers becoming the popular trees of a not so distant future, with a public which takes them for granted. If the present trend continues, in the course of time the green fir forest may conceivably have become as essential a feature of the Devonshire landscape as of the many southern counties. Already in districts away from the moorland it is coming into its own. Around Eggesford, for example, where some of the first governmental affore-stations in England took place, noble woods now stand. Afforestation upon varying scales is extending all over the country and nature, which always helps the alien, is proving a strong ally. For miles around the plantings, seedlings spring up to mingle with any indigenous woodland growth that remains, and the more extensive the artificial plantings, the wider the natural propagation. In the neighbouring parish of South Tawton is a large abandoned limestone quarry with old workings spread over a wide area. Much of this is covered by fine soft-wood trees of many species, ranging from cypress to larch. Since they now form an impressive wood, I always assumed that they had been planted as a means of utilizing the otherwise derelict ground. In a recent talk with the owner, however, I was astonished to hear that every tree on the place had been self-sown or, more correctly, sown by birds which must have carried the seeds from plantations a mile or so away. This occurred over a period of some sixty years, and Devonshire's natural woodland may conceivably present a very different aspect sixty years hence.

Of individual trees I have said little, for although the county is well provided with its famous oak patriarchs, they are of mainly local interest and often prone to be figures of exaggerated size and tradition. Many were listed in the *Devonshire County Book*, and of these several have since gone the way of all wood which, like all flesh, has a common destination. One notable example is the Pascoe Oak, the preservation of which was made a condition of sale when the property upon which it stands changed ownership a few years ago. And since tree celebrities are not all oaks, there is the mighty yew in the churchyard at Stoke Gabriel, mentioned by Baring Gould in 1909 as the second largest of its kind in England.

On the little village green of Meavy still stands the shell of the celebrated oak, even now bearing some resemblance to the tree within the hollow of whose once immense trunk tradition affirms that local greybeards formerly congregated and, like Ossian's old heroes, discussed the deeds of long ago. Very little imagination is required to realize that it would have been quite the last place selected for such a purpose, owing to its restricted outlook, facilities for observation being a primary essential. Any village gossip of the past or present would willingly shiver in the open all day rather than miss the first glimpse of some interesting passerby. Today, at any rate, the vicinity of so venerable a relic is avoided by its human representative for fear that it might fall on him, since fall eventually it must. Indeed, the apprehension of such contingency is sometimes carried to excess.

Fronting the churchyard steps and the old Church House at South Tawton, upon a walled pedestal, stands a great elm, which has been subjected to periodical drastic pollarding. None the less, fears that it eventually might fall on somebody continued to trouble the nervous.

South Tawton was divided into two camps over the issue. It was obvious that the poor mutilated old stump could damage no property, even in the most improbable event of its fall, being separated from the nearest cottage by a space trebling its own height. The aesthetically-minded, therefore, urged the preservation of so venerable a feature;

Cold East Cross with its modern signpost

the practically-minded, on the other hand, had little use for sentiment and none for an old stump. The majority verdict was "get rid of it" and it only remained to carry out the sentence. The tree had acquired so hostile a press among its adversaries, that nothing short of complete uprooting seemed sufficient. No vestige of it must remain, and to achieve this end all available forces were mustered. The formidable demolition force duly assembled, while the out-voted objectors looked on like unwilling spectators at an execution. A high-powered traction engine had been requisitioned, and for this an unbreakable chain soon encircled the condemned but still resolute-looking trunk. The fateful signal was given. The engine pulsed and roared; the strong chain creaked and strained to its utmost stretch, but the actual state of things continued. The engine doubled its efforts and noise, finally rearing upon its hind wheels. The earth literally shook with the vibration or blast until a part of the churchyard wall, a few yards away, collapsed. Yet that old elm-stump, the imminent fall of which had been so dreaded remained as immovable as the Rock of Gibraltar.

South Tawton thought again. Since all the Queen's engines and all the Queen's men were incapable of making that stump budge one inch, the danger of its fall was dismissed as remote. If nothing could move the tree, obviously it must be allowed to remain and after the cracked and damaged wall that encircled its roots had been restored, a plaque was attached bearing this inscription:—

CROSS TREE

A TREE HAS STOOD HERE SINCE

THE DAYS OF QUEEN ELIZABETH

THE WALL AND SEAT WERE REBUILT

TO COMMEMORATE THE CORONATION

OF QUEEN ELIZABETH II IN 1953

No perceptible smile wrinkled the scarred bark of the old stump, so presumably mere wood has no ironical sense.

The old oak tree at Meavy

VIII

AGRICULTURE

1. Crops and Stock

IN Devonshire most roads and railways either lead to or diverge from Exeter, the nerve centre of the great web. In the former case the destination is obvious, but from Exeter—where? Excepting places along the coasts, such as Exmouth or Torquay—these being essentially holiday resorts, or Plymouth, Tavistock and Tiverton which have other industries, most of Devonshire's towns and villages live directly or indirectly upon agriculture. Apart from taking in one another's washing, so to speak, most of the inhabitants derive their livelihood from the country-people. Garages cater for the farmers' cars, shops for the needs of the agricultural community; from the principal stores, travellers—or roundsmen as they are now called—tour the surrounding villages, canvassing orders for goods which their vans deliver, while agricultural subsidies provide the banks with cash from which overdrafts are granted to people engaged in less lucrative branches of industry.

Farming is lucrative because subsidized, the existing conditions having produced the modern farmers, very largely ex-service or ex-professional men, comparatively few of whom could make a living off the land without state aid. There is a current convention that in order to get the right man for any job, he must be paid big money. The argument is applied to everyone in turn from the highest to the lowest. As often as not, however, the principle works the other way, high remuneration being always liable to tempt people with no particular flair or aptitude. In Devonshire, perhaps, the type of farmer has altered more than elsewhere, partly because it is a county which attracts people when retiring from the forces or from jobs overseas. Retirement is earlier than was once the case. Men still active need some occupation that will augment their pensions, and nothing seems simpler than to buy a farm, particularly since to do so has become the fashion. This has happened extensively in the Dartmoor district, which offers many inducements to men who think of adopting an agricultural career as a supplementary source of livelihood. Though, comparatively speaking, far from the madding crowd, it is "residential" country—picturesque and full of people doing the same thing.

Formerly, by general convention, West-country farmers were classified under two categories, the "working farmer" and the "gentleman farmer"—the latter term not necessarily bearing any relation to social class, but merely distinguishing the man who, under ordinary circumstances, did no manual labour. Naturally the distinction was largely determined by the size of the farm, which when big necessitated more supervision than actual work on the part of the boss. Also, the working farmer was recognizable in other ways. He came to market in a muddy "trap" drawn by a carthorse. The gentleman farmer arrived in a smart turn-out or, as standards rose, in a car. "This isn't like on the red land where the farmers drive their cars," was a remark once made to me by one of the "working" description. The working type came to market invariably attired in breeches, with black boots and brown leggings polished like glass by his toiling wife since in the agricultural community of the old kind, no male ever cleaned his own boots. The "gentleman", on the other hand, appeared in flannels and a tweed coat, with nothing to denote his occupation. "Do I look too smart for a tenant farmer?" was an anxious inquiry once heard from a young representative of the order, fearful that his appearance might influence the prices demanded of him. Now, of course, all has changed except in the cases of a few old-timers, regarded as quaint back-numbers worthy of notice because linked with the past conditions. That all farmers, excepting a few of the eminently primitive and fast disappearing school, now attend market in the family car, goes without saying. One peculiarity characteristic of the industry still persists. A complaint was recently lodged that in Okehampton on market days, the side streets are blocked to the inconvenience of the public, with the cars of farmers who will not pay the modest sum charged at the official and quite commodious parking-place.

There are very few large farms in Devonshire as compared with the general standard throughout the country. At the end of the Second World War, out of a total of 18,000 agrarian holdings only twelve exceeded 500 acres, and anything approaching that amount is considered large. Since the war there has been a great deal of reshuffling, with a tendency upon the whole to split the larger farms, rather than to increase their acreage. On the other hand, there has been a certain amount of amalgamation, and the frequency with which land changes ownership makes the position so fluid that figures become out of date almost as soon as supplied. The general position remains much the same however, the sale of old estates making little difference, as the farms are usually bought by the occupiers.

Concerning agricultural estates the position is much the same. Some time ago, I was discussing the question of wild bird protection as opposed to shooting interests with a friend who inquired how our big land-owners reacted to the problem. When told that we had none, he looked astonished if not incredulous; but such in the main is the position. Speaking for my own district in mid-Devon, I can think of no estate comprising 1,000 acres within an area covering a good 500 square miles. A few remain in other parts of the country, but they tend to disintegrate one after another as the old squires pass on, and throughout the country generally the "owner-occupier" farmer has become the rule rather than the exception.

The price of land, like that of wayside inns and house-property generally, has rocketed during recent years to a height which within easy memory would have been considered beyond sheer economic possibility. To mention one fantastic example among many—a 400-acre farm in this parish was bought just before the Second World War for £5,000. The purchaser sold it in 1956 for £14,000 and changing hands again in 1960 it realized £26,000. In 1964, this same farm, now reduced to 289 acres, was bought for £37,000. In general the values have multiplied by at least 500 per cent and in the case of one little inn not far away, the purchase price rose from £1,800 to £30,000 in a succession of sales spread over twenty years. This, of course, might be considered a purely fancy price and few land-sales could show so artificial an increase. Yet the general scale has been remarkably high, often apparently unrelated to the quality of the land.

The character of Devonshire soil varies almost as much as the landscape, including the best and the worst from a productive point of view. Indeed, it could scarcely differ more, ranging from the rich fertility of the sandstone areas, the South Hams, the Exe valley and the red heart of the county, a vein of which pierces the culm until checked by the Okement at Exbourne. The culm area extends over the greater part of North Devon to meet the wide shaley belt surrounding the Dartmoor granite. The moorland farms are mainly of the kind now described as "marginal" intakes and can only be brought to high productivity at a cost which leaves at best a narrow margin of profit, owing to the need of continual outlay. "We can grow as good crops up here as on the red land if we dress them:" was the remark of one hill farmer. "But they want so much of it:" he concluded. And "dressing" is so costly that it almost amounts to buying the crop, rather than cultivating it.

One notable development within recent years has been the definite improvement in pasturage. Formerly there was a convention to the effect that a sheep was the best manure cart, and on farms where large flocks were kept good grass grew as a matter of course. I have always remembered an answer given by the tenant of a rough hill holding to the owner's agent who complained that the land had deteriorated during his occupation of about five years. "You'm wrong there, sir. I've kept more sheep on it than anyone did before, so the ground *must* be better." Such was the view held among farmers of every type, and upon land of every quality. Fashions change, however, and nowadays procedure is largely governed by the subsidizing systems, and the policy directed for the time being by the Ministry of Agriculture. Farmers are encouraged to concentrate upon first one line of production, then another according to the prevailing need of the moment. A decade or so ago for example, milk production became the official policy and throughout the West Country, except upon the high moorland, sheep went off the map to all intents and purposes. Indeed, in the course of a journey from Swanage to Okehampton, passing through the best of two counties, I saw nothing in wool whatsoever. Cattle of every description were there, from the alien Friesian to Devon's own "Red Ruby" but when commenting upon the absence of sheep to a farmer on the Dorset downs, he replied with an air of complete finality—"Oh, nobody keeps they now." That was in 1949, but now, over twenty years later, the fields are again covered with them. My nearest neighbour, who in 1950 had given up sheep-farming ostensibly for ever, was shearing 300 a few days ago. These were confined for the following night in a field adjoining my garden, and since the weather was cold and the sheep expressed their discomfort in interminable vociferation, I found myself regretting his change of policy.

A sheep is a sheep wherever it may be but each county, or even each district specializes in some particular variety. In Devonshire, where such widely different conditions prevail, several more or less distinct breeds may be seen. Devon Close-Wool and the Devon Long-Wool are popular, while the South Hams—which produces the finest type of cow native to the county—can also claim an outstanding sheep, usually known as the South Devon. It is somewhat higher in the leg than most others of its kind and is easily recognizable. Dartmoor sheep, so termed from long custom since they have predominated for half a century, are strictly aliens, being mostly of the Scotch hill variety—little, lithe, heavily-fleeced animals which might now be regarded as natives of Devonshire. They are mainly notorious for their aptitude at breaking bounds, having seemingly inherited the Scottish Highlander's propensity for descending from the mountains to raid the surrounding lowlands. A fence that can exclude almost anything else on four legs—or two for that matter—does not necessarily deter a Scotch sheep for a moment, and since around Dartmoor commons the law which obliges a farmer to enclose his own stock is reversed, land-occupiers often have their work cut out if they wish to preserve their property. My own garden is protected by the river Taw and a thorn hedge. From a Scotch sheep's point of view, however, a mountain stream with its protruding boulders is merely a stage set for long jumping practice; as for a bank, thorns or no, there the slogan is "Excelsior". Despite the long fleece, where a black head can penetrate, the rest will follow, and to find two or three on the lawn, quietly accepting all the hospitality offered, is a common occurrence. Stout galvanized iron netting, of the type known as pig-wire, is the only form of fence that effectually excludes them and this is largely used along the moor boundaries today. It is safer than barbed-wire however close and tightly strained, since the push and go policy which is the Scotch sheep's method of dealing with any obstruction frequently gets it into difficulties. I have extricated many from both wire and briar entanglements and as the sheep persistently pushes and does its best to "go", even during rescue operations, the process leaves much to be desired.

It is rather curious that being the country showing the largest sheep population and six breeds of its own, with so many traditions and so much of its commercial background associated with wool, sheep rearing in Devonshire has never acquired quite the same romantic atmosphere that clings to the South Downs, the Pennines or the "Owd Bob" country. The "shepherd" of Devonshire has never been the picturesque figure who as described by Tennyson "gazed on the evening star"; indeed upon Dartmoor there has never been such a personality in the conventional sense. The individual who earlier in the century made prison if not actually political history, under the title of the "Dartmoor Shepherd", acquired it by a combination of accidents. The man who runs sheep on Dartmoor is a flock-owner who merely herds them or rounds them up now and again for some special purpose, and there is no "shepherding" about it. In Devonshire no "drowsy inklings lull the distant fold" as could be heard in many counties, for even upon high Dartmoor—where such a practice might have been considered essential—no sheep wears a bell. Again, sheep-herding has never attained the high standard of art found upon the northern Fells, where sheep-dog trials are taken more seriously than hunt-races in the South.

Sheep-dog trials have indeed been introduced into local fairs or shows held on the fringes of Dartmoor. These, however, lack the genuine local colour that would be found in a ploughing match or sheep-shearing competition, most of the competitors coming from far afield and bringing their own atmosphere—which may not necessarily be that of the Fells. The West-country, or particularly the Dartmoor, dog deals with different situations, is accustomed to different handling, and responds to a different language, not always literally. In a ploughing match, on the contrary, a man is doing his habitual work and there is nothing artificial about the proceeding. Also it should be mentioned that sheep-herding upon Dartmoor differs from that upon the lowland farms, since it is "herding" pure and simple. There is no folding, or close attention paid to the flock which runs virtually wild. The "shepherd"—so termed for the sake of convenience—rides upon his round, which may be made two or three times a week, and there is no walking among the sheep with the conventional crook. I only knew one man who ever went afoot, which would indeed be beyond the ability of many. He was probably the nearest approach to the picturesque shepherd of tradition seen upon the moor within living memory. Crook in hand, he walked from choice many miles over the hills, accompanied by a dog who would follow no other. This man eventually met his death crossing a moorland stream by some strange mischance which only the dog witnessed.

To obtain a realistic picture of any county or country, one must look not so much at its past which is over, but rather at its present state which is the outcome of its past. Devonshire is a county of mixed farming, two-thirds of its agricultural area being pasture. In the main it was never a wheat growing county, wheat only forming about 4 per cent of the cereals grown, the South Hams and the Exe valley being the districts where the best crops are produced. Over the hilly country and the culm area, which might be described as the central and western plain of Devon, the land of clay and molinia grass, oats have always predominated, and such is still the general picture, with the addition of barley and of more modern crops, such as kale and sugar beet.

Kale, as a more or less general food for stock, has been perhaps the most notable innovation. Formerly disregarded or little known, its value is now so widely recognized that it is grown upon most of the larger farms, five out of six being the present ratio. Its main purpose is to supplement hay for milk production. Upon a rough average a quarter of an acre is expected to provide enough kale for one cow's consumption during the winter months. Apart from its use to the farmer, kale has acquired a national reputation among sporting people, owing to the cover that it affords for foxes, but more about that in another chapter. On the other hand, the few people who still walk on Devonshire by-roads, and indeed at times the exploring motorists, regard kale—or at least its transport from field to farmyard—without unmixed enthusiasm. When carried by tractor from well "paunched" clay land, its passage along the roads is marked by layers of mud shed from the wide wheels, to clean which before entering upon the highway, is a legal obligation more frequently neglected than honoured. Possibly the farmer, like the seller of lewd postcards, finds it more profitable to pay an occasional nominal fine and continue business as before.

The most significant change perhaps in modern farming, is the general increase of milk production and sale throughout the county, this being the main reason for the wide introduction of Friesian cattle and blood into the dairy stock. The famous South Ham breed in many districts is still popular, but a notable example of the changing fashion has been the sale of the famous Dartington Herd of South Devons. It is understood that Friesians and Ayrshires will take the place of the tawny cattle which were once so characteristic a feature of the landscape.

Years ago, the dairy farmer took large baskets of butter to the nearest depot daily or every other day according to the season, and this, apart from the calves, brought in the main profit. £10 per annum was supposed to reach the household exchequer via each cow's udder, the yield being skimmed and the cream churned by hand—a most laborious process in hot weather. The skimmed milk went to make swill for pigs, or as supplementary food for the older calves. Now the big butter-baskets are forgotten, and few of the young farmers of today have ever seen one. Now the milk is piped direct from the "parlour" into a Milk Marketing Board's sterilized container, driven up to the door. Outside more isolated farms, or at crossroads, small wooden platforms are still used for standing the regulation churns to await official collection. There are still farmers of the old school who cry in the wilderness, deploring the changed methods, declaring that each gallon of milk carried away represents that equivalent of nourishment taken from the land. Formerly, they say, everything was fed back to renew fertility; now most of it goes away, with only artificial fertilizers to take its place.

None the less, whatever veteran agriculturists may think of changing policies and methods, their successors, in Devonshire at least, seem to be full of enthusiasm and efficiency. Nowhere has the Young Farmers' movement made more satisfactory headway. In competitions, at any rate, its members have excelled. The cup annually presented by the National Farmers' Union to the county gaining the highest maximum points in national shows was won by the Young Farmers' Clubs of Devon eight times during the first ten years of the competition, and this in a county that has always been regarded as slow in abandoning tradition or adopting modern innovations.

The "working farmer" always worked far harder than any of his labourers, since with him there was no downing of tools at any recognized time. If possible, today he works harder still having fewer employed hands to help him, while his modern representative of the new class takes life even more seriously. The work seems to grip him, like golf grips the golfer, or fishing the fisherman, to the exclusion of everything else. One sees men, who were once keen on field sports for example, gradually relinquishing all their former relaxations, giving up their hunters and settling down to an existence which neither they nor their wives would have considered conceivable not so many years ago. Nevertheless, hard as the work may be, the primitive character of the farm-house and life within it has mainly passed away. The younger workmen no longer "live in", to sit around the kitchens on hard benches or settles during the long winter evenings. They live in their own homes, usually marrying early, and come to work by motor cycle or even car. The old cobble floors over which hob-nail boots once clattered and the crude but efficient cooking facilities have given place to floors that polish easily and stoves of the latest design; the stiff benches or settles to easy chairs from which the television screen can be watched. Gone too are the days when milk pails were washed in the nearest stream, when water was carried by bucket to the bull in his stall, and a bathroom was considered a luxury. I have referred to the very active interest taken in Dartmoor streams by various Water Boards, and when distributing the flow of river and brook over the county by

other than their natural channels, neither the bull nor the milk pails—
not to mention the much-needed bathroom—have been forgotten.
No area is considered too remote to be beyond the reach of an adequate
water-supply; new taps are running—often to waste—in numerous
farmsteads and cottages where such privilege was not only unknown,
but would have been considered quite beyond the housewife's wildest
dreams, twenty or even ten years ago.

In 1960, the North Devon Water Board alone laid eighty-six miles of
main pipe-line, connecting 265 farms, and unless a nuclear bomb renders
any further provision for human needs unnecessary, the programme
envisages an annual average addition of 250 farms during the next few
years. Clearly, should such an estimate not prove too optimistic, there
should be few agricultural holdings in the county where the teapot
need run dry, or ablution in any form present difficulty. Yet misgivings
there are, not all concerned with possibilities from behind the Iron
Curtain. Many pipe-lines have still to be laid, each increasing the drain
upon a reservoir capacity, and already the supply does not appear to
be inexhaustable. One particular shortage I remember occurred in July
1961 when drought prevailed and loud-speakers paraded the village
urging the necessity for restraint in the use of water, while posted
notices, expressed more forcibly, could be seen on any hoarding. When
inquiring of my barber, a keen fisherman in Okehampton, whether he
had been out lately, he replied bitterly—"What's the good! No water
in the river."—and a glance at the Okement, a hundred yards away,
amply justified the complaint. The Taw, winding down its valley,
trickled forlornly around its boulders—and all this in July, October
being regarded as the month when normally streams are low. This
state of affairs was far from being solely due to the amounts as yet
extracted; all streams at that point were low, and the demand was still
in its minimum stage. There will be more dry summers, and with
future consumption many times multiplied while pipe-lines spread
like a spider's web over the county, one wonders whether even the
crystal rivers of Dartmoor can transform agricultural Devonshire into
a land flowing with milk and, as a means to that end, water.

Innovations have not been confined to water schemes, and in the
"cream country" even as elsewhere, both the principle and technique of
farming have so completely changed that few of the old methods and
crafts remain. I should here diverge to mention that in spite of a convention to the contrary, cream remains an indispensable item on the
Devonshire bill of fare. It no longer appears in the harvest field, how-

ever, since harvest teas have passed out of custom with the conditions which they accompanied. The old waggons, the waggon-loaders, the pitcher and the rick-maker have gone and with the horse-drawn waggon and plough went also the horse. A few survived for a while, being used for odd jobs at which a tractor seemed too much like applying a sledge-hammer to a hazel nut. As each went the way of all flesh, however, it was not replaced, and I have not seen a heavy horse at work or in action for many years. One, indeed, still lived, or rather existed, in the parish, a retired minister very much without portfolio. He could be seen any day, supporting his weight in a field within slow-walking distance of a gap in the hedge, over which a "burn-ropeful" of hay was occasionally thrown as supplementary subsistence allowance. The venerable creature suggested Kipling's "mountainous mammoth, hairy" and very much "alone" with his recollections. His labours came to a sudden end one day, when the shaft of the even more ancient cart which he drew detached itself from the remainder of the vehicle. That remainder lay on the wayside where the brambles enveloped it and the sole task left to the old horse was to support the weight of his own head —a task which he appeared to find more than sufficient. After a while he found another pastime, having been transferred to a meadow adjoining the main arterial A30 road. From this he was separated only by a low wall, over which his head hung comfortably while he watched the traffic, moving at a pace so unlike his own. That his head blocked the pavement, obliging the pedestrian to digress, was immaterial from his point of view, and the passerby gave him a benevolent pat before stepping into the roadway. Picturesque as it was, one cannot regret the passing of horse-labour, so toilsome to man and beast. Homewards was not the only "weary way" that the ploughman plodded, and the miles that he trudged behind his team through earth and dust in the course of an eight-hour working day need only be calculated. Little wonder that his successor prefers the seat of a tractor, with the dust behind rather than all over him.

Farm-work now means the use of the latest mechanical devices, and fields too small or rough to make their employment possible are merely abandoned to pasturage, or in the case of the more primitive Dartmoor holdings, they just revert to the wild. The old wooden five-bar gates, over which the ambitious fox-hunter jumped and courting couples dallied, have gone, replaced by wide iron structures to accommodate moden implements. Iron fences eliminate the necessity for hedge-trimming and electric wire replaces the hurdle.

I have remarked that Devonshire has always been slow to adopt innovations, but curiously enough it was the first Western county to introduce one of the latest. This happened at remote little Hatherleigh, mainly noted as a holiday centre for fishermen. It took the form of an imposing erection known as a Harvestore, standing sixty feet high, in a steel frame with glass-lined interior. Its main function appeared to be the manufacture of "haylage", a hybrid form of fodder embodying hay and ordinary silage. It claimed a storage capacity for feeding seventy cows during the winter months. Regarded as a nine days wonder upon its first appearance, it does not seem to have become as essential a feature of the farmstead as some of the more elaborate installations which have revolutionized agriculture throughout the country generally.

It is to be hoped that people who live appreciably near a "Harvestore" in the years to come will find haylage less odoriferous than silage without the hay. From living in an old farm-house, with the buildings which once belonged to it at a distance not always sufficient, I know from experience that silage can have one definite disadvantage. The discovery was made during the last war when my neighbour, who fed his cows in the yard, decided to try the form of fodder so highly recommended by the Ministry of Agriculture. The preparation of silage, however, requires experience, lacking which, it can diffuse a smell both penetrating and atrocious. We were living at the time in nightly expectation of air-raids, with the possibility of poison gas always on the agenda. The gaseous attack from which we actually suffered, however, seemed scarcely less obnoxious since it permeated the house, even to the extent of tainting the strictly rationed provisions in the larder. My neighbour assured me that—"It wouldn't be so bad when the wind changed." But the wind was unco-operative, and under the circumstances we could do no more than grin and bear it—or rather bear without the grin.

For every branch of farm-work, excepting perhaps the singling of roots, or the surgical treatment of animals, there is now some modern contrivance as revolutionary as the self-binder was considered, when it made its appearance early in the century. It was considered as wonderful as the modern combine harvester, and the farmer long-sighted enough to buy one, found himself and his machine in wide request, being hired to cut all the corn in the district before he had time to think about his own. The usual consequence was that the machine broke down under the strain and my boyish impressions of self-binders in Devonshire was rather of their being themselves bound or otherwise repaired in some corner of a field. That was long ago, and the three-horse self-binder is now almost as antiquated as the ancient waggon or the sickle.

With the old crafts have passed the men who excelled at them, the broadcasters or hand sowers, the scythesmen, the hedgers, the hurdle-makers and many more. By a somewhat curious convention in the West-country, it was customary for the head "waggoner" or horseman on a farm always to sow the crop, when done by hand. Better broad-casters might be available, none the less, it was the waggoner's or carter's special job, and upon that one occasion while he scattered the good seed on the land, a substitute worked his horses up and down, harrowing the newly sown ground.

Today there is no such person as the agricultural labourer once so freely caricatured in comic songs as a figure of primarily bucolic tradi-tion. He has passed with the primitive conditions to which he belonged, even as modern farming bears little resemblance to that of half a cen-tury ago. The old fashioned labourer was highly skilled in his own department, but his craft was mostly of the manual kind, the qualifica-tions required of him being comparatively simple. The agricultural worker of today, however, needs to be a skilled mechanic with the standard ever rising as more and more complicated machinery comes into use. Some knowledge of scientific farming is also considered essential and most youths contemplating a career upon the land attend an agricultural college as well as undergoing a course of practical training at some garage where the most up-to-date implements are repaired and maintained.

From this comprehensive and specialized education, the boy emerges with qualifications higher than those required for merely elementary work. The inevitable consequence is that more seek jobs as farm managers than as tillers of the soil, in which latter subservient position few are content to remain for any length of time. One might visualize a future in which more farm managers are available than men requiring management. The same principle, however, applies to modern industry generally, and the problem will doubtless provide its own solution.

The principle of communal harvesting or cultivation generally, under which groups of farmers combine their mechanical resources, so far has not been as widely adopted in Devonshire as in some counties. Cultivation not being so intensive, the crops are dispersed over wider areas. The machines available are fewer and as an inevitable consequence too many are needed at the same time in places far apart. While crops upon one farm are harvested, those upon another have to wait and favourable opportunities in the way of weather and the condition of corn or hay are lost. On the whole, therefore, farmers who do not possess the most modern machinery, find it more satisfactory to employ contractors who will come when required and bring full equipment—at a price. The agricultural columns of local papers contain frequent advertisements issued by firms prepared to undertake work of every description, and cultivation as well as harvesting by contract will certainly become more customary as time goes on. It may be, and is, costly at the time, but upon the other hand it obviates the running expense of labour, which often amounts to mere "retaining fees", and over long periods may be quite unprofitable.

Upon a reverse but somewhat similar principle, one sees crops of standing hay grass or corn offered for auction or private sale, to be harvested and taken away by the purchaser for consumption elsewhere. To this the die-hards might well take exception, and with every justification, since a more blatant system of land robbery could scarcely be conceived. It is reminiscent of the days during the First World War, when the Government requisitioned the best available ricks, to provide fodder for the vast number of army horses and mules then in use, not to mention commandeering every reasonably sound light horse which could not be hidden by its owner. That was regarded as a temporary policy, admittedly undesirable and only employed as an emergency measure. Old farm leases almost invariably contained clauses providing against such practices. They prohibited tenant farmers from selling hay, roots other than potatoes, straw unless in the form of reed for thatching, or any cattle fodder. The prohibition, of course, only applied to sale for removal. A tenant was at full liberty to sell any kind of "keep" to be consumed on the spot, and it often happened that in the case of impecunious farmers, or those who employed little labour, their crops were eaten by cattle—and particularly sheep—other than their own. As far as fertilising the land was concerned, it mattered little to whom the sheep belonged. In general a farm benefits mostly from stock perennially kept upon it; again, upon the whole, it is more likely to deteriorate under an owner-occupier who is at liberty to adopt short-term policies, and is responsible to nobody but himself. This applies not only to cultivation but to the general upkeep of a holding and in my own locality, where almost everyone owns the land that he farms, one may see examples of misuse and deterioration that would be unthinkable on any tenancy.

Such instances, however, are only here and there. Upon the whole, the owner-occupier, mostly of the modern type, is enthusiastically busy upon his farm, employing all the methods that the new age has produced. In many cases he is fresh from an agricultural college, with all the latest technique at his fingers' ends. Watching the "young farmers" at work and listening to their eager discussions on the radio, it is a curious thought that so many of them cannot remember other conditions, nor visualize a past when there were no combine harvesters, harvestores, electric fences or milking parlours; when cows were milked by grubby hands and toxic sprays on fields devoid of hedges and grazing beasts were unknown. The transformation is like a new building upon an old site, but bearing no resemblance to that which it has replaced.

2. Rabbits

The change of outlook is also as different as the change of method. One type of agriculturist that will be seen no more is the rabbit-shooting farmer. Once prevalent in Devonshire, he is now virtually an extinct species, and his decline had set in long before the rabbit—for the time being, at any rate—had ceased to be a problem. Indeed, the decrease of rabbit-shooting was the main reason for the rabbit's increase, inconsistent as it may seem. The younger men found ferreting tedious and when, as the big estates were sold, the farms with full sporting rights came into their possession, pheasants and partridges proved more attractive game, as long as any remained. "I wish the rascal would ferret some hedges, instead of going after those wretched snipe all day," was the remark of one farmer, referring to a younger brother, and the complaint was general. The rabbit, indeed, has lost its niche in the agricultural scheme. Once taken for granted, desired or otherwise according to point of view, it was turned to as profitable an account as possible, and upon waste ground—of which there was, and still is a great deal in Devonshire—it undeniably paid well for its keep. When sold by the million, during periods of meat scarcity occasioned by the two wars, it more than justified its existence. Always abhorred by the Ministry of Agriculture, its elimination almost overnight by myxomatosis was regarded as a national deliverance. The aim was to prevent so grave a danger to the country's very existence from ever again raising its long-eared head. The tendency to proceed from one extreme to the other appears to be a part of human nature, and Devonshire never did anything by halves. The county, over whose green surface rabbits had swarmed like locusts, was declared a prohibited area to the entire race, £50 being the maximum penalty to which a land-occupier became liable if he harboured even one enemy of the state. I actually knew of a case in which a solitary rabbit seen by an "informer" near a private wood occasioned a visit from an inspector, enquiring as to measures taken for dealing with so serious a public danger. But in the main the "£50 a rabbit" policy was short-lived; indeed it proved as impracticable as the Black List to curb drunkenness. Only one or two isolated cases ever came into court and the most recent instance cost the rabbit-harbourer not £50 but £5.

As in other counties, Rabbit Clearance Societies have been formed to deal with pockets of resistance, but the response to these could not be described as generally enthusiastic. The position, legal and otherwise, was curiously involved. For one thing, farmers were by no means unanimous in desiring the complete extermination of the rabbit. Those of the new school, fresh from agricultural colleges or the services and well steeped in conventional propaganda, had no use for it and agreed that the last should be killed in the national interest, even if doing so cost its weight in paper currency. Some unenlightened die-hards, however, preferred to see a few rabbits about for sport if nothing else, and even tried to get one or two pairs to restock completely depleted areas. Others who had none on their land were reluctant to join Rabbit Clearance Societies since doing so meant subscription without obvious benefit. Meanwhile, when unwanted rabbits appeared in any numbers upon ground not covered by "clearance" arrangement, the disease also mysteriously reappeared. Part of anti-rabbit propaganda had been that descendants of animals that escaped myxomatosis would be immune against further outbreaks, although the reason why it might be so were not convincing. Artificial introduction of the disease had, of course, been declared illegal, but Devonshire is Devonshire and whether artificially or naturally infected, the new generation of rabbits seems unaware of their alleged immunity. That is how the situation has developed. Some people of the sporting type trying to preserve a few rabbits, others, recollecting the former plague-like conditions on many farms, endeavouring to reintroduce the disease.

According to official estimates, six rabbits consume as much valuable fodder as one sheep, and nobody would be surprised if in course of time the figures became reversed. If so, they would be no more fantastic than many of the accusations levelled against the buzzard not so long ago. How such estimates are reached one does not know, but to the un-

Network of hedgerows round Widecombe-in-the-Moor

initiated they merely suggest the more than doubtful value of statistics. Since one sheep, upon an average, easily outweighs thirty rabbits, the allegation that it eats no more than six, taxes one's credulity, both animals being insatiable nibblers. One lifelong farmer, who specialized in sheep but also made an annual income of £500 by the sale of rabbits, dismissed the estimated ratio very briefly—"If that was true," he said, "I could have been lambing another thousand ewes all these years, and that's just about five times as many as my farm can carry, rabbits or no rabbits." He sold the farm soon after, and since the myxomatosis epidemic there has not been a rabbit upon it—but his successor keeps about the same number of sheep.

In spite of frequent representations to the contrary, one might add that the rabbit of today differs in no respect from the rabbit of ten years ago. One often reads that it has now largely adopted the habits of the hare, lying mostly above ground where it cannot be assailed by myxomatosis. In reality, of course, numbers always lay above ground, scuttling for their burrows when disturbed, and this is the precise policy of their descendants. At any rate, every rabbit that I have scared up since has taken rapid steps for his home in the nearest hole, and the burrows are worked in the same proportion as they always were. Indeed, the rabbit is still the rabbit, once as generally accepted a feature of the countryside as swallows around old buildings or foxgloves alongside hedgerow banks. Once it figured largely in every West-country larder, from that of the squire to the stone-cracker. Once bought for sixpence, with its skin carefully preserved for resale to the hawking gipsy, it now costs at least ten times as much. Now the story must be reversed. A blot on the landscape, the rabbit's presence is considered as an indictment of the land-occupier and it is seldom seen on any country table, its flesh having become abhorrent since the myxomatosis epidemic. An ex-trapper, who recently caught a rabbit by accident in a gin illegally set for a fox, related the incident to me as characteristic in more ways than one. "I sold 'un for six bob," he chuckled, "and that was for the cat to eat!"—a trivial incident indeed, yet providing a curiously apt illustration of changed outlook and changed values.

The rabbit era, together with all that it involved—even amounting to an industry in itself, has passed, and with 633 Rabbit Clearance Societies in operation throughout the country, it is unlikely to return upon any extensive scale. Yet human reaction, rather than actual history as runs the proverb, has a remarkable tendency to repeat itself.

7

A typical South Hams landscape

When early in the present century, rabbits became extinct over the red-lands of Devon, they were reintroduced with general approval. They were quite as destructive then as now, but such expressions as "pest" and a popular sport, and rabbit-pie both inexpensive and palatable. The pendulum, however, is slowly swinging back. Since the government's withdrawal of subsidized cartridges for rabbit and grey squirrel shooting, Rabbit Clearance Societies have collapsed, with the result that both animals are staging a come-back. After the myxomatosis holocaust, it seemed that modern children might know the rabbit merely as a fairy-tale figure having no reality. Now, after all, it may be seen again, not only in picture books, but as a living creature in its natural setting. One hopes that this time another population explosion may be avoided by a less horrible means of control.

IX

DARTMOOR

1. The National Park

DARTMOOR's place in the agricultural history of Devonshire cannot be assessed with any certainty. Clearly much would depend upon the definition of the terms "Dartmoor" and "agriculture". If Dartmoor embraces the country over which the heather originally spread and outcrops of granite still defeat all attempts at cultivation, and if "agriculture" also covers the grazing of flocks and herds, then Dartmoor was probably once the centre, if not of cultivation, at least of pasturage. Its pastoral value, however, was not recognized by the compilers of Domesday Book, but it was reserved as a hunting forest under the Norman kings.

It acquired commercial importance when the demand for tin attracted attention to any district that could provide minerals. As a source of mineral wealth, began the long story of Dartmoor's utilization. It has always been the district to which everyone turns for anything needed—china clay, fuel, granite, space sufficiently grim in which to house prisoners, a terrain suitable for military training, scope for water-schemes and afforestation, free pasturage, a happy hunting ground for archaeologists, a holiday centre and finally a National Park.

I have mentioned that the A30 road to the West cuts through our village. That road for some distance also constitutes the boundary between the National Park and less privileged parts of the county, one effect being that there are gardens half in and half outside the prescribed area. The National Park area is not conspicuously different, and speaking generally, the most unsightly innovations within recent years have sprung into being on the park side of the division. "Agricultural buildings" they are termed, and in the interests of agriculture anything is permissible. It is indeed, a little difficult to discover what Dartmoor has gained from her National Park status. It did not prevent the erection of a lofty television mast on one of her conspicuous hill-tops. It has led to no curtailment of military exercises, nor has it restricted the extension of the china clay workings on her southern fringe. Any or all of these and other forms of exploitation may be essential but are quite incompatible with every preconceived idea of an area, the distinctive natural beauty of which is to be preserved for all time. That was the avowed purpose of a National Park, and if still open to exploitation of every kind under one pretext or another, the park status becomes a farce, the inevitable question being—"Why declare it as such at all?" Parodoxically, in a National Park one recognized condition seems to be that the actual state of things continues, and if this involves continued utilization, any positive distinction becomes hard to trace. It might be possible to dictate the type or colour of a new private house, but what after all is the colour of a house, which soon tones down in any case, when compared with a great dam, a television mast, afforestation, and all the installations inseparable from such schemes? All that may be counted safe from utilization is that which cannot be utilized, and even as England since 1066 has many times been saved from invasion by the Channel, so the Dartmoor country has retained as much of its character as survives, by its inaccessibility and sterility.

Perhaps when urging the preservation of Dartmoor as nature made it, we are a little liable to forget that, apart from the high granite peaks and blanket bog, the moor has been since prehistoric days a scene of intermittent human activity. The principal features that antiquarians desire to preserve are themselves artificial, the interest lying in their antiquity and direct connection with an unknown past. The ancient hutments and monuments, together with the extensive remains of surface mining extending over centuries, themselves prove that Dartmoor has been "exploited". Traces of early activities now considered picturesque, at the time were doubtless as sordid and unsightly as modern work is today. Indeed, whereas the promoters of modern schemes do their best to restore the landscape as far as possible, the "old men" or tinners had no such scruples, leaving their slag heaps and trenches as scars upon the face of the moor, which time has covered but cannot efface.

One of the main difficulties in arousing the public conscience concerning an area such as Dartmoor lies in its comparatively limited appeal, for since one must be realistic—that appeal *is* limited. The actual number of visitors to the area provides no criterion. Crowds go everywhere because they must go somewhere, and people who find portable radio music essential while sitting beside a Dartmoor stream can scarcely be very appreciative of their surroundings. To the majority of sightseers the new television mast on North Hessary Tor is certainly more impressive than the stern grandeur of Great Links; and the artificial beauty of Burrator reservoir would seem to be more attractive than the wild reaches of the Okement or Rattle Brook. Actually very few people who live in the district ever set foot on the moor for the joy of doing so. Visitors take the conventional drive from Tavistock to Moretonhampstead, visit Cranmere Pool or perhaps climb Yes Tor and High Willhayes—the highest point in southern England—because each is the customary thing to do. Little general concern would be aroused, however, were every height crowned with a mast, every river dammed or every ancient monument removed.

Another reason for the constant encroachment upon Dartmoor is the lack of similar facilities elsewhere. If realities must be faced, densely populated England is just not big enough to afford the reservation of any really extensive area in its entirety, upon the pattern of the Yellowstone or Kruger National Parks. Dartmoor, being unique of its kind, offers so much that no other tract of country in southern England can provide. It was always so. Even as the industrial North has been blackened and defaced for the production of coal, so Dartmoor was seared and scarred in the search for tin and copper. Now it is her further resources, including the very character of the country, that are in demand.

There is no other ground so suitable for military training. There are no hills so convenient for television installations, no other wild valleys down which boundless waters flow so invitingly. Where else is so much open space that could be afforested? Where else can so much china clay be quarried to help the export drive? Surely, so it is argued, positive and obvious benefits to the many should outweigh aesthetic considerations which affect only a comparative few. After all, it is the same everywhere. One sees old buildings demolished to facilitate road-widening schemes or to allow new erections upon a modern scale. The same precept has applied all down the centuries, otherwise all that is old in England would remain much as it was in Norman times. The ancient oak-scrub that clothes the slopes of Dartmoor valleys may be characteristic of the country, but so were the reeds that covered every undrained marsh, or gorse and brambles growing profusely over "marginal land". If the brambles should be cleared for growing corn, the rushes eliminated for the cultivation of fine grasses, why should not the useless oak-scrub be uprooted and replaced by much needed timber which yields quick profit? That is the utilitarian point of view, as it applies to every question that arises, and the protesting voices which cry in the wilderness—or the little that remains of it—are as ineffectual as an appeal for restraint in wage claims, or anything else of which little notice is taken.

2. Forest and Fire

Of the many schemes for utilizing Dartmoor, afforestation has probably provoked the widest controversy. So far it has applied mainly to intakes, or ground already privately owned and enclosed. The principal objection has been to the alien character of the trees planted. What could be more out of place than a Sitka Spruce forest in country to which only the dwarf oak and mountain ash are indigenous? So it is truly urged, but would similar objections be raised, one wonders, were the same land cleared with bulldozer and tractor to be planted with some artificial crop such as sugar-beet or kale to feed great herds kept on the surrounding moors? One doubts if the same outcry would arise. Yet the crops would be equally foreign to the landscape, and public access to the ground even more restricted.

The truth, of course, is that afforestation has acquired a "bad press". This is partly due to the regimented appearance of the trees, as well as to the incompatibility of conifers with the character of the country. Actually nothing combines better than Scotch pine and heather, provided that the combination is natural, as on the wooded slopes of Surrey or—adhering to Devonshire—upon Woodbury Common. Were much of lower Dartmoor covered with self-sown, or rather bird-sown trees of any species, the effect would be considered beautifying or softening to the stern landscape. Curiously enough, before they were afforested, tracts of the moor were often condemned as "featureless". Indeed, when repeatedly blackened by fires they were downright ugly, yet when that objection is removed by planting, the complaint is louder still. The appearance of afforested ground from a distance is at least green and pleasing to the eyes, whether the trees are indigenous or not. A hill-side perpetually devastated by fires is a scene of unrelieved desolation, in no way mitigated by the knowledge that the scorched bare boulders represent the skeleton of the real moor.

In general, when the principle that the actual state of things must continue applies equally to abuses, the conception of a National Park loses its meaning. An area set aside as one of outstanding natural beauty, and therefore protected by the State, should automatically become

State supervised, in the same way as property held under the National Trust.

Dartmoor Forest was described in a recent survey of Devonshire, as owned by the Duchy of Cornwall, the surrounding commons belonging to the respective parishes to which they are attached. Actually that is a somewhat misleading version of the situation. Each parish has special rights over the common that bears its name, but it could not, upon its own authority, enclose or appropriate a yard of the ground. Over Dartmoor as a whole, the lordship of the soil with all that ownership involves, is vested in the Duchy of Cornwall; in most cases there are no visible boundaries between the commons and the Forest, and for the purposes of the National Park there should be no distinction. One aim of the Duchy has always been to preserve both "the beauty and utility of the moor" and the same principle could be rigorously enforced upon the commons without contravening any rights, or causing injury or loss to anybody. There is no reason why the moor should be strewn with the corpses of animals which die from sickness, neglect or under-nourishment, and are left for the ravens and foxes to bury in their own unsatisfactory way. There is no reason again why every approach to the moor and every accessible hill-side should be rendered unsightly by fires, lit, not to provide pasturage—which is the conventional excuse—but merely for amusement. The right to burn gorse or heather, in season and within reason, is vested in every commoner, this term being generally interpreted as meaning a householder. The right is not transferable, and the vast majority of fires—often highly destructive—are lit by village youths and even children who have no right whatsoever to set a match to anything.

Fire "raising" in Devonshire has long been an issue which authority for some unaccountable reason has always been reluctant to face; therefore no firm measures for its repression are taken. Visitors from other parts of the country often express frank incredulity at the position. The idea of little boys and "teen-agers" setting the countryside ablaze with utter impunity, while the fire service is kept busy running round dealing with one conflagration after another, seems too fantastic to be believed yet such procedure is more or less taken for granted. Little effort is made to trace the culprits, and police action—when taken—is seldom supported. Occasionally press reports contain a casual announcement to the effect that the cause of the fire is unknown, but more frequently there is no comment whatsoever. By general convention, which actually amounts to taking the line of least resistance, the conflagrations are treated as "accidental", the inevitable cigarette end being the customary and most convenient scapegoat or red-herring, to distract attention from unwelcome realities. Actually, not one forest fire in a thousand is accidental.

Published accounts are often purely ridiculous. There was the story of two children left in charge of the bungalow where they lived. They occupied their time raking up garden weeds, which, in the language of the press, "caught fire". Whereupon the children rushed to the telephone and summoned the fire brigade, fearing that the blaze would reach the bungalow. They were highly commended for their perspicacity nor did the question as to *how* weeds "catch fire" appear to arise. So convenient a tendency has escaped the notice of most gardeners.

Another typical example occurred when the fire brigade was requisitioned to deal with a gorse blaze on Torrington Common. While this was being done, a second fire "broke out" on another part of the common, demanding attention in its turn. The sceptic may well raise his eyebrows and accuse me of exaggeration. Such were the actual accounts given, however, incredible as this state of affairs may seem. In any case, whether the conflagrations are "authorized" or mischievous, the idea of starting a blaze and then summoning the fire service to extinguish it when "out of control"—never having been under control from the outset—seems illogical enough and quite impossible outside Devonshire.

I began the subject by describing the custom of excessive burning upon Dartmoor commons as deplorable from an aesthetic point of view. It is also disastrous upon purely practical and economic grounds. As the heather is gradually destroyed, not only on the commons, but also in many parts of the Forest, in its place springs up the far stronger and indestructible bracken, less decorative, and useless to man or beast, except perhaps to a few small-holders who still cut a certain amount for bedding. This is recognized, but the fires continue, the temptation to burn being irresistible, even as the drug habit persists although known to be lethal. If ever drastic control was needed, it is certainly here. During the past year or so, the position has improved to some extent, owing to the law which prohibits the burning of gorse and heather between 31 March and 30 September, this regulation being more or less observed by responsible people. That in no way checks wild orgies during a dry March however; indeed, it rather invites enthusiasts to make hay while the sun shines. Nor does it prevent the application of the surreptitious match, which has been far too much in evidence whenever dry conditions have prevailed. Fortunately the new Society known as "The Dartmoor Commoners Association" appears to be taking a balanced view on the question of "swaling", as this type of heather-burning is incorrectly termed in Devonshire. The result has been a decided—if belated—improvement in the situation.

3. Commons and Commoners

The title "Dartmoor Commoners Association" in reality is somewhat of a misnomer. It should more correctly be the "Dartmoor *Graziers* or *Ranchers*", the society consisting entirely of people who run sheep or cattle on the moor. The proportion of residents who do this is very limited, comprising at most one commoner or rate-payer in three hundred, upon a rough average. Since the vast majority of commoners never use their rights, appropriation of the whole by the few who *do* is inevitable and has become customary. In effect, a parish common, together with adjoining parts of the Forest, has developed into a ranch usually monopolized by one or two men who take complete possession.

I remember when a particularly possessive ranch king forbade the foxhounds to approach his territory during the lambing season. This would have been perfectly legitimate had he owned or rented the moor, but since many people with equal rights wanted the hunting, the man should obviously have been required, for the one occasion, to collect his sheep upon ground where they were not likely to be disturbed. After all, this is done regularly when the ranges are cleared for artillery practice.

The case may be trivial in itself, but is merely one of many examples which might be cited to illustrate the manner in which the commons are appropriated by individuals. One might reasonably ask why it should not be so, since others do not avail themselves of the privileges, and anybody in the parish could do the same if he liked. In theory, of course, he could; but in practice it would be impossible. In a moorland town which possesses a common there might be five hundred rate-payers or commoners, and if each exercised a similar right and ran a thousand sheep on the moor—as two or three may be doing—the common would be stocked with half a million sheep, a number many times beyond its capacity to maintain. All, therefore, could not use their rights upon the same scale, even if desiring to do so, and in reality only a mere few derive any advantage from them. While the many get nothing, therefore, the few nowadays make fortunes, circumstance having placed them in a position to do so. Yet the main burden of the rates, including the provision of gates and grids and any other expenses involved, falls upon the many. The position does not seem equitable, nor is it a case of it always having been so, since monopoly is an abuse which has developed during comparatively recent times. There are men who would be glad to run a few cattle or sheep upon the hills as a sideline, but they complain that their animals are crowded, if not actually driven, off the best pasturage by the "big" men. That the moor should be turned to useful purposes is, of course, both desirable and essential in the public interest, but the whole matter needs revision and reorganization from top to bottom. The much-abused, misapplied and too often unnecessary State subsidies for moorland beasts have been described as the "biggest racket in the country", and is openly ridiculed even by those who benefit from it. "Money for jam," was the contemptuous comment of one sheep-owner, who would have gladly paid for pasturing his flock if necessary, since it was profitable enough without State assistance. Subsidy rackets, however, are mere side-shows quite apart from the main issue of common land generally and the Dartmoor commons in particular.

The truth is that they have long out-lived their original purpose, which was to benefit the local community *as a whole*. In most cases now, the only right claimed or exercised by the villagers is to kindle fires for the fire brigade to extinguish, or to shoot game which they are not entitled to do in any case, holding no game-certificate. Justification is claimed under charter conferred by King John, although much of this was rendered obsolete by subsequent legislation; on the other hand, restrictions imposed by Plantagenets and later rulers are dismissed as "out-dated". Actually the entire position is as "out-dated" as it could be, conditions having changed somewhat since the reign of King John. Rights vested in a community, in this case represented by a parish, should be the property of that community and not merely remunerative privileges to be appropriated by individuals. It is difficult to find a parallel situation, the position being indeed unique. Imagine such a state of affairs either on a seaside beach or river-mouth, where remunerative rights are acquired at a price—by arrangement—as they should be. As matters now stand with fantastic prices for meat and wool and even more fantastic subsidies, free moorland pasturage has become so profitable a public right, that those to whom in reality it equally belongs are entitled to at least a share. By all means let the few who, through the accident of circumstance, are enabled to use the privilege, do so. But since they also avail themselves of unclaimed rights belonging to the many, fairness suggests that they should pay for the privilege upon a proportionate scale. The proceeds could be used to ease local rates or help towards parochial expenses. The idea may seem revolutionary, but the old conditions have gone in any case and reorganization will become imperative sooner or later.

Until within comparatively recent years the rights of *turbary*—the cutting of turf and peat—were more generally used upon Dartmoor commons and forest than those of pasturage. Many commoners who owned no sheep or cattle found it helpful at least to get their fuel from the moor, and the pungent but pleasant smell of peat-smoke, which prevailed in villages such as Belstone or Postbridge, indicated their close association with Dartmoor. The surface turves or "vags" were cut in flat blocks, rather larger than bricks, and set up to dry in pairs, like a child sets up playing-cards. At one time during the summer months, accessible peaty slopes would be covered with these little erections grouped about like miniature primitive villages. Pannier donkeys were once used to bring in the fuel, but their capacity was naturally limited, horse-drawn turf carts being the rule. Wheel tracks to the turf "ties" or the more remote peat-cuttings led from every entrance to the moor. Some were deep from long usage, and many of these may still be traced, although the moor, helped by winter storms, is fast reclaiming them. The last of the donkeys was released from servitude half a century ago; and no turf cart is now in use. The peat-cuttings lie mostly derelict, and although for a few years a lorry or two went out to the more accessible places to collect the odd load, even this somewhat revolutionary method of gathering peat has now been virtually abandoned. The reasons for the decline of so old a practice—for it could scarcely be called an industry—are compatible with the times. The horses have gone and the carts which they drew fallen to pieces. The approach lanes, always rough and rocky, have been washed out by winter floods and nobody now troubles to repair them. More significant still, the turf-cutters of the past have either died or grown too old for the work, which does not appeal to their descendants. Again, the villagers now have so much more money to spend that they can buy coal or logs, both of which provide more satisfactory fuel than dusty moorland "vags" or peat. The last peat that I saw in this village had been brought from Sedgemoor in Somerset, and suggested the proverbial coal offered for sale in the "Black Country".

The same applies to surface granite or "moorstone", the collecting and shaping of which for gate-posts, buildings, monuments and ornamental work provided a definite, although limited, industry. Split boulders, still bearing the marks of the chisels, may be seen anywhere on the moor today, and the fact that they were never ultimately taken away tells its own story. Stone-masons, and even ordinary builders requiring shaped stones of any kind, now find it easier to obtain them from the great quarries at Tavistock, while granite gate-posts, which were once the rule, are now replaced by iron "standards" for the wide gates needed to accommodate modern farm implements. Thus, the ring of sledge-hammer on chisel, described by Trevenna as characteristic "moorland music", is not likely ever to be heard on the Dartmoor hills again, and in years to come the scarred stones will be regarded much as the kistvaens are today, indications of a bygone era. So of all the purposes the moor once served, only pasturage remains, and that is now a privilege used by comparatively few Dartmoor people.

Black Galloways head the cattle list of the four-legged inhabitants of the moorland. Scotch sheep are most numerous but Welsh sheep have lately been introduced and are gaining popularity among hill farmers. Cattle of many breeds are brought to the hills during the summer months, from the dainty little Jersey to the ample-bodied South Hams, and the number of ponies that roam the hills has considerably increased during recent years. A pony is now worth as many pounds as it sold for shillings during the period between the two wars. When no longer required in considerable numbers for the mines, the only market was for slaughter—a depressing destination, although perhaps almost preferable to a dreary and laborious existence underground. Now, since riding has become so popular among children, particularly girls, ponies are in great demand, and the idea of getting one "from the moor" has great attractions. Conventionally, but quite incorrectly, all ponies that run on Dartmoor are called "Dartmoor ponies", but in reality the true moorland breed will be seen on the hills no more, unless special and drastic measures are taken to reinstate and conserve the strain, which is unlikely. The comparatively few survivors are now kept in private enclosures, since if released upon the open moor the purity of the strain would be quickly lost. There is no restriction as to the type of stallion running free over the unenclosed areas, and the inevitable result has been the nondescript type of animal seen there today.

The remarkable hardihood of both the true Dartmoor and Exmoor pony has always been recognized. In the olden days, both these strains were freely introduced for breeding pack-horses, the largest animals, of course, being selected for effecting the cross. Moor blood might conceivably have been desirable if the pack-horse was really required to perform the acrobatic feats attributed to it, such as crossing streams by means of the old cyclopean bridges. Since this feat was in reality manifestly impossible to any animal carrying a balanced load, the real qualities needed were endurance and sureness of foot, traits which would certainly be derived from the hardy moorland strains. Horses of almost any serviceable description were doubtless used as "beasts of burden", just as any nondescript mongrel can become an "official" sledge dog in northern countries today.

Breeding of animals big enough to carry a sufficient load, whether in peace or war, always appears to have been a difficulty, and this was officially recognized in the days of Henry VIII. Even then, the problem of "mongrel" stallions running uncontrolled, troubled horse-breeders of the period. In Henry's opinion the breed was—

"now much decayed and diminished by reason that in the Forests, chases, moors and waste grounds, little horses and nags of small stature and little value were suffered to pasture thereupon."

To correct this state of affairs, a *Bill for the Breed of Horses* was passed, which at the time, no doubt, had considerable effect. Obviously this was aimed at the small native breeds of hill ponies, of which His Majesty disapproved. So Clause 2 of the Bill decreed that no stallion under 15 hands was to be allowed to run on any moor or common. The height of a Dartmoor pony, by the way, is about 11 or 12 hands, a hand being 4½ inches in measurement. The Bill also sanctioned the confiscation of a horse "of unlawful height"—a provision which nowadays would have given rise to more than acrimonious argument. In Tudor times, however, it is improbable that anything in the way of argument was permitted, since it would have been a policy of mere might. Official horse-measurers were appointed, and anyone who refused to have his horse subjected to the test became liable to a penalty of 40s.

Next, to ensure that the regulations were not evaded, all forests, chases and commons were "driven" a fortnight before Michaelmas, every horse, mare and colt that showed no promise of growing into a "serviceable animal" being sorted out and killed, no matter what views its owner entertained on the point. But Bluff King Hal was nothing if not thorough. If he wanted a new wife, he had one—or rather, six; if he wanted a new breed of horses, he took care that he got it. As an additional precaution, he commanded all owners of parks and enclosed grounds one mile in extent, to keep two mares of 13 hands each, for breeding purposes. If a man had four miles of parkland, he had to keep four mares, and if his wife wore a velvet bonnet—a mark of high social standing—he was obliged to have a saddle-horse of 15 or more hands in height.

Old documents show that these enactments were strictly enforced on Exmoor. Since they applied to all forests, chases, moors and wastes in the country, there is no reason for supposing that Dartmoor was excluded. Being Crown property it could scarcely have escaped any such regulations. So in the sixteenth century, the Dartmoor pony was "improved" according to Henry VIII's standards, and now, four centuries later, the breed is again becoming "decayed and diminished", and the running of the wrong kind of stallions on the moor is once more attracting official attention.

The Dartmoor ponies of today, like those of the New Forest, are periodically in the news, as being a source of danger to speeding motorists. They are always liable to cause accidents by crossing roads at the wrong moment, and they approach rather than avoid cars, owing to the tendency of people to feed them when picnicking by the wayside. Appeals against this practice circulated by radio and press, with notices posted at every possible vantage point, have met the customary, or rather complete lack of, response. Indeed, they seem merely to incite deliberate disregard—upon the "agin the Government" principle; nor has an actual by-law prohibiting the feeding of ponies under penalty, been treated with any more respect. In the middle of Princetown not long ago, I saw loose ponies being fed by visitors close beside one such notice, and within view of a policeman who, apparently, preferred to look another way. Admittedly, it is difficult to resist the solicitations of an engaging little animal, which approaches a picnicking party with every confidence of getting some edible recognition, but it would be far more difficult to avoid the accident which the same animal might cause, when familiarity with cars leads to dangerous contempt. The pony can read no notices and may therefore be exempted from blame. A more responsible attitude, however, might be expected from the public who should possess sufficient intelligence to realize that laws are seldom made, or appeals issued, without some strong reason.

Casualties upon the road crossing Roborough Down finally reached such proportions that after much controversy, the road has been stoutly fenced along both sides, affording mutual protection to motorist and beast.

Although every pony running upon the moor is branded, each, of course, belonging to somebody, the fantastic idea that they are "wild" still persists. This belief was actually pleaded, when a charge of horse-stealing was recently brought against a man who had somehow managed to get a pony on board a van, and was taking it away when stopped on the road by the police. Ignorance of the law is not normally a valid defence, but surprising as it seemed, when the case came to court the plea was accepted. Clearly if naïvety of this practical description could be permitted upon a big scale, Dartmoor ponies would soon cease to be a problem upon the roads or anywhere else.

X

WILD DARTMOOR

1. Spirit of the Moor

So far I have written solely about the utility and natural resources of Dartmoor and the extent to which they have been exploited. There remains, however, the principal reason why this land of mists and mires, "grand old hills" and wild mountain streams was the fourth area in Great Britain to be set aside as a National Park—an area of outstanding beauty. I have said that the moor does not appeal to everyone; but to those sensible of it, that appeal is unique.

> "England, thy glories are tame and domestic
> To one who has roved o'er the mountains afar.
> Oh for the peaks that are wild and majestic";

wrote Byron when describing country upon an even grander scale, and although there is nothing specially arresting about these lines, in a minor degree they express Dartmoor's secret. It is the extraordinary contrast between the gentler beauty of "England's green and pleasant land" and the stern magnificence of a landscape in atmosphere and general character untouched by time. Upon those great wild wastes of granite and blanket bog, where grandeur and silence reign supreme, anything "tame and domestic", any sign, indeed, of human activity seems insignificant and out of place. There, one might think, "only man is vile" since his activities can do nothing but deface.

One often hears the contention or complaint that remote and inaccessible country, however beautiful, is useless because so few people can penetrate it to enjoy its charm. That, however, is rather the attitude of the fictitious schoolboy who, when forbidden to climb a mountain, wished that it were "rolled flat and planted with potatoes". It is, of course, that same inaccessibility and remoteness which constitute Dartmoor's character—the suggestion of the unconquered and unconquerable. If intersected by easy roads or paths and sign-posted, with refreshment bars in every valley, all character would be lost. The man who loves the mountains best is not necessarily the greatest

The Erme valley. Sharp Tor in the background

climber. Indeed the two have little in common. One friend, who has
walked hundreds of miles with me over the moor, always complained
of the desolation, yet felt impelled to scramble to the top of every
rock and tor.

One is often asked to select the grandest or most impressive of
Dartmoor's tors, but it is scarcely a matter of comparison. Each of
the giants has characteristics of its own, and among the minor heights-
while distinction is never lacking, there is also a great deal of similarity.
Often one decides in favour of the peak upon which one happens to
be standing, only to reverse the decision when visiting another.
Indeed, all are magnificent. The highest parts do not always carry the
most outstanding granite crests, with the exception of Yes Tor, where
height and rock effects combine. The character of Yes Tor, however,
is somewhat marred by the military flagstaff, like that of Snowdon
by its railway and snack bar. One might add that upon High Willhayes,
the highest point in southern England, the tor is quite insignificant.
Haytor Rock, happily has lately had its handrail removed. Yet, due
to accessibility, its imposing character loses much from the inevitable
assembly of coaches, cars, ice-cream and fried-fish vans that collect
below, imparting a sort of Stonehenge atmosphere.

In my opinion, the most sinister, and for that reason one of the most
impressive of all the tors, is grim Great Links, between the Lyd and
the turbulent Rattle Brook, round which the abandoned peat workings
add to the desolation rather than detract from it. They suggest the
ultimate triumph of the moor over human endeavour. Even the ruin
appropriately known as Bleak House, standing below the great rock
pile, adds to the sense of wildness, having been taken possession of by
enterprising ravens who often profit from man's abandoned work.

One might mention many more—the famous rocks of Hound Tor,
Staple Tors' grotesque formations, and the loftiest pile of all, the
apparently insignificant Vixen Tor, which figures so much in Eden
Phillpotts's novel *The Mother*. Vixen Tor loses most of its effect by
its low position under the Staple Tor's ridge; only its head is visible
above the ravine, over which the main pile towers on the southern
side. If the importance of a hill or tor can be judged by the view that it
commands the northern heights of Dartmoor must claim precedence in
this respect. On some hill-tops, the ability to view the county from
coast to coast is claimed, but there is no point upon the moor from
which the Atlantic can actually be seen. From Cosdon Beacon and
Yes Tor the whole northern coastline can be traced, beginning with

8

Dartmoor ponies sheltering at Sharp Tor

the Exmoor hills and reaching almost as far west as Tintagel. The high
cliffs bound the horizon, however, and there is no glimmer of sea
beyond. On the other hand, the Channel, being so much nearer, is
overlooked by most of the southern heights, and from the Staple Tors,
for example, it is even possible to classify ships afloat on Plymouth
Sound.

I compared the atmosphere of Haytor Rocks with that of Stonehenge, the effect produced by the numerous sightseers being much
the same. Actually the position is very similar at any Dartmoor beauty
spot which cars can reach. Accessibility upon wheels, however,
constitutes the limit beyond which few visitors penetrate very far. A
walk recently taken down the East Dart, between Bellever Bridge and
Dartmeet, suggested a stretch of railway lines between two crowded
stations. The empty line was represented by the wild river, sweeping
along a course as undisturbed as in the days when pack-horses crossed
the fords which the bridges now span. The bridges and their immediate
approaches might have been the stations, thronged with cars, and with
the "music" of transistor radios drowning the song of the stream.

It should be noted that most of Dartmoor's famous antiquities are
reasonably accessible, even according to modern standards and ideas.
In really remote areas, such as the great northern blanket bog or the
wilds of Dart Head, there are no hutments, avenues or other signs of
early human activities. The late Hamlyn Parsons, an eminent moor
authority whose activities were tragically hampered by physical
disability, always claimed that he could guide visitors to any object of
interest within half a mile of a motor road. Actually this left very
little beyond his reach. The circles and kistvaens at Merrivale; the
avenues and menhirs at Drizzlecombe on the Plym; Grimspound,
Ryders Rings, and the comprehensive relics on Shovel Down might all
be listed as being reasonably accessible. By contrast, Erme Pound and
the outstanding hutments on Watern Oak above the Tavy, the Grey
Wethers near Teign Head and the numerous circles around Cosdon
Beacon are not easily approachable and therefore seldom visited.
On Lec Moor the great china clay workings are being insidiously
extended, the Cholwich Stone Row having recently been engulfed
by their creeping spoil heaps. These, for many years, have created
a great white excrescence on the landscape, bleaching the waters of
the Plym to such an extent that the area might be a land flowing
with milk, if not with honey. Incidently, the Plym during this stage
of its course is known as the Cad, even as the Thames at Oxford

becomes the Isis. It might well change its name, since the white flood
which passes under Cadover Bridge bears little enough resemblance
to the clear Plym, which threads lonely Drizzlecombe and was flowing
there when the prehistoric men set up their mighty menhirs, thousand
of years ago. Those ancient stalwarts, with their crude equipment and
imperishable materials, left their traces for all time, and until now the
evidence of their work has been regarded as inviolate. Here and there,
indeed, circles were robbed and avenues depleted by countrymen
scarcely less primitive and certainly less aesthetic than the ancient moor-
dwellers. They were people who merely wanted granite slabs for walls
or gate-posts, and to whom a monumental stone was just a stone, and
if erect, the more easily removable. This practice was later discouraged
and today, officially, antiquities are strictly preserved. None the less,
when utility is weighed against sentiment, practical considerations
usually tilt the scales. The needs of the many, the importance of export
—in the china clay case—the national food supply, the scarcity of
timber, water for increasing needs, each in its turn is a familiar slogan
raised when some new venture is launched against Dartmoor's
amenities.

Dartmoor is often depicted as a region of mystery and even terror,
and those who know it best can the more readily understand its effect
upon strangers. The spirit of the moor is not a friendly spirit; she
knows no gentle mood; nor can one wonder that "cruel" is the adjective
which time has allotted to the indescribably beautiful river Dart.
The attitude of the moor towards those who invade her fastnesses is
rather that of the enchantress who lures to destroy. The desire of the
rambler is always to penetrate farther and farther, to explore the
mystery of the distance, and often enough it pleases the enchantress to
punish his temerity. The warmth and sunshine of her smile may be
flooding the landscape, when upon some colourful hill-side there
appears a wisp of white vapour, no more than the smoke from a
cartridge. It looks insignificant enough but its significance is profound.
Without further warning, and all in a moment as it seems, one realizes
that every landmark has been blotted out. Visibility has gone, sound is
muffled and a vast opaque, grey gloom envelopes hill and coombes
alike. A bewildering unreality distorts even the few near objects that
can be seen, making an ordinarily inconspicuous hummock look like
a mountain, and to crown everything, all sense of direction is lost.

Such is the "black mist", actually pearl-grey, described by Davis as
the most "dreaded of Dartmoor's terrors". So formidable is its reputa-

tion, even today, that people suddenly entrapped in its coils often lose their heads completely, although they may be following a well-defined track and therefore in no danger. Unable to recognize their surroundings and bewildered by the distortion, they become obsessed with the idea that they are on the wrong track, and are walking into unknown country. Under this impression they strike blindly off in another direction, seeking the very path which they have left. This happens often enough and one might fill a chapter describing the almost incredible wanderings of mist-confused ramblers, with now and again, the story of one who has never returned.

As we know, fog in some shape or form occurs all over the British Isles, but upon Dartmoor it is the difficult terrain which aggravates the trouble. There are the mires and the clitters, those expanses of tumbled rock hard to negotiate under the best conditions. There are the blanket bogs with their terrible mazes of natural dykes, from three to twelve feet deep, among which a lost man may wander interminably. For that matter the rugged surface of even the open moor often presents difficulties enough to an exhausted pedestrian, when stumbling over it hopelessly for hours.

How best to act when caught in a fog is a question often asked, but of course there is no hard and fast line to suggest. Everything depends upon the particular circumstances, and the best policy in one case might be the worst in another. The main essential, although it may sound like advice more easily given than followed, is to keep cool, and with a clear head some plan usually evolves. Even though visibility in technical language may be nil, any knowledge of the country is a help. There are numerous places or objects which cannot be mistaken by anyone to whom they are familiar, and knowing where you are goes a long way towards knowing what to do. A stream can be a useful guide as to direction, so long as one knows what stream it is; but blindly to follow the first that one strikes, when lost, is a policy of despair. Dartmoor rivers always take the most difficult course for a pedestrian, since all thread rocky coombes and by no means necessarily take the most direct course off the moor—often indeed the longest and quite the worst. Following a river can only be recommended as a last resource, when one knows the stream and where it leads. In that case, however, one is not really lost, the difficulty being merely one of picking the easiest way. A compass can be helpful. I carried one for many years, but actually seldom used it, since on the moor a straight line to a required point is rarely the best way of getting there. Perhaps the wisest course for an amateur rambler when overtaken by mist is to make for the nearest track that he knows, before he loses his bearings, even if doing so involves a detour. Unlike a stream, a track will at least lead him into no difficulties.

That again is advice easily given but sometimes impossible to follow. A man familiar with the moor may also be aware that there is no track of any description within many miles. So placed he can do nothing but avoid panic and use his wits to their best advantage. There is an old saying to the effect that anyone who has never fallen off a horse is no rider, and upon the same principle, when a man claims that he has never been inconvenienced by a Dartmoor mist, one may rest assured that his experience of the moor is very limited. Mists are as closely associated with the Devonshire highlands as sea-fog with the sea, or dust-storms with a desert, and it is impossible to know the moor well without also becoming familiar with her most characteristic mood.

Mist is not the only natural phenomenon capable of baffling those who wander far into the trackless moor. The featureless bogs or marshes sometimes have a deceptive appearance which often induces people to walk in circles even on a clear day. That is what the older moormen meant when they talked about being "pixy-led". I do not think that the genuine country people ever believed in the existence of pixies as actual beings. Baring Gould referred to them as out of date nearly a century before even his time, and so no doubt it has always been. When a moorman speaks of being "pixy-led", he merely means that he has lost his way, attaching no superstitious meaning to a purely picturesque expression. Even more curious tricks are also played upon the imagination or vision by the peculiar light effects, sometimes incorrectly described as "mirages", which distort distances so that a rock a quarter of a mile away appears to be within a stone's throw, or on the other hand, comparatively near objects may look remote. Hills again may be dwarfed or magnified, a mountainous ridge appearing almost flat, or an insignificant tor enormous. Sunlight reduces height; gloom magnifies. Much of this would apply to great spaces anywhere, but upon Dartmoor one sees the effect of both space and height, upon plain and mountain alike, the combination being unusual.

2. A Touch of Mystery

Being such a land of mystery with its prehistoric past, the area is not as rich in legend and folk-lore as might be supposed, the reason

being that its background is actually too old. The unknown past left
no figures around whom legend could take shape, and it is too remote
to offer much scope even for fiction. The "old men" or tinners, again
never had much popular appeal, and very few stories of their activities
have been written; indeed, Baring Gould's little-known book *Guavas
the Tinner* is the only one dealing with this subject that comes to mind.
Yet the "mystery" of Dartmoor is not confined to her unknown past,
and although the countrymen may never have believed in pixies
which mainly originated from fiction of the *Puck of Pook's Hill* type,
they do hold strong belief in strange influences abroad on the moor,
about which little has been heard or written.

Up to the present day, people relate curious experiences which
are frequently too unexpected to be dismissed off-hand as merely
arising from imagination or suggestion. Intelligent and responsible
individuals describe occasions upon which, for no apparent reason,
they have been gripped by a mysterious sensation of fear or even terror,
shared in at least one case by a companion. In one instance this occurred
in a place to which no superstitious associations whatever were
attached. A former rector of a neighbouring parish, who spent a great
deal of time on the moor, has told me of one such uncanny experience.
Once, when walking over quite familiar ground, he was suddenly
seized with such fear and consciousness of malignant influences all
around him, that only by repeating prayers could he gather enough
courage to proceed on his way.

Curiously enough, some of the modern stories actually concern
motorists. A great deal has been heard within comparatively recent
years of the mysterious hand, seen—or so it is alleged—to take possession of a steering wheel and divert a car, with tragic consequences.
This is said to happen on a stretch of road between Moretonhampstead
and Princetown where many accidents have occurred, some before
the days of cars and probably for the same reason—whatever that may
be. It is interesting to remark, that Eden Phillpotts in one of his novels,
chose this stretch of road as the scene of a fatal horse and trap accident.

Animals, as well as human beings, appear to be affected by these
influences. Not long ago, a lady motorist, when following a road
which crossed a reputedly "haunted bridge", had an experience for
which she has never been able to account. The road being familiar,
she was thinking merely of ordinary matters, when she became con-
scious of an icy chill, as one feels when starting a high fever. She
thought, indeed, that such must be the case, and stopping the car, she

looked round for a coat left on the back seat beside her sleeping terrier. Until then she had considered her own state as something purely physical, but the sight of the dog put a fresh complexion on the matter. It had withdrawn into a corner, where it crouched trembling, every hair erect, every tooth bared as in desperate self-defence, its attitude one of abject terror. Shivering almost as violently herself now, the lady—not unnaturally—drove on without waiting to put on the coat, which however she did not need, as after driving a little way, the cold fear passed and she felt perfectly normal. She even pulled up again, bracing herself to return and solve the mystery if possible. She was discouraged from doing so, however, by the condition of the dog which, having presumably seen more than its mistress, continued to shiver and display intense fear, until the place was left far behind. She has passed the same spot many times since, without experiencing any unusual sensations.

There is an old belief that animals are nearer to the occult than human beings, and their behaviour at times certainly suggests perception that we lack. There is one place near some old tin-workings, on the western flank of Cosdon Beacon, which a locally bred horse could never be induced to pass. The case is not unique, a possible explanation being that the animal has suffered some previous *natural* fright at the same spot and has never forgotten it.

I should perhaps mention one extraordinary belief current among old-time moormen, They endowed animals with a dual personality, rather upon the were-wolf principle, talking about "sheep which were not sheep". This ancient superstition, Celtic in origin, is akin to one formerly prevalent in the West Highlands. There, the water-horse and the water-bull would rise from a loch at times to join the normal herds, disappearing or changing shape at will. Upon Dartmoor, these dubious animals mingled with the flocks and roamed the hill-sides in sheep-like guise, but behaved in a suspicious manner incompatible with anything that walked about in a genuine fleece. That they were considered to be malevolent is clear, but how the genuine wool-bearers were distinguished from those which had assumed their likeness, is not so plain. Possibly, in cases of doubtful identity, inspection was carried on from a discreet distance, flock-owners being content to leave non-essential points to supposition. Whether any such consideration would deter a modern grazier from trying to collect anything that wears wool, is very doubtful. Sheep most definitely *are* sheep on the hills today, the only question being—whose?

XI

WOOL AND ITS LEGACY

IN life generally, many interesting things are taken for granted, not least among them being the evolution of the domesticated animal. The earliest accounts of man depict him with his flocks and herds, the manner in which he acquired them being left to the imagination. Their presence is just "given", as in a Euclid proposition. Balaam's ass, like all other livestock, was merely there, doing her duty to the best of her ability, as presumably her ancestors had done before her, and further examples might be traced into a very remote past. No past could be more remote or obscure than that of Devonshire's prehistoric inhabitants. The hut-dwellers, who alone left records of their presence, suggest other problematic spectres, in this case four-footed—although not supernatural like the sheep described in the last chapter.

Whether the Stone Age or Bronze Age men scratched the earth for tin is a question which I will not reopen, but most antiquarians agree that they must also of necessity have been "pastoral" people, from which assumption arises the natural enquiry—"What did they pasture?" If not the pioneers of the tin industry, were they the pioneers of the wool trade? In brief, did they or could they have kept sheep, with so many predators, biped or quadruped, against which to compete? If so, the question as to how the sheep got there is another of the many that cannot be answered. Presumably they arrived upon their feet, but by whom shepherded matters very little.

If tin constituted Devonshire's oldest industry, wool was certainly the most profitable. Its benefits were so much more generally distributed. Tin mining was localized, and therefore also the earnings derived from it. Sheep could be kept anywhere. While first introduced upon a big scale by the Cistercian monks of Buckfastleigh, or their predecessors the Grey monks, flocks soon appeared all over the country wherever suitable grazing could be found. Some time must have been required for the monks to rear the immense flocks eventually pastured on the moorland slopes. The sheep is not a prolific animal, and unless local stock was available, which seems improbable, importation could have been no easy matter. Actually, of course, the building up of

great flocks was a gradual process developing with, and largely contributing to, the growing prosperity of the monasteries, as far as
Buckfastleigh was concerned at any rate. A prosperous industry soon
creates a demand, and with increasing demand the supply also grows.
A century is a short time when related to history, and the full benefits
of initiative are often reaped by succeeding generations.

Roughly the story of wool coincides with that of tin. It appears to
have received national—which meant royal—recognition during the
twelfth century, and the same monarchs who encouraged and
facilitated the output of tin also supported the wool trade, and for the
same reasons—to provide revenue for foreign enterprises and to
stimulate commerce. Needless to say, the trade was nation-wide, but
Devonshire had a good start. The county was better stocked with
sheep than any other in the early days; also it was singularly well
adapted to carry on the industry. Running water, so essential for the
preparation of wool, presented no difficulties. Indeed it achieved a
value never before recognized, and for several centuries Devonshire
became one of the most industrious counties. By the time the trade had
reached its height, there was scarcely a town without its tucking and
fulling mills, scarcely a village that could not boast of one or two;
scarcely a cottage to which Macaulay's line "The goodwife's shuttle
merrily goes flashing through the loom" would not have been applicable. It differed from the tin trade in one marked respect. While every
tinner procured his own metal, every villager engaged in the combing
and spinning of wool was not necessarily a sheep-owner, dealing with
his own fleeces. The position was much the same as now. Fleeces were
produced on a big scale by the farmers or land-owners, then sold to the
manufacturers who distributed them locally for treatment. People
undertook the spinning and carding in their own cottages, as later
they "took in" washing before central launderies monopolized that
task.

In Devonshire the industry followed the customary pattern. Each
of the larger towns such as Barnstaple, Tiverton, Ashburton, Bideford,
Crediton and many others dominated its own area. Each claimed
superiority in some way, usually without any specific reason other than
local pride or prejudice.

As with everything Devonian, however, Exeter eventually became
the hub and centre of it all. When not preoccupied with supporting
kings at war or sustaining sieges, the city supported the national
exchequer by carrying on a highly thriving commerce. Exeter's

woollen industry, with all that it implied, became a pattern of commercial organization, which operated under the supervision of its famous guild known as *The Worshipful Company of Weavers, Fullers and Shearman of the City of Exeter*. This formidable and, for the most part, beneficient body of city magnates legislated for the woollen trade and its interests, very much as the Stannary Parliament did for tin. While the rule of the Worshipful Company was not devoid of bias, it worked upon the whole for the common good—at least within the industry. There were "restrictive practices" and monopolies even in those days and tricks of the trade certainly abounded. Wool is adhesive stuff, as everyone who has handled fleeces knows, and the amount which adhered to the hands of those who manipulated it was usually more than enough to be serviceable. In other words, the combing was liable to be drastic, and when measurement rather than weight happened to be the standard, the elasticity of wool proved helpful.

Legislation to curb some of these undesirable practices became necessary at various times, and a few of the measures passed are interesting enough to be quoted. There was one order that no wool was to be bought "by fraud to abate the price", this being an obvious provision to prevent what we should now call "under-cutting". In those days, high prices had to be maintained, not, as now, to preserve the level of wages, but to provide enough revenue for the Crown.

Another enactment debarred any person from buying wool for his own use. All wool was required "for export only"—an expression familiar enough today. Weavers, apparently, were not above reproach, being ordered to produce their cloth "without deceit". This necessary provision was to curb a tendency to include hair, lambs' wool, flock, or cork, and if the finished product fell short of standard, it should be forfeited to the King. Dartmoor sheep enjoyed special privileges. On their cold pasture ground they were still liable to grow coarse fleeces containing too much hair, after the manner of their prehistoric ancestors. So the people of Lifton, Tavistock and Roborough, after sending a petition to the King, were allowed "by reason of the grossness and stubbornness of their district", to mix as much lambs' wool and flock with their wool as may be required to work it. And no doubt, the commoners of all the other Dartmoor villages took advantage of this concession.

The next statute, passed in the reign of Henry VIII, was certainly an essential piece of legislation. It forbade a clothier to sell any cloth that would shrink more than one yard, when wet. This obviously must have referred to a full bale, otherwise there might have been very little left of a short piece of material. Another statute was required to check the monopoly of pasture rights. This laid down that the price of wool having been forced up by sheep-owners, no man must keep a flock numbering more than 2,000—a somewhat inconsistent measure at first sight, as it gives the impression of curtailing production.

From time to time laws were passed, ordering people to wear certain garments, an indirect method, of course, of creating a demand and helping the Crown revenues at the same time. In the reign of Elizabeth I it was made compulsory for "every male person over six years of age to wear a woollen cappe on Sondaies and Holy days". Anyone appearing without his "cappe" was fined 3s. 4d. I rather fancy that on hot Sundays most of the men and boys must have left their thick headgear at home, for in old churchwardens' accounts there are entries of the whole parish being fined "for not wearing of cappes". Just as Edward III had needed wool subsidies for his French wars, so Elizabeth needed all the wool taxes she could get, for carrying on the war with Spain—hence the Sunday "cappes". A century later, Charles II needed all the wool money *he* could raise for fighting the Dutch. So the "Merry Monarch" devised perhaps the strangest of all the wool laws—the well-known *Burial in Woollen* Enactment, which made it compulsory to wrap every corpse in no other cloth than woollen, before burial could take place. The officiating clergyman at a funeral was obliged to sign a declaration to the effect that the law had been observed. Among the registers of most old churches may be found an *Affadavit* or *Burial in Woollen Book* signed by the parish priest of Charles II's reign, after an interment.

Another statute has a decidedly modern ring, being yet one more example of recurring situations. We read that 225 years ago punishable offences on the part of workmen engaged in the woollen trade included demands for advancement of wages or shorter hours, as well as for "quitting service before time" or producing bad work. So once again, nothing in the industrial situation today lacks precedent—trade-union abuses, higher pay, shorter hours, absenteeism, and restrictive practices, the same old list of complaints in the reign of George I as now.

The woollen industry, as it affected Devonshire and particularly Exeter, was exhaustively described in my book *Devonshire*—written for the County Book Series—and Dr. Hoskins gives all available statistics in his later work, *Devon*. I will not, therefore, enter into elaborate details here. The trade enjoyed a good run, extending well into the middle of the nineteenth century, subject always to intermittent fluctuations and adverse periods, caused largely by wars at home and abroad, and all the other customary influences which affect trade at all times. The final decline was due to causes very characteristic of Devonshire. These were partly conservatism and a tendency to adhere too rigidly to old customs and methods, but even more to the geographical position of the county when its main industry could no longer depend upon its own resources. Barnstaple was one of the first towns to lose trade, even in the earliest days, owing to the unsuitability of its port which made transport difficult; and when steam supplanted water power, Devonshire generally could no longer compete with the industrial North. Coal, by means of which modern machinery worked, was too far away and too costly, while in any case the old factories were not adapted to steam power. They were like the wooden Chinese warships at the end of the last century, when pitted against the up-to-date ironclads of Japan. The horse-plough cannot compete with the tractor, nor bows and arrows with rifles, and when Devonshire at long last realized that "old times were changed, old manners gone" the bulk of her industry had drifted northwards, never to return. Nevertheless it still lingers today in isolated pockets, but only to any appreciable extent in the Buckfastleigh and Ashburton districts, where oddly enough it first came into being under monastic organization. The last mill now left at Buckfastleigh still spins wool, producing yarn which goes to Axminster for carpet manufacture.

Those early Cistercian monks, although little credit has been paid to them, nevertheless played a bigger part in shaping the county's history than any other influence before or since. By introducing Devonshire's most profitable industry, they laid the foundations of a long prosperity which left many enduring marks. In those days wealth was not acquired and dissipated overnight. It went into something solid, and very solid forms it took in some cases. Everyone who has read West-country topographical works is familiar with the claim that the proceeds of wool built Bideford Bridge, and probably its rival structure at Barnstaple. It also founded Blundell's School and various benevolent institutions, while many stately homes and fine estates came into being upon the strength of fortunes provided by the trade. The noble and the great dabbled in commerce as freely during Plantagenet and Tudor times as they do today. Big business would be impossible without wealth and brains behind it. In the case of the wool trade, it was the land-owners who provided the raw material, since they alone had the means of rearing sheep upon a big scale, and as far as they were concerned the industry in all its stages offered ample scope for shrewd investment. Many old families and historic demesnes have only retained their status by pursuing commerce in some form or other, while the new nobility is largely composed of "merchant princes". We have newspaper peers, manufacturing peers, and now life peers, the honour being bestowed either for national service or the acquisition of wealth. It is in no way remarkable therefore that wool or tin magnates arose in their day and laid the foundations of a subsequent aristocracy.

Another notable bequest left by the industry to posterity was the unparalleled number of occupational surnames. These, or the families which bear them, are mainly of West-country origin, suggesting that the custom of adopting surnames had been generally established before the trade moved northwards. One imagines that such names were *chosen*, rather than so repeatedly thrust upon a man by virtue of his calling, that when required to make a selection he could think of no other. Even now, when a name is unknown, a person may be addressed by his or her obvious profession—a policeman as "Constable", a taxi-driver as "Driver", a uniformed nurse as "Nurse" and so on. In some cases erroneous spelling did indeed creep in, as "Dwyer", an obvious corruption of the more usual "Dyer", but whether this was done for the sake of variety is another question. Alternatives indeed were popular, and every branch of the trade, with all its technical terms, figures in the directory, which lists at least twenty-three occupational surnames of unquestionable "woollen" origin.

We find Tucker, Fuller, and Weaver, Carder and Cardmaker; Webb Webster and Walker—the equivalent of Fuller—occur frequently. Shearman and Sharman were there, so the great Sherman of American military fame apparently had more peaceable ancestors. Comber and Cumber speak for themselves, and one assumes that the first Woolcombe deserved a complete specification of the craft at which he excelled. Woolman must have been something of an all-rounder and a streak of originality appears in Dyson and Dyster. I have never come across the simple and comprehensive name "Wool"—except as a Dorset place-name—but possibly that would have covered too much and suggested monopoly. It is a curious reflection that in centuries to come, present-day occupations will not be commemorated in a similar manner, when they too in their turn have become things of the past. There will be no "Tractor-drivers", "Electricians", "Broadcasters".

Possibly lunar or Martian names will have crept into the directory if the tendency to mix races is still popular in the future.

One might add that in modern Devonshire it is not unusual for a man's surname, or the name by which he was generally known, to be prefixed by his calling, I can remember Butcher Cook, Postman Harris and many others of the same description. Apple-tree Jack was a nurseryman; Parson was the frequent prefix to a village clergyman's name, while the title Farmer So-and-So was still prevalent until the modern type of agriculturist superseded the old-fashioned order. "Farmer" does not attach readily to a colonel or a major, and in this case the occupation is assumed. Again a district nurse is still "Nurse" whoever she may be rather than Mrs., Miss, or her Christian name. "Doctor", of course is universal, and in a different category since denoting degree. Much of this again applies everywhere, but old customs persist longer in rural Devon than in many parts of the country.

The gradual passing of the wool industry from Devon's countryside to the northern towns, left the county with very little in the way of trade or employment for its inhabitants. After a somewhat prolonged period of doldrums, however, new light industries are being encouraged by government grants in specially selected areas. Modern factories gleaming with glass and with hygiene are rising on the outskirts of towns, pleasantly situated and "landscaped" into their countryside surroundings.

XII

TIN

In general, the tin-producing area of England was confined to the Cornish peninsula extending as far eastwards as to include Dartmoor, or roughly—the granite country. If there is any foundation of truth in the supposition that the unidentified Cassiterides, so often mentioned in ancient history, were the islands from which the earliest Phoenician tin-traders procured the mineral, those traders must have been clever, or fortunate, to strike the one corner of Britain where tin could be obtained. That, of course, applies to the discovery whenever made, but south-western England's identity with the Cassiterides is a theory which does not bear critical analysis. If true, the early inhabitants must have been more advanced than is generally supposed, besides possessing methods of communication which make almost any theory possible.

Whatever the truth may be, it would be interesting to know how the pioneer traders first discovered that the newly found island contained tin, or how they established contact with that section of the population which could provide it. It seems more than improbable that the primitive people living on the coasts of either Devon or Cornwall would have known anything about tin, or where to obtain it, even if shown samples. On can only assume that the first Phoenician traders must have done their own prospecting, by peaceful means or otherwise, and so set the industry afoot. In that case they must also have been the first open-cast miners, subsequently known as "tinners", otherwise the aborigines would never have known what to look for or how to get to work. In all likelihood prehistoric tinning, if it ever took place, was a form of piracy, akin to ivory or slave hunting by Arab traders, although upon a minor scale. In that case, Cornwall and perhaps Devonshire, may have suffered a form of Phoenician occupation, before commerce upon purely business lines became established.

It seems scarcely realistic to imagine that St. Michael's Mount, even if inhabited, was used for shipment, the inconvenience of so remote a point being obvious. Indeed, every practical consideration renders the idea most unlikely. The comparatively minute island would have offered no inducement as a base of any kind, when once contact with the mainland had been established, and common sense suggests that whether Phoenicians or Britons delivered the tin, the vessels upon which it was eventually loaded came to the nearest points possible, rather than the farthest and least accessible. All that, however, only leads to further questions. If trade with the Mediterranean countries was ever established in the early days, when and why was it discontinued? Why did it not become a matter of history, rather than mere speculation? Were the Ancient Britons unable to maintain the supply with their primitive tools? Or, assuming that the traders helped themselves to the mineral, was it merely a case of finding more profitable scope elsewhere? In the latter case, the still semi-savage Britons might conceivably have been incapable of commerce upon their own account, a complete collapse of the trade being the inevitable consequence. It all amounts to surmising much and knowing nothing, except that, as far as Devonshire is concerned, tin was eventually found on Dartmoor. The industry certainly originated in Cornwall, advancing into Devonshire from the west, even as agriculture developed with the Saxon infiltration from the east, As for establishing the real identity of the Cassiterides, the controversy might be compared with that concerning the college at which Sherlock Holmes graduated. The only difference is, that whereas the Holmes problem might have been solved by referring it to Conan Doyle, explicit information from Herodotus as to the Cassiterides, is not available to modern inquirers.

I have already remarked that research can prove more baffling than enlightening, and this is certainly the case with the long story of Devonshire's tin industry. Periodically, in all matters concerning history largely based on legend or tradition, discoveries are made which seem to refute theories until then regarded as gospel. It is now considered questionable whether the world famous "death-shaft", alleged to have killed Harold at the battle of Hastings, ever fell—there being as much evidence to suggest that a battleaxe, rather than an arrow, brought the Saxon dynasty to an end. Possibly in years to come, historians describing the tin industry will refer to the alleged sessions of the Stannary Parliament on Crockern Tor as picturesque romanticism comparable with Arthur's Round Table.

So much has been written about Dartmoor's tin industry that it is difficult to find a fresh angle of approach apart from the stereotyped or purely statistical. Since tin is inseparable from Devonshire history, however, a summary of the part it played through all its known vicissitudes is essential. Its probable or improbable connection with the

Harford Bridge, relic of pack-horse days

Bronze Age has already been discussed. All questions as to its beginning can therefore be dismissed in the words of the late Mr. Hansford Worth who, in his authoritative work on Dartmoor, pronounces that "the origin of the tin works in the West of England is hidden in prehistoric obscurity". Tin must certainly have been produced in Cornwall during the Roman occupation, but whether the industry extended from Cornwall to Dartmoor is another matter, and the ensuing period until the end of Saxon times remains a blank in this respect, as in so many others. The trade, revived in early Plantagenet or late Norman days, was at its height with fluctuations until the end of Elizabeth's reign after which its importance gradually declined. The last Devonshire tin mine at Vitifer in the centre of Dartmoor closed to all intents and purposes in 1912. An attempt to reopen it was made as recently as 1930, but proved a short-lived venture.

Historians, who discredit the idea of any connection between the ancient hut settlements and the tin trade, regard the omission of Dartmoor from Domesday Book as an indication that the mineral potentialities of the region had not been discovered at that date. Up to a point the argument seems logical enough. Clearly the compilers of William's comprehensive survey were unaware that the moor contained a liberal store of a commodity in which they would certainly have been keenly interested. That does not necessarily prove, however, that the existence of tin upon the moor was unknown to local inhabitants. The conquered Saxons were anything save co-operative, and if the Normans regarded Dartmoor merely as a barren district, to explore which would be mere waste of time, the country people were scarcely likely to point out the mistake. The less they saw of the Conqueror's surveyors the better, and their policy would certainly have been to withhold rather than impart information.

How or when some early Norman or Plantagenet king first discovered what he and his predecessors had been missing, would make a good story, if known. Records show that the tin industry, with many of its laws and regulations, was an organized institution in 1198, with everything to suggest that it had then been functioning for a considerable period. The evolution of the famous Stannary Parliament with all its uses and abuses—the latter predominating in the main— must have been another interesting phase in the history of the industry, but apart from the first mention of it in 1494, nothing is known of its development or in whose bright brain the plan originated.

The Stannary Parliament derives most of its picturesque notoriety

9

Haytor, most frequented of Dartmoor rock-piles

from its alleged sessions on Crockern Tor, an inconspicuous but definitely breezy eminence near Two Bridges. I use the word "alleged" deliberately, for while there is no doubt about the connection between Crockern Tor and the primitive so-called Parliament, legend has so enwrapped the entire proceeding together with the grain of truth upon which it is founded, that the two have become inseparable. The Parliament consisted of ninety-six members, each of the four Stannary towns, Chagford, Ashburton, Tavistock and Plympton, contributing twenty-four representatives. Crockern Tor was the central point at which the four divisions joined. It was also accessible, for although the main road which now passes near the little hill was not constructed until centuries later, one assumes the existence of ancient tracks along the routes eventually followed by the present road system. There the members met, presumably in much the same way as modern hunt-followers, or villagers for a bound-beating ceremony assemble at an appointed spot. Some ritual may have involved ascending the tor, but common sense dismisses the idea of any important or lengthy business being conducted upon so singularly unsuitable a place. One would go so far as to suggest that the entire idea originated from the curious formation of the rocks, in which imagination can trace some resemblance to crude benches. Imagination indeed, can trace resemblance to many things in granite formations, but the picture of ninety-six staid or portly legislators sitting in solemn conclave on eminently uncomfortable stoney "benches" when there was not the slightest necessity for doing so, strains credulity to snapping point. One has only to think of them shifting about on their hard chilly seats, with the wind whistling as it always whistles round a Dartmoor tor, taking possession of somebody's headgear, or scattering the minutes of the last meeting insecurely held in the warden's numbed fingers. The proceedings must have been diversified by many a paper or hat chase, or by the sudden eruption of some member seized with cramp.

In all seriousness, however, one cannot visualize the legendary hill-top sessions as ever actually taking place, and any sense of realism suggests that they never did. The rocks were as cold, wet and hard and the human body as susceptible to chill in 1494 as today. Presumably the delegates assembled to discuss serious matters but discussion upon a bleak hill-top in a bitter east wind would have been too uncomfortable to be possible, so before imagining so unlikely a situation it might be as well to think again. Later records mention adjournments to Tavistock for the conduct of business, and one may safely assume that something of the kind always took place. In his book *Guavas the Tinner*, Baring Gould depicts any kind of social gathering connected with the industry as taking place in the building beside the trackway under Crockern Tor, known as "Tinners' Hall". Although the description is admittedly fictitious, it was none the less based upon tradition, for undoubtedly a building of some kind once stood upon the specified spot. As recently as 1897 a coaching inn, of which no trace now remains, occupied the site and it seems only reasonable to suggest that "Tinners' Hall" and the Stannary House of Parliament were more or less one and the same, with the consequent country inn as its descendant. Crockern Tor being so near, the building might indeed have borne that name—like the Cawsand Beacon Inn in South Zeal today. By way of final simile, when hounds are advertised to meet at, say, Lamberts Castle, they do not assemble among the ancient earthworks, but at crossroads which bear that name half a mile away, and so it may well have been with the Crockern Tor Parliament.

The tin trade, together with its accompanying and elaborate organization waxed and waned all down the centuries. Its prosperity depended largely upon its importance from the national point of view, or the policy of the reigning monarch. The more warlike or progressive the régime, the more metal was required either to provide armaments or to stimulate commerce. and the industry experienced its final boom during the reign of Elizabeth I, who needed funds for both purposes. Long after the decline set in, the Stannary Parliament continued to meet, like directors of an insolvent modern trading company to declare "no dividend" and give some semblance of justification for their own high salaries. The last members sang their swan song at the beginning of the eighteenth century, but since—unfortunately at least in this respect—there were no tape-recorders at that time, nobody will ever know whether the refrain expressed joy in emancipation, or lamented good times "gone for aye".

History, which means the past, can never "repeat itself", the expression being merely a literal inaccuracy. None the less, events frequently follow old patterns, and many resemblances might be traced between the protection of "indispensable" labour today and the privileges enjoyed by the tinners when their output was in great demand. Like coal mining or agriculture in war-time, tinning was a "reserved occupation" and those engaged upon it were granted special concessions in the way of tax relief and exemption from feudal service. The Stannary Parliaments—like modern county councils—made their own by-laws, many of them as iniquitous and as one-sided as imagination could devise, while the reigning powers at Westminster preferred to turn a blind eye to abuses and injustices, even if aware of them at all. To get the metal was all that mattered, and even as today almost anything is condoned under the pretext of necessity in the interests of food-production or export, so the tinner could do much as he pleased provided that he produced the mineral. The only difference was that the tinner acted within the law, monstrous as that law might be, whereas his representatives of today—labourers engaged in essential or "key" industries—take illegal action to enforce their demands, covering themselves by the proviso "no victimization" when their demands are ceded.

Even as, when at war, private property is requisitioned in the national interest, so at all times, for the benefit of the national exchequer tinners were legally empowered, by a loosely-worded statute, to "seek and dig" for the metal wherever they pleased; and if it happened to be their pleasure to select an unpopular neighbour's garden or even the floor of his sitting-room as suitable for mining operations, it was "just too bad" as far as the unfortunate neighbour was concerned. They could even divert water-supplies to facilitate their "streaming" if so disposed, and against such high-handed policy no action could be taken since it was covered by Stannary legislation. One would have expected counter action of a very definite kind in those rough and tumble days. The prospecting tinner might conceivably have been buried with his own pick and shovel, or at least have been obliged to abandon his tools while he fled to save life and limb. Unfortunately, however, for upholders of the principle that "an Englishman's house is his castle" the ruling made a special exception in the case of tinners. To "trouble" or hinder one of the fraternity in the exercise of his profession, whatever forceful course such exercise took, was a highly criminal offence, which at the very best landed the offender in Lydford gaol where he was likely to remain indefinitely.

Here again, no doubt, one must allow for inevitable embellishment and the growth of legend over the years. Probably few houses were actually demolished, if indeed a single authenticated case ever occurred. It would be far easier to dig elsewhere, and it is more than likely that coin of the realm persuaded a prospector that tin of superior grade lay on the outside of a garden wall, rather than within the enclosure. Indeed, the worst form of the abuse may have been the means that it obviously offered for extortion. One can think of few tin-workings that could have been anywhere near "built-up areas" and the only person likely to have suffered from the exercise of such a "privilege" would have been the truculent occupier of some remote tenement who had got himself disliked. Again while the powers granted to, or appropriated by the industry, since it legislated mainly for itself, were excessive to iniquity, there was another side to the question. Tin, or the revenue that it provided for the exchequer of a country often at war and always impecunious, was urgently needed, and mining for the Crown, unless backed by authority, would not have produced very much. More often than not, advice to try the infernal regions would have greeted an applicant for permission to dig in another man's intake. Without a legal right of access when desirable, it might conceivably have been impossible to work ground over which any question of ownership arose. Actually, although such things may have happened, interference with private rights must have been at worst, infrequent.

Since nothing is new, parallels might be traced between such conditions and situations in modern life. Within the past year or so, two excavating schemes—the laying of drainage and water-supply pipes respectively—have passed through this village, in effect as devastating to private rights and property as any of the alleged incursions by tinners. For that matter, the modern representatives of the "old men" appeared to lack any sense of property whatsoever. Incidentally, concerning the drainage scheme, which passed through my garden, I was unaware of the impending menace until discovering that part of my tennis court had been pegged out as a convenient site for a new village cess-pit. In that case, naturally, strong objection was upheld by a Government representative who pronounced the spot to be "unsuitable", but under a Plantagenet régime the matter might conceivably have ended otherwise.

The activities of modern officials or engineers have nothing to do with tin however, and were only mentioned by way of comparison between procedure of the past and present. Human nature does not change, as one may gather from many Old Testament stories, and the tin miners of Plantagenet or Tudor times were ordinary countrymen, in reality differing very little from their descendants, the rural labourers of every type, whom we knew before the social revolution obliterated their order for ever. The tin-workings were only forerunners, upon a minute scale, of the great granite quarries, china clay operations, water-schemes, and all the activities that mar the face of the moor today. Everything is merely relative. During the old days, there were frequent and well-justified complaints that the sludge from tin-streaming operations silted up the streams and harbours. Today one looks askance at the waters of the Plym, milk-white from contact with the china clay workings, while other streams, polluted by the discharge from factories, not to mention sewage, present never-ending problems to all concerned.

Even the numerous modern marketing boards ring a bell which in many respects has a definite "tinny" note. Under the Stannary laws tin was tested, graded and tested in the receiving centres, very much as agricultural products—eggs providing one outstanding example—are graded and stamped at the present time, the main difference being that while the tinner had to get his metal to the centres as best he could, such things as eggs and milk are now collected from the producer by lorry.

Upon the same principle, distressing pictures have been painted of the hardships endured by the tinners, particularly after the surface supplies had been exhausted, and "open cast" work was replaced by crude underground mining. This must certainly have been tough toil, nor could one imagine work more arduous than driving shafts among granite boulders where the metal deposits lay. It is hard enough to dig a ten-foot trench even with the aid of modern machinery to remove the heavy rocks. The same applied, however, to all mine work of the period, and the manual labourer's lot was harsh the world over. Upon the whole and considering the times, the tin-miners, although always poorly paid, enjoyed many advantages, and the industry only came to an end when it could no longer be carried on upon an economic basis. Agitations for its revival upon modern lines are frequent, but revival upon any extensive scale is improbable, although at the moment prospects of a large increase in the price of tin imported from Malaya, where it is now mainly produced, have again drawn attention to supplies which may still lie untapped under Dartmoor's surface. There, however, they will probably remain, for the same reason that they have done so since the beginning of time; that reason being that Dartmoor will only relinquish her deeply buried treasures at a price which nobody can pay.

XIII

FROM COPPER TO CLAY

THE story of Devonshire copper differs from that of tin in almost every material respect. The latter provides the antiquarians with as much food for controversy as his heart could desire, while the former is mere modern history, devoid of any mystery whatsoever. Copper had no past either picturesque or romantic; enjoyed only a brief although eminently sensational present, and even the most sanguine do not allow it any prospect of a future. Many private fortunes were made through tin. None the less since Devonshire tin was mostly extracted from Crown lands, it was a product over which the Crown claimed prior rights, the main purpose of its production being to swell the national revenue. Copper-mining, on the other hand, was a matter of "private enterprise" over which the State exercised no direct control.

Whereas the tin story has no known beginning, that of copper dates from early in the nineteenth century, and another hundred years saw its virtual end. It enjoyed a short life but a gay one, and a "boom" which during its heyday had probably no parallel in British history. Few mines were sunk actually into Dartmoor soil, but many into ground over which the moorland once extended. The only one actually within the Forest whose story I know was a mere speculative venture and yielded, according to local accounts, just as much copper and no more than had been secreted in the soil to encourage the enterprise. In this immediate neighbourhood there are the visible remains of two extensive mines in which many of the older villagers whom I remember had worked. Of these there is now, I believe, only one survivor, and but for the still open, dangerous pit-heads and ineradicable slag-heaps, there remains no evidence of the part they played in local history. This "spoil", once in great request for gravelling drives and paths, owing to its weed-killing properties, has now lost its sterility, and the mounds excite no further interest. Each shaft, one near Belstone, one near South Tawton, was originally sunk upon a high ridge, which to the inexpert practical eye suggests an uneconomic line of approach, particularly as in each case deep delving proved necessary to find the mineral. About a quarter of a century later the waterlogged recesses of the abandoned Belstone mine must have been jarred by new vibrations when a large county council stone quarry was opened on the side of the same hill, and worked for many years through ground under which the old tunnels must have penetrated. The quarry was eventually abandoned, much to the relief of local residents whose houses, not to say nerves, were repeatedly shaken from the effects of the blasting—although this was not the reason for the closure. It became apparent after all the upheaval and expenditure, that road metal could be procured more economically from the immense quarries at Tavistock, so road metal quarry and old copper mine never came into positive contact.

No spectacular fortunes were made either at Belstone or South Tawton, nor was it a story of shares rocketing to fantastic heights almost overnight, as in the case of the Great Consols and other mines in the Tavistock area where most of the copper-mining was carried on. At one period as many as forty pits were working in the parish of Tavistock alone. A mine was known as a *wheal*, the word being derived from the Celtic *huel*, a mine; and each had its distinguishing name, the origin of which sometimes offers scope for romantic speculation. To titles such as *Wheal Betsy* or *Wheal Emma* one naturally ascribes some direct feminine connection; but whether they were merely facetiously bestowed under the necessity of providing a name of some kind is another question. A lady who officially "opened" a mine —if they did such things in those days—might have given it her name with her blessing, but *Wheal Friendship*, on the other hand, rather suggests a philanthropic enterprise and an atmosphere not always obvious in mining relations.

Discounting tin, most of Devonshire's mineral wealth was drawn from the country lying roughly between the Tavy and the Tamar, Bere Alston and Bere Ferrers being the main centres. This belt then extended northwards to Coombe Martin, where in the period between the late thirteenth and late nineteenth centuries silver and lead with the accompanying arsenic were sporadically mined, and as in the case of tin, the output fluctuated according to the demand. Like tin again, silver-mining was conducted under royal supervision, the Crown claiming the lion's share, and the proceedings were governed by legislation much resembling the Stannary laws upon a minor scale. So again the tin-mining conditions were not unique, being actually representative of the times and the manner in which industry was organized at any particular period. Concerning places such as Coombe Martin and North Molton, both centres in their time, North Devon's share in the mining history of the county is liable to be overlooked. The lime-light has mainly concentrated upon the Dartmoor area, about which most records are available and where more evidence remains. Again Devonian topographical writers with few exceptions have been southern men, naturally giving most publicity to the district with which they were best acquainted. Over North Devon, too, mining operations wherever they took place were more sparsely scattered, fewer generally and farther between, owing to the limited potentialities of the soil.

None the less, both Coombe Martin and North Molton have a long mining record, although North Devon's claim to a prehistoric overseas commerce does not seem very realistic. Like the theoretical tin trade with the Phoenicians, it again presupposes a standard of civilization improbable in Ancient Britain. Had the Cornish peninsula figured in world markets, the knowledge could scarcely have escaped the Romans, who appear to have been unaware of any such thing. Indeed, from a purely historical standpoint the record of North Devon mining is much the same as in other parts of the county, except that the production of iron ore around North Molton in particular enjoyed a run which, although spasmodic, was one of the longest in the history of West-country mining. Discounting frequent attempts to revive output, which happened to many Devonshire and Cornish mines with the same negative results, the iron ore epoch virtually came to an end with the nineteenth century. Its record, indeed, more or less coincided with that of copper. The story of Coombe Martin's silver and lead mines was shorter. Sequestrated by Parliament during the Civil War, they never again made profitable headway, although when in full production their output had been the highest in the country.

Exmoor has never really come into Devon's mining picture, lacking in this respect the geological potentialities of Dartmoor. The absence of granite meant no tin for which to delve, so the less rugged Exmoor slopes escaped that form of early exploitation, remaining also apart from the controversial publicity which tin acquired. The fringes of Exmoor have frequently been probed for iron, particularly during the eighteenth and nineteenth centuries when the trade experienced intermittent flashes of prosperity. Unlike the Mendips, however, the district was never conventionally associated with mining, and when R. D. Blackmore attempted to introduce the atmosphere into some of his books, the efforts never struck a life-like note. A mine seemed misplaced in the Lorna Doone country and quite incompatible with the background of the story.

If Devonshire mining ever revives to any appreciable extent, it will be upon nationally subsidized lines, to a degree hitherto unprecedented, and any prosperity that it might enjoy could only prove artificial and ephemeral. The last copper mine closed early in the present century. With the mines went also the old mine "captains", somewhat mystifying figures to anyone unacquainted with mining terminology. My first personal impression of one of these "captains" was of a man whose personality suggested neither naval, nautical, nor military status. It was some time before I realized that the rank to which, by convention, he considered himself entitled, was actually equivalent to that of foreman in a quarry or factory. We are frequently told that the end of coal-mining also is in sight, as one after another of the old seams becomes exhausted, and we can only hope that no hitherto untapped store will be discovered under our western fields and moors. Less likely things have happened, for Somerset has black spots on its eastern boundaries; but so far the nearest approach to coal in this county is the lignite—often incorrectly called "brown coal"—once produced in the Newton Abbot district at Bovey Heathfield. There are no lignite "mines" in the sense which infers a deep subterranean system of shafts, the term "pit" being really more applicable. As the value of the product is limited, descent to greater depths in search of it seems improbable.

Upon the whole, the story of Devonshire's industries is one of decline, since most of them were rooted in conditions that have passed. Of course there are exceptions such as quarrying, the demand for road metal being on the increase and the supply inexhaustible. Upon the other hand, granite as a building material is being supplanted by the more convenient brick and concrete blocks. Meldon, near Okehampton, still provides a considerable amount of both granite and limestone, being indeed one of the largest quarries in the country. Many other quarries, such as Tavistock, Burlescombe, Drewsteignton, Petrock-stowe, Beer and Oreston, some abandoned, others still working, are scattered over the face of the county.

Lime is no longer so freely used upon the land, but one branch of "quarrying", if so it can be termed, which has increased and continues to extend on the southern slope of Dartmoor is the excavation for china clay already mentioned. Its broad, white and ever-widening scar provides the most conspicuous landmark, and certainly not the best impression of Dartmoor, as first seen from ships entering Plymouth Sound. Indeed, in a fading light, these ghostly mounds suggest a lunar landscape, the "dead white mountains of the moon" rather than Dartmoor's swarthy flank, purple-crowned in the sunset. Nothing could be more inconsistent with the National Park principle, but here again the claims of aestheticism and utility come into direct conflict with the scales weighted in favour of the public advantage—in other words the export drive. And still again, the situation does not lack precedent with the abandoned "white works" of Fox Tor glimmering not so far away, as an ineradicable reminder of activities, probably deplored in their day. Certainly the Lee Moor workings have reached a magnitude in no way approached near Fox Tor, and with the increased facilities for transport and export from Plymouth, they have achieved a far greater importance in the national economy. Lee Moor is now Devonshire's main source of china clay, as Dartmoor has always been.

Other clay products, defined as "pipe" and "ball" or under the more general term of "pottery clay", are still produced extensively in Meeth and other areas, notably in the Bovey Tracey district. Known as the Mid-Devon Ball Clay Industry, "mining" of this description has been carried on since early in the eighteenth century. Planning permission for further extensions has recently been granted and a considerable increase of output is expected in consequence. This has led to some alarm in the district, residents fearing that the story of Lee Moor may be repeated in the picturesque district of the Bovey. Assurances have been given that very little defacement will take place, since the mining will be of the deep shaft type. The ultimate effects, however, remain to be seen.

Formerly, a large proportion of the clay was used more or less upon the spot for the manufacture of the famous Bovey pottery. Since this industry has now come to an end, the main output goes for export, this being facilitated by the greatly improved road haulage system, not to mention modern machinery. Export of Bovey clay involves no transport problems being made easy by the proximity to the sea.

The general tendency is to regard Teignmouth purely as a pleasure resort, with a sandy "front" densely covered with deck chairs and holiday-makers. That is correct as far as it goes, but the importance of the place as a port during two or three centuries is usually overlooked. The wealth of a port depends upon its commerce and even as wool built Bideford Bridge, so clay laid the foundation of Teignmouth's prosperity. Since the output of clay, Teignmouth's main export, has increased a thousandfold during the past two hundred years or so, the figures, in this case, speak for themselves.

Devonshire was never a great manufacturing county, as compared with the industrial Midlands and the North, although some of the local products have become world-famous. At the present time the Tiverton "lace factory" as technically termed, with a far more comprehensive output, remains one of the most prosperous in the county. Indeed, with its atmosphere of contentment and co-operation, it provides a pattern which might be followed with advantage throughout industry generally. Axminster carpets have remained a name with which to conjure, but during a long and periodical intimacy with Axminster, I only heard them mentioned as products of an affluent past. Carpets are still made there from Buckfast wool, but whether there is any resemblance between the original Axminster carpets and carpets now made in Axminster is a question upon which the carpet experts must pronounce.

The last of the Devonshire "smitheries", where iron tools were forged by hand, closed some years ago. Described in the book *Devonshire* as a remarkable institution still to be seen at Sticklepath, near Okehampton, it started business early in the nineteenth century, and continued as long as skilled men could be found to carry on the craft. It passed without obsequies, its swan song being protracted over a long period, as one by one the anvils ceased to ring and the "trip-hammer" to thud. Nobody realized when the last blow was struck, or when the famous "trip-hammer" relapsed into silence for ever. It was just heard no more, nor was it even imagined that the once familiar thud would never sound again. Demolition and reconstruction are progressing together. Meanwhile, the old building with its reconditioned water wheels is being given a new look as a museum of Rural Industries. As many of the interesting features as possible, however, are to be preserved, although one can only regret the relegation of the "Foundry", as it is called locally, to the museum machinery or big scale production, even were the craftsmen still available. Gone are the old Devonian hurdle-makers, the scythesmen, the hedgers, the stone-masons (as distinct from the builders), the blacksmiths, the wheel-wrights, and many more familiar figures. They are no more needed now than coach-builders or ox-harness makers. As far as I know there are none even of the once indispensible village cobblers left today. There are still a few men tucked away in the side streets of smaller towns who bear a wraith-like resemblance to their village prototypes. Their "cobbling" is not so much derived from the personal customer as from the shoe shops who collect and pass on repairs. Large town stores have their "instant heelers"—possibly an intentional *double entendre*—who slap on a new heel while you wait. But this is a far removal from the genuine village cobbler, whose small, and usually dark, workshop was seldom lacking a customer or two merely "passing the time of day". It is a curious reflection that within a comparatively short space of time nobody will be alive who can remember other conditions.

XIV

THE STATELY HOMES OF DEVON

THIS is not an attempt either to enumerate or to describe all Devon's stately homes. To do so fully would need a long book in itself, whilst a brief summary would be little more than a dull gazetteer. Also it would be difficult to draw a line without insidious distinctions constantly occurring. The term "stately homes" suggests noble, historic mansions "amidst their tall ancestral trees" and with traditions as deeply rooted as the great oaks, limes and beeches which guard their approaches. Most of them were of the smaller manor house type, which have, in many cases, degenerated into rough farms. With the advent of the "new" farmer, however, a considerable number have been well restored to something approaching their old status. Other counties possess more mansions of the "palatial" description, such as Blenheim in Oxfordshire or Longleat in Wiltshire, but Devon has been mainly content with those of less magnificent character.

Comparatively few can claim to be the birthplace of a great national figure—naval, military, political or even literary. Among those to which an illustrious name and long tradition still cling, one of the most outstanding is Powderham Castle, appropriately commanding the sea-ways to Exeter with whose fortunes those of the Courtenay family have been so closely associated throughout history. While so many ancestral mansions have passed into other hands, or undergone change in character and use, Powderham is still occupied by the Earls of Devon. A long line of Courtenays, men and women, from Elizabeth I's reign to the present day, rest beneath the little red sandstone church at Powderham. Upon the walls, memorials of shining brass record their dates and names, including those of many other illustrious families, such as Bohun and Baldwin, into which they married. Indeed, a visit to Powderham Castle might be regarded as a lesson in history, reaching far back into Devonshire's past. Admittedly the Castle has lost a certain amount of its private or feudal character, being among those regularly open to the public for visits on prescribed days. None the less, while it is still the home of the Courtenay family much of the traditional atmosphere remains. Being a Royalist stronghold, the Castle did not survive the Civil War unscathed. It suffered heavy damage, rising again from its wreckage with the restored fortunes of the Stuart line, which it has so long outlived.

Many of the old semi-feudal manors, whether famous, or missing the accident of fame, very much resembled ancient villas. They were little communities in themselves, largely self-supporting in the days when requirements were simple, the big house and its estate providing most of the local employment. Among people who remember the days before the social revolution, the attitude towards the "big house", when in its heyday, is nostalgic, almost without exception. Nothing that has followed is quite like it and nothing since has taken its place. In many respects the old-fashioned country estate had the main advantages, without the drawbacks, of "communal" farming which has been tried and found wanting, in this country. The manor organized and shared the responsibilities of its tenantry, the interests of the one being those of the other, and there were few tenant farmers who did not regard the collapse of the manorial system, when it applied to themselves, as a calamity.

Even when an old mansion becomes a benevolent institution, as so many have, the sense of loss remains, for change always means that something has gone. Also, while stately homes were usually ideal as such, under the old conditions they often proved unadaptable to other uses. Maristow, where the Lords of Roborough once lived, occupies a situation which in earlier days left nothing to be desired. Standing in its own park-like grounds overlooking the wooded valley of the wide-flowing Tavy, its setting could only be described as beautiful. Beauty indeed is there and peace, but Maristow also stands in splendid isolation, and when, some years ago, the house was converted into a home for retired clergy, many of the new inmates found their retirement only too complete. The nearest towns, Plymouth and Tavistock, are both several miles away, and clergy subsisting on pensions are not always the possessors of cars. To board a bus involved a long uphill walk. The same difficulties applied to maintaining an adequate domestic staff, while the place generally possessed too many social disadvantages. Eventually fire brought an end to its use as a retirement home, and the house is now being run as a school for backward children.

In the same locality is Buckland Abbey, once the home of Sir Richard Grenville, and subsequently of Sir Francis Drake, such a residence providing ample proof that maritime adventure was profitable. Buckland Manor, upon which the Abbey eventually rose, was

one of the many bestowed by William the Conqueror upon his grandson, Baldwyn de Bryonis, eventually coming into the possession of
Amicia, Countess of Devon. By her the early monastic establishment
was founded and presented to the White or Cistercian monks about
1278. It developed upon the customary lines to become a thriving
institution, deriving most of its wealth from agricultural sources. Its
immense "tithe barn" with its wonderful roof in the construction of
which no iron nail was used, and wide imposing entrance, both suggest
the enormous amount of produce that a thriving monastery acquired
and stored. That the great tithe barn housed a vast deal more than the
tithe if ever full to capacity, is also obvious. One may safely assume
that on the Abbey lands golden fields stretched far and broad, and that
the fleeces of sheep which roamed many hills were piled high in that
capacious storehouse. All the same the tithe must have been substantial,
since it was the Cistercian policy to establish a generally high standard
of agricultural prosperity; the better the times, the higher the tithe
being an approved maxim.

Buckland Abbey witnessed nearly three centuries of monastic
ownership before suffering the fate of all similar establishments under
the general dissolution. The property was bought by the Grenville
family in 1541 and so began its remarkable maritime connection. The
first three occupiers holding the distinguished name died in sea warfare,
and after them came the great Sir Richard by whom the mansion, very
much as it stands today, was actually built. Sir Richard did not enjoy
the results of his work for very long. At war with life—or with its
treatment of himself, as he visualized it—he threw in his hand and
acting upon angry impulse, sold the estate just forty years after his
family had acquired it. This deed, committed in haste, was certainly
repented at leisure. Sir Richard eventually discovered that the purchaser,
acting through an intermediary, was in reality his rival Sir Francis
Drake, the one man into whose possession he least desired that the
property should fall. But such was the price of precipitation. Thus
Buckland Abbey passed from one sea dog to another, continuing its
maritime association, but it is the spirit of Drake rather than that of
Grenville which haunts the place today. Indeed, taking the word
"haunt" in its literal sense, it is interesting to find that in later versions of
the Wish Hounds legend, Drake is substituted for Dewer, the ghostly
huntsman. He is said to follow his phantom pack along that stretch of
the old Abbots Way which leads to Buckland Abbey—an example of
the evolution of folk-lore extending into comparatively modern times.

Bowerman's Nose. A conspicuous feature

Whether the money which purchased Buckland came from Drake's "earnings" or State grant for services rendered does not transpire. Glory was its own principal reward in Elizabethan days, and Drake was probably in a position to buy the property for himself. Whether given or self-acquired, however, Buckland Abbey has always been regarded as an appropriate home for Devonshire's and England's naval hero, and it seems regrettable that Drake left no descendants to perpetuate the direct succession. The property remained in his family, however, actually under the same name, until about 1792, and in the possession of Drake connections on the female side, for many subsequent years. Buckland Abbey did not come on to the public market until 1942, being finally bought four years later by Captain Arthur Rodd, who presented it to the National Trust as an establishment too big for private occupation under new conditions, but too splendid a national monument for demolition.

Still maintaining the maritime tradition, the spacious buildings were most appropriately used during the Second World War to house naval stores, and this naval association is still carried on by the Plymouth Corporation, to which body the property has been leased. Buckland Abbey is now open to the public as a museum which, as might be expected, specializes in displaying souvenirs of Drake and his era, together with other relics of West-country interest. This, of course, has involved certain adaptations to meet the requirements of visitors, and there is a note of startling constrast as one passes from a busy white-washed restaurant into the sombre dignity of rooms where Sir Richard Grenville or Drake once sat, pondering problems the outcome of which may have made history, but quite as frequently, no doubt, concerned the ordinary affairs of mortal men. The great sea dogs were very human and the last years spent at Buckland by both Drake and Grenville were not the happiest of their lives. Such a place in such a setting is in itself a museum, the main contents being associations and suggestions far more realistic than the souvenirs or relics that have been accumulated. When a stately home becomes a museum of its own past, it cannot escape a hint of melancholy. Old houses which have been converted into benevolent institutions or even adminstrative offices strike a completely different note, owing to the lack of all direct association with their historical background.

An outstanding example of such an adaptation is Bicton in the Vale of the Otter, near East Budleigh—Raleigh country—although this particular house was built long after Sir Walter's time. It is a remarkably

10

Buckfast Abbey, cradle of the woollen industry

fine Georgian mansion, formerly a seat of the Clinton and the Rolle families. There are the "ancestral trees" and the "pleasant land", so symbolic of the descriptive poem by Felicia Hemans. In some respects, the general setting of the house resembles that of Dartington Hall with its proximity to the old and now disused church, of which, in each case, only the square tower remains. Although lacking a long historical background, Bicton in its day was a mansion of distinction with a past so completely irreconcilable with its present use that no feudal associations remain. It is now an agricultural school under the Devon County Council, a sign-post indicating the drive entrance from the main road being ornamented with a picture of a cow. As though further to demonstrate the break with the past, the depicted beast is a Friesian, nor could a more efficient exorciser of ghosts have been devised. While Bicton has become an agricultural school, North Wyke has recently been acquired by Fison's Fertiliser Company. It is now changed from a private residence into a centre for comprehensive agricultural experiments on grassland research, and in the panelled rooms where centuries ago the Wyke family once entertained royal visitors, today white-coated young scientists study very different problems from those of state. Concealed from view behind the old quadrangle, are up-to-date farm buildings, housing every type of modern agricultural machinery and equipment, with new dwellings to accommodate employees. Upon the whole, the North Wyke of today has very little in common with the same North Wyke in its tranquil setting, even a quarter of a century ago.

Lew House, of Baring Gould fame, with all its qualifications to the manor house status, is now a hotel, although still in the possession of the author's descendants. The original site was acquired with the estate by the Gould family during the early Stuart period, subsequently undergoing various additions and renovations, some of them made by the Reverend Sabine Baring Gould himself. "Manor House" hotels, indeed, are many and to enumerate them all would be tedious.

Upon the whole, the purposes to which some famous residences have been relegated are as varied as imagination could conceive. Stover, for long a seat of the Templers, is now a girls' school. Poltimore, with its reputed 365 windows and spacious setting, is a private hospital. Flete, overlooking the picturesque Erme valley, has already experienced two changes since the comparatively recent and tragic death of its former owner, the last Lord Mildmay. Serving for a short time as a maternity home, for which it proved too remote, it has now been converted into a block of flats, the success of which scheme has yet to be tested, the flat being still an innovation not quite compatible with the general idea of country life. Endsleigh, the Devonshire home of the Dukes of Bedford, situated on the county's western fringe with only the Tamar to separate the estate from Cornwall, has been bought by a syndicate, consisting of fourteen members, mostly West-country residents. Their interest in the property appears to be largely riparian, the avowed intention being to use the house as a lodge for fishermen. "Lodge" perhaps, seems a scarcely appropriate title for a place of such dimensions, but it never ranked as a "mansion" in the generally accepted sense, being actually called a "cottage", and has no historical background.

Dunsland House*, dating from early Tudor times, was bought in 1954 by the National Trust, a final destination shared with many other Devonshire estates in similar case. In many instances the sense of loss is based upon sentimental grounds or those of association, rather than upon the disappearance of ancient architectural masterpieces. Comparatively few of the mansions which have outlived their original use, or become white elephants to their owners are really old as they stand today. A great deal of rebuilding and renovating took place during the nineteenth century and many ancient manor houses were completely replaced by more ambitious edifices, sometimes upon the original site, but quite as often upon entirely new ground. For the most part architectural "gems" or buildings of outstanding historical interest have been acquired by the National Trust, or are maintained by other public bodies upon payment of a nominal rent to owners who do not wish entirely to relinquish possession. Of those which had no special claim to preservation at the public cost but could no longer be kept in habitable repair, some have relapsed into ruins, or have been sold and demolished for the sake of the material which they contained. Among the latter, Trebartha Hall, although situated on the Cornish side of the Tamar, was a typical example.

Fire solved the problems of many large houses, such as Oaklands, near Okehampton, since rebuilt to provide council offices, while no trace now remains of the once fine mansion at Eggesford, where the late Earl of Portsmouth maintained his magnificent sporting establishment during the closing years of the past century. Few people now would imagine the "glory that was" when visiting the former site of

---

* This historic mansion having been recently restored and refurnished at great expense was completely destroyed by fire in November 1967. As with Eggesford House no trace now remains. All debris has been cleared, the site levelled and grassed. Only a few rhododendrons and a white magnolia recall a long history utterly obliterated.

Eggesford House, around which azaleas bloom as might exotic plants to mark the tomb of some Eastern potentate.

Ruins, which in themselves cannot fail to strike a melancholy note, no matter how beautiful they may be, alone commemorate the colourful, but not particularly eventful Berry Pomeroy Castle. Expressing fewer vicissitudes of fortune and ownership than many of its contemporaries, the castle or mansion, in its picturesque sylvan setting, was abandoned to the bats and the owls long before others of its period gave up the struggle to maintain their status. Also, beside the Dart, that Rhine of western England with its feudal atmosphere and old-time associations, still stands Dartington Hall, anything save a ruin and providing, perhaps, the most notable example in the county of a former "stately home" successfully adapted to eminently modern use.

Yet Dartington Hall might conceivably have suffered a fate similar to that of Berry Pomeroy, Eggesford and Stevenstone—another mansion of which ruins only remain. After an early chequered history, Dartington was acquired by the Champerownes during Elizabethan days and remained in possession of the family until well after the First World War, although much of it had fallen into disrepair for the reasons all too common in the records of old mansions. Eventually, however, when Dartington Hall appeared to have no future other than as an interesting relic for antiquarians to visit, the property was bought by Dr. L. K. Elmhirst who foresaw the possibility of founding an institution unprecedented in Devonshire. This materialized into a community, self-contained and largely self-supporting, comprising scope for developing rural crafts of every description, with centres for music, drama, art and education. Now the movement has been extended into North Devon, Dartington having recently established a second cultural centre at Beaford, with similarly gratifying results. Achieving unqualified success, and drawing its personnel from all sides, Dartington Hall has gained a wide reputation; and so from the imminent ruin of one stately home arose an institution, perhaps the most beneficial and generally useful that the changing conditions have witnessed.

Little need be said of the old castles, in the literal sense, such as Okehampton, Totnes and others. Some have been preserved as interesting architectural monuments for sightseers to visit upon payment of an entrance fee; many have been left for time's slow hand to obliterate. These did not linger into modern times as "homes", or centres of rural life with long manorial associations. But perhaps I might close the chapter upon a somewhat unusual note, by referring to a communal building or block of buildings, more famous in Devonshire than any mansion, but in no sense either stately or providing a home which anyone would desire to occupy. It is imposing enough, however, and appears to have acquired an entirely new social value.

Until quite recently, Princetown prison had been considered and represented as a bad blot upon the landscape, if not upon the national escutcheon. The hardship endured by everyone obliged to live in so harsh a climate, and so remote from all social amenities was depicted in moving detail. A campaign for the demolition of the prison and its removal to a more desirable site was so zealously maintained that success seemed assured. Then when this end appeared to be attained, almost overnight the local attitude changed. Residents suddenly awoke to the realization that the removal of the prison would also mean the end of Princetown's main source of livelihood. Not only did the prison provide a great deal of local trade, but it also brought a vast influx of visitors eager for a glimpse of so celebrated an establishment. Without it, all interest and therefore all attraction would be gone. Princetown, it was urged, would degenerate into a ghost town, deprived of the one reason for its existence, its prosperity a mere matter of memory. Agitation to retain the prison became more vehement than the campaign for its abolition had been and apparently achieved its end. Those upon whom the responsibility for removal would have fallen were glad to be spared the necessity of finding another stately home for delinquents, or a better place to put it. As matters now stand, the old buildings of Sir Thomas Tyrwhitt fame will disappear indeed, but Princetown will not suffer the loss of revenue and attraction, as a new prison, complying with modern standards, will arise not far from the original site. One can foresee no corresponding change in the harsh moorland climate or any lessening of Princetown's remoteness from "amenities", yet everybody appears to be satisfied. However, a somewhat illogical change of view when disadvantages are realized does not lack precedent.

XV

SOME LITERARY FIGURES

NOT long ago, at a West-country meeting convened by the Society of Authors, I had a subtly humorous but none the less typical experience. After talking for some time to two fellow writers, when opportunity occurred I was asked by each in turn—*sotto voce*—whether I could tell him of anything that the other had written, the information being required for tactful use in possible further conversation. It is always difficult to define an "author" since in some cases the publication of a short local guide book qualifies the writer to be ranked under that heading. Devonshire has produced many writers, some who have become famous and doubtless others as talented who have missed the accident of fame.

Numerous Devonshire names come to mind, yet whom can one select as having left the most permanent mark upon the county's literature? The test of an author lies, not so much in his temporary sales or temporary "press", as in his characters, which, if great creations, far outlive him. This applies to fictitious personalities whose names occur in the ordinary talk of educated people, without a thought being bestowed upon the writer who invented them. The White Knight and the Mad Hatter are figures of speech, but who thinks of the uninspiring Lewis Carroll when either is mentioned? Anyone could place John Ridd or the Doones, but they conjure up no picture of the self-effacing Blackmore in his quiet garden. It often becomes a question of which is famous, the writer or his book, or which has achieved fame upon account of the other.

Among the literary giants of Devonshire, as a general rule, it has been the writers who have become famous, or recognized pillars of their profession, rather than the popular fictitious character, or even the classical works that they produced. There are, of course, exceptions. *Dewar Rides* would not necessarily bring L. A. G. Strong to mind, while *Tarka the Otter* stands forth as a masterpiece of poetical prose and literary technique. Yet, upon the whole, Devonshire authors have created few, if any, characters with real world-wide or even national appeal. No book issuing from a Devonshire pen has brought to life individuals equivalent to Jane Eyre, Tess of the D'Urbevilles, or many that have figured in the pages of Dickens. None have achieved an atmosphere comparable with that of *Wuthering Heights*. Dartmoor has produced no *Owd Bob*. *Reynard the Fox*, perhaps the most realistic animal poem with an obvious West country setting, was the work of a recent Poet Laureate. The most outstanding animal character that has emerged from Devonshire literature, arousing most sympathy because so accurately and beautifully described, could only be Fortescue's wild red stag. He was given no name, however, so never attained the individual reputation on the strength of which many four-footed heroes have survived.

With Eden Phillpotts passed Devonshire's grand old man of letters, dying as he did at the age of ninety-eight, metaphorically with pen still in hand. His work might be regarded, in the main, as a long series of portraits, depicting country life, largely with a Dartmoor setting, backed by intimate personal knowledge of his subject in all its aspects. Unlike his Dorset contemporary Hardy, who disguised all place-names, Eden Phillpotts set his characters in villages or even houses that could be found on any ordnance map, often using old family names still common in the districts about which he wrote. This gave his stories a real-life quality which few writers achieve, there being no room for doubt—as in the case of the fictitious Sherlock Holmes's college—as to the place that the writer had in mind. His command of language, picturesquely descriptive, was unsurpassed, and no eye surveyed the wide colour scheme of moorland and summer sky more appreciatively than did his. He knew how to create atmosphere upon paper with words and similes entirely his own. Sometimes indeed, a reader who knew the scenes portrayed might be inclined to consider the frequent word-pictures a little over-done, but any such momentary tedium was always modified by the thought, "a fine description all the same".

There are those who consider that Phillpotts exaggerated the native speech, by making too much use of expressions long out of date—even if ever customary, or that he made the talk of country people too flowery, as at times he certainly did. It must always be remembered, however, that nothing is more difficult to render upon paper than convincing dialect, and a great deal had changed materially throughout the seventy years during which he wrote. One cannot live for a long period among the moorland people whom he described without realizing how excellent and accurate his characterization was. Very few writers, for that matter, excelled at village public-house talk— a trap into which both he and Thomas Hardy frequently fell.

Like Baring Gould, Eden Phillpotts seldom, if ever, idealized. He presented people as he found them, even as he correctly described the country in which they lived. In consequence they were the more life-like, if not always men or women whose personal acquaintance one would have sought. In my own opinion his *magnum opus* was one of his earliest works *Lying Prophets*—a story with a Cornish setting—containing two of his most pleasing characters, in shape of the attractive Joan, the non-conformist fisherman's daughter and her benevolent farmer uncle, a perfect representation of his type. The story also presents a woman of very different mould, and on the whole, perhaps, the feminine characters created by Phillpotts were more convincing than his men. At least perhaps, they were more outstanding, such as "the Mother" in the novel so entitled, or Avis in the book which bore her name—both characters being remarkable mainly for strength of will. There are few of his characters, howeyer, who would be remembered were their names mentioned in literary talk, while that of Phillpotts himself will always remain a household word wherever books are read.

Whether or not Phillpotts and Baring Gould were known to one another I cannot say. Up to a point they were contemporaries, although Phillpotts survived the Lew Trenchard rector by a great many years. They shared the same field with its background of moor and country life, and although Baring Gould extended his scope to the study of antiquities and subjects other than fiction, none the less the two had much in common. When referring to some book, the question: "Was that by Phillpotts or Baring Gould?" is not uncommon, even though the style of one bore little real resemblance to that of the other. They wrote from different angles, owing perhaps to different circumstances and environment. Phillpotts was possibly the better naturalist, a better artist; Baring Gould the more experienced moorman, with the greater wealth of country outlook and tradition behind him.

Possibly Baring Gould is better remembered upon the whole for his topographical and biographical books than for his many novels, although his grim powerful *In the Roar of the Sea* paints vivid pictures and catches an atmosphere which can only be appreciated by anyone who has heard the Atlantic breakers thunder on the terrible coast of north-west Devon. Yet curiously enough, if one chose the character that stands forth most prominently from his writings, it would certainly be the real-life figure of "The Vicar of Morwenstowe". His was a personality whose remarkable qualities, not to say idio-

syncrasies, would probably never have received so wide a reputation
had it not been publicized by Baring Gould. The Reverend R. S.
Hawker, described in the book mentioned, actually lived just inside the
Cornish boundary, so although so closely associated with the adjoining
county, he cannot be claimed as a Devonian.

All considered, no literary figure has attained the stature reached
by Baring Gould in the West Country. A categorical list of his works
is not required here, particularly since his full biography has recently
been published. As already mentioned his canvas was wide, embracing
besides fiction his notable contributions to the hymn-book, and much
concerning the history, topography, folk-lore and music of his
county. Of the various old songs and ballads which he collected, the
most famous is certainly "Widecombe Fair", adapted from a much older
and very different version which had never been set to music. It was
acquired and first jotted down by him at an old moorside farm-house
near Belstone, where he carried out a great many of his Dartmoor
investigations. The Lew Trenchard author possessed a strong individuality, and the inevitable fabric of legend grew up around him.
Typical among these was the convention that he did not know his own
numerous children individually. This is mainly based upon the
anecdote which doubtless gathered much in repetition, of his meeting
a young daughter on the staircase and inquiring her name and
parentage. The actual incident, by the way, has been recently confirmed
by the daughter in question. Since the little girl was dressed up for a
children's party then in progress, the mistake was perhaps compre-
hensible—particularly if "papa's" thoughts were otherwise occupied
at the moment. Owing to defective sight, I have failed to recognize
my own mother in the road, and once familiarly accosted a stranger in
mistake for my wife—the sequel emphasizing the need for more careful
identification ever after.

Baring Gould died, if not many times, at least more than once
before his death. I remember one such occasion, when an obituary
notice with biographical details having appeared in the press, my sister
wrote to one of his daughters, a former school friend, expressing the
customary sympathy. For this the girl returned the equally conventional thanks, but added that "Papa" was still very much alive and
deeply touched by all the complimentary tributes that had been paid
to him.

He lived and worked in a Devonshire that has gone, in the picturesque
era of Jack Russell; when Davis wrote his *Dartmoor Days*; when first-

rate hunters stood in the country parson's stable and the village rectory or vicarage was a well-staffed mansion. Lew House where he lived was an appropriate setting for one who wrote so much about the beauty and romance of a countryside which changing conditions had as yet affected so little. The pixy, he was wont to say, had retired into the world of fantasy at least eighty years before his day, but Lew House had not entirely lost its atmosphere of old-world superstition, as an anecdote told to me by the daughter of the staircase incident more than suggested.

One dark winter evening the great man was standing at his desk— he never sat when at work—his fingers driving the prolific pen, but his ears alert for the sound of carriage wheels, his wife and daughters having gone out for tea. He heard the expected sound distinctly at last, and pen still in hand, hurried to open the front door. To his surprise, steps and drive were empty, but as he looked about, puzzled, above his head there sounded something which he could only describe as "a ghastly gibbering laugh", as though to say, in his daughter's words this time, "sold again". It must certainly have been both an eerie and startling experience. Ornithology, however, was not Baring Gould's strong point and I could not but wonder whether a passing herring gull, itself even more startled by the sudden light below, had voiced its protest. Needless to add, the suggestion was never made. It would have lacked tact. Besides, there remained the puzzle of the ghostly carriage wheels which had ground so audibly upon the gravelled drive.

Another novelist who emulated to some extent both Phillpotts and Baring Gould was John Trevena. In his writings he usually disguised names, but presented characters so true to life that they bore too close a resemblance to living people, who considered them unflattering caricatures of themselves—sometimes not without justification. Trevena was as unpleasantly cynical as Beatrice Chase, John Oxenham's "My Lady of the Moor", was sentimental, and it was mainly to John Oxenham that the Widecombe authoress owed the popularity which she enjoyed for a considerable time. She worked to deserve it, however, and in *The Heart of the Moor* she achieved her best. In her heyday she did not lack a public of both sexes, but despite her guild of "White Knights", virtuous young men whose high standards and ideals qualified them for enrolment like those admitted to Arthur's Round Table, her following was mainly feminine.

For many years she played the part allotted to her in Oxenham's novel. As "My Lady of the Moor" she frequently accosted visitors walking on the hills, welcoming them with a sprig of white heather—when in season—and more or less graciously conferring upon them the freedom of the moor. In keeping with her love of sentimental tradition, over a long period she secretly made herself responsible for the fresh flowers regularly placed upon "Jay's" grave, the much romanticized wayside mound near Hedge Barton. She delighted in the touch of superstitious mystery that became attached to these flowers around which grew the legend that so impressed sightseeing tourists. Incidentally, this practice has been continued since her death by some kindred spirit upon whom her mantle has fallen.

In spite of her idealism, she was a lady very much disposed to take her own line, as I discovered upon our first personal acquaintance. Meeting far out on Dartmoor, and unknown to one another except by correspondence, she inquired the way to Cranmere Pool. I supplied the information, only to be told that it was incorrect according to her calculations. Her imposing and resolute figure, as she strode off in the wrong direction, left an impression as indelible as it was mildly humorous.

Her real name, of course, was Katherine Parr, and as such she always signed her personal letters. Unfortunately her last years at Widecombe were far from happy, and both Beatrice Chase and her work are now virtually forgotten, belonging, as they did, to an era which has passed for ever. At one time her chapel and cottage were indicated to the tourist, whom she always welcomed, "lime-light", as she called it herself, being something to which she was far from averse. To the tourist of today, however, her name would convey little; souvenirs of Uncle Tom Cobleigh being the main attraction at Widecombe in the Moor—a further tribute to Baring Gould's more enduring influence.

Few classic novels have created a more realistic atmosphere than Charles Kingsley's *Westwood Ho*. It is essentially Devonshire's own, even though so much of its setting is spread elsewhere. The scent of the wayside honeysuckle clings to its pages as Amyas Leigh walks home after his eventful meeting with Salvation Yeo and John Oxenham on Bideford Quay. The Torridge gathered much of its romance from Kingsley's "Rose", even as Marsland Mouth has ever since suggested its witch. Personally I read the book too early in life fully to appreciate its magic, as so many read Lewis Carroll and Walter Scott. None the less it gripped the imagination, investing Bideford, the placidly flowing Torridge and Barnstaple Bay with the glamour of Elizabethan adventurers, historic figures such as Sir Richard Grenville and the ghosts of other tough seafarers who might have manned the *Revenge*. No poetical line, in itself so simple, has stirred the imagination more vividly than Tennyson's "men of Bideford in Devon", but much of its appeal is certainly due to Kingsley's *Westwood Ho*.

The real Devonshire background is difficult to reflect, and various writers have been prone to exaggerate native characteristics or eccentricities. A new resident can seldom make his work realistic. Charles Garvice, who lived in the county for several years, despite his fluency found the task beyond him. He only attempted one Devonshire book *A Farm in Creamland*, and being unable to provide essential local colour, eventually surrendered the work to a literary friend better qualified to undertake it. Margaret Pedler, another prolific writer of the Garvice school, produced novel after novel from her home in the heart of the red land, but none of her liberal output, whether printed or filmed, suggested its Devonshire origin, and few of her readers ever associated her with the county.

Ecclesiastical writers, historians and archaeologists drop into another category. As Dr. Hoskins points out, Hooker can only be claimed for Devonshire by the accident of birth, his work having no other connection with his native county. A similar qualification applies to Raleigh, most of whose work was done in prison. Here, however, the ranks divide. Dr. Hoskins, author of *Devon, Two Thousand Years in Exeter, Devon and its People* is himself a Devonian, while Rowe, Crossing, and the Worths—father and son—do not need the status of native to localize their work. To Crossing's books no further tribute can be added than the general appreciation paid to them. His guide books, each dealing with one section of the moor, are as useful and highly prized today as when they were first written. They have been less affected by the passage of time than might be supposed, since he mainly described the unchangeable. Allowing for the difficulties under which he worked in days when transport was slow and limited, his exhaustive study of Dartmoor was astonishing. It would be safe to say that over the 130,000 acres that he surveyed, scarcely a hut circle or anything at all resembling an ancient relic escaped his careful inspection. It is true that with the passing of another half-century much that he described has disappeared. Old trackways have gone, afforestation schemes, water-supplies, and other exploitation have altered the landscape. Old farmsteads have been abandoned to the hill sheep and foxes, but the moors over which he traced his routes remain, and one still turns to Crossing when in doubt about the correct name of some lonely little brook, or the best point from which to reach an unfamiliar objective. One has heard men claim that they know every inch of Dartmoor, and accepted the assertion with very definite reservations. Both Crossing and the late Hansford Worth, however, come as near as anyone ever has to deserving such a distinction.

There are, of course, contemporary writers, such as Alan Jenkins, Dr. Margaret Lambert, and Victor Bonham Carter, much of whose work has probably still to come. Of these Dr. Margaret Lambert is the most essentially Devonian by birth and long tradition, as daughter of the first Viscount Lambert, who for fifty years represented the South Molton, which eventually became the Torrington Division in Parliament. He published no biography, having always resolved never to do so, although his daughter was more than equal to the task, and her various literary works to date have dealt with public affairs and economy rather than matters of purely Devonian interest. To her also fell the work of translating and filing a vast accumulation of German documents which came into the possession of the British Government after the last war. A woman of letters, indeed, but one whose sphere has lain far beyond the limits of the little mid-Devon village where her childhood was spent.

The books by Alan Jenkins, whether adventure or travel stories, cover a wide field. He has stretched his canvas from Lapland to India, his subjects ranging from elephant to domestic cat. It is a far cry from India or Lapland to his home on Dartmoor's fringe within sound of the Taw as it plunges from the hills to the lowland, passing the cottage where John Oxenham lived and wrote more than half a century ago.

Victor Bonham Carter has found his inspiration in the rural village and life on the land, while E. W. Hendy, apart from his poetry, specialized in natural history. Although Hendy wrote on the further side of the Somerset boundary, his connection with Devonshire is unchallengeable. An active foundation member of the Devon Bird Watching Preservation Society he was also, like Blackmore, a Blundell's School boy, with early roots deep in the county. I realized this upon one occasion when travelling with Hendy on a Devon General motor-bus. He was returning with me to spend a weekend after a meeting of ornithologists at Exeter, and by chance we fell into talk with a countryman who, it transpired, had frequently played football against Blundell's and Hendy himself. Soon the two were away on reminiscences of Tiverton and a casual listener would scarcely have known which was the Devonian.

There is no doubt about the work of Ernest Martin, the question being the category and not the county to which it belongs. Unaided by extraneous circumstances of any kind, he found his literary feet by individual effort and took his own independent line. It seems somewhat ironical that he should have lived in the parish of which the famous Jack Russell was the incumbent, and to whose reputation he appears to have taken pronounced exception. The biography of Devonshire's famous hunting parson is still read, his character, however likeable, little resembling those of the fictitious country clergy depicted by Blackmore. Baring Gould, on the other hand, evinced no disposition to idealize members of his own profession, although he never let down the cloth by creating such figures as Whyte Melville's "Abner Gale" or Daphne du Maurier's "Vicar of Altarnun".

The literary list of country clergy contains no second Gilbert White; nor, for that matter, has such a figure arisen elsewhere, but less, perhaps, for lack of the mantle than shoulders which it might have fitted. Gilbert White was a pioneer, the first real field naturalist, unique in his time and therefore in his appeal. Posthumously he acquired numerous disciples and emulators, but each was one of many. Without for one moment decrying his indisputable greatness, there would be little room for his work today. Devonshire county clergy, like Thornton, Hobbs and Keble Martin, have possessed a similar love of nature, powers of observation and aesthetic sense, but without achieving popularity. The Reverend Francis Hobbs, the same man, incidentally, who came to the rescue of Garvice, and often collaborated with Thornton, once told me that early in his life he wrote a number of articles upon the wild birds that he loved. They were printed and very good, but after publication his editor advised him to "give birds a rest and write about people". He was an ardent disciple of Gilbert White and under different circumstances might have become the Selborne naturalist's Devonian successor.

Into much the same category falls the equally well-founded charge that Dartmoor has inspired no classic poem, the verse of Davis scarcely qualifying for such a distinction. Here, however, the case is reversed, the rhymer rather than his subject being required, since few great poets of any time have known the country. "Meet nurse for a poetic child" it should have proved, but in all probability to men such as Herrick and even Coleridge, Dartmoor meant nothing but a ragged blue line bounding the western horizon, a region of grim repute to be avoided rather than sought. There is nothing to suggest that Herrick ever wandered far from the flowery meadows of the South Hams in search of themes, or even desired a wider field. He defined his scope simply but comprehensively:

> "I sing of brooks, of blossoms, birds and bowers,
> Of April, May, of June and July-flowers
> I sing of May-poles, hock-carts, wassails, wakes,
> Of bridegrooms, brides and of their bridal cakes."

For him the daffodil had more appeal than Scott's "dark mountain heather", and in any case a setting of crag and tor and upland torrent creates an atmosphere requiring the muse of a Wordsworth or Byron to capture its spirit. Unless Herrick's dislike of the county in which circumstances had placed him was more assumed than real, Devonshire streams must have been the veritable waters of Babylon, and the great blanket bog of Dartmoor, had he seen it, the Slough of Despond. However that may have been, it is noteworthy that after his temporary eviction under the Commonwealth, he reclaimed his Devonshire benefice and ended his days in self-imposed exile, if such it was.

There is always a tendency to bracket Herrick with Coleridge, although two centuries divided them. Diametrically contrasted in some respects as were their life stories, they do not altogether lack similarity. While Herrick was born in London and did not arrive at Dean Prior until he had reached the age of thirty-nine, Coleridge was born at Ottery St. Mary in south-east Devon and died in London. While one was a clergyman, the other figured for a time as a Unitarian preacher. Herrick was a bachelor; Coleridge was not adapted to idyllic marriage. While the Londoner Herrick wrote in his Devonshire vicarage, the eminently Devonian-born Coleridge wrote little that reflected the atmosphere of his native county. Even "The Ancient Mariner" took shape, not in some Plymouth or Bideford tavern where wild sea tales were told, but in the unlikely setting of the Quantock Hills, overlooking the sea indeed, but an inlet of the Atlantic singularly devoid of romance. Only one line in "The Ancient Mariner" suggests the author's youthful environment. "Like one who on a lonesome road doth walk in fear and dread" is a simile which might easily reflect the mental attitude of an imaginative boy when crossing ghostly Woodbury Common on some owl-haunted winter night.

"The most wonderful man I ever met," was Wordsworth's comment upon Coleridge during the period of their mutual hero-worship, and Wordsworth's influence was certainly apparent in the best of Coleridge's work. That his achievements might have been greater or that his premature decline was self-precipitated cannot be denied, yet how frequently is genius the measure of frailty. The loftiest peaks are those most wrapped in clouds and snow, and had Coleridge possessed a more balanced temperament he might never have set pen to paper.

The life story of most men, however, would read very differently had they been other than they were. Up to a point we make or mar our own destinies, but circumstance plays a large part and we are all subject to limitations.

Dartmoor's wool-bearers, mainly Scotch sheep

XVI

WILD LIFE OF DEVON

1. How the Buzzard made History

IN the matter of wild life study Devonshire has been progressive. The Bird Watching and Preservation Society was inaugurated more than forty years ago by twelve ornithologists meeting informally at the old Deller's Café in Bedford Square, Exeter. The old meeting place has gone, victim to 1942 bombing, but the society has grown progressively with the years, its present membership being well over a thousand. Its spheres of activity also are ever widening, one of the last being the launching of the Lundy Field Club with support from the National Trust.

Broadly speaking, the wild bird life of one southern county is very much like that of another. Below the grouse line and the Norfolk Broads there are few natural features with outstanding attractions for any particular species. A thrush is a thrush whether it sings in the Kent or Dorset twilight, and when endeavouring to describe the birds of a county, there is very little point in talking about those which may be seen anywhere. Devonshire on the whole is not teeming with feathered life. Indeed, Charles Dixon, writing eighty years ago perhaps somewhat disgruntled at being obliged to exchange a Yorkshire home for a Devonshire one, declared that the southern county could not claim a single species that might not be found north of the Tweed in greater abundance. In the main the charge was true, although giving perhaps a somewhat misleading impression of the general situation. Actually the avifauna of the county is remarkably varied, by no means sparse, and possessing in some cases a peculiar ecological interest. Once again, even in the matter of wild bird population, the geographical position of Devonshire is a disadvantage. It lies below the grouse line and the breeding range of many species, also westwards of the nightingale country, excepting a few areas where the bird has become established within recent years. Again the lack of natural freshwater lakes or extensive fens comparable even with the lowlands of Somerset means no inland habitat for wild fowl or waders, and in

The mouth of the Teign, from which clay is exported

the main, it must be admitted that as a wild bird county, Devonshire's scope is limited.

Excepting perhaps the Exe estuary, Braunton Burrows and Slapton Ley, where a hut for bird observation has recently been set up, I know of no section of Devonshire's two coastlines where the feathered life could be described as unique, or even remarkably outstanding. There is, for example, no Poole Harbour, no Tintagel where night and day the crying of multitudinous sea-fowl provides an auditory background even more perpetual than the voice of the sea itself which abates when winds are hushed. Lundy is in a case apart, lying so remote from the mainland that its presence is scarcely realized unless clear visibility renders it more than usually conspicuous. Excluding Lundy, therefore, and the other places mentioned, along the coastline generally one sees the ordinary birds of the cliffs and shore and few others. These are mostly the common but always decorative herring gulls—indeed the more numerous an ornamental species, the greater its beautifying value. There are the inevitable and ubiquitous jackdaws, a few heavy-winged cormorants, the occasional raven and peregrine falcon, the more frequent kestrel. In general, however, one goes westwards from Devon to find the shag, the guillemot, the razorbill or possibly one of the few surviving choughs, while Lundy is the main Devonian home of the puffin.

Apart from the coasts, Devonshire's interest from a purely ornithological point of view lies, not so much in the abundance, which is not very great, as in the distinctive character of bird life. Like Cornwall, within the latitudinal and other limitations, the county provides a habitat for almost any British species from the highest in the avian scale to the lowest. Here indeed a curious parallel might be drawn, for even as the Devonshire of national and political history often proved a rallying centre for lost or desperate causes, so in the case of wild life, the county has provided a last stronghold for birds whose names had become little more than legendary elsewhere.

Whether the story of old-time industries will find its parallel in natural history remains to be seen, and one can only add regretfully that the indications are not too hopeful. Old sportsmen of a generation ago referred to Dartmoor as a teeming land of black-game within their own experience and it was hoped that the afforestation of large areas in former favourite haunts of this fine species would give the blackcock a new lease of life. It is a bird of the conifers, but the planting of spruce or pine came too late to save Dartmoor's once abundant indigenous grouse. It was indeed somewhat ironical that whereas a pine-loving species had held its own for centuries on the open moorland, the planting of wood growth suitable to its economy seemed to help it very little. A few old birds which had escaped the shot-guns, sought sanctuary in Fernworthy Forest, when the cover had become dense enough to offer protection, and one or two lingered until 1960. They appeared to be non-breeders, however, and unless the species is re-introduced it seems unlikely that the rolling call of the blackcock will again be heard in Fernworthy or any other Dartmoor forest. That the red grouse can live upon Dartmoor has been shown beyond question by periodical introductions. The bird was never given a chance to become really plentiful, however, and any attempt to repeat the experiment could only end in failure under existing conditions.

Writing in 1891 the ornithologist Charles Dixon, already mentioned, described the range of the buzzard as then restricted to certain Welsh cliffs and the Scottish Highlands where he had "seen its great nest in the crowns of the fir-trees". True, wild bird study was not so far advanced in those days as now. The same impression with regard to the buzzard was general in southern England. Indeed, until well within my own time, the species was virtually unknown east of the Exe, except as a rare visitor difficult to identify. When a ten-year-old boy living in West Dorset, a gamekeeper's son little older than myself, described the bird to me as a rare phenomenon. One had appeared over the plantations of which his father was in charge, near the great Pen Wood of roe-deer fame, mystifying everybody. "It looked like a great fowl up in the air," my much -impressed informant assured me. "We couldn't think *what* it was. Then Father shot it, and we found it was a buzzard—and as fat as butter!" That Father *would* have shot it, in complete ignorance as to its harmfulness, utility or aesthetic value went without saying, but that is incidental,

I still regarded the buzzard as virtually extinct, until, coming to live in mid-Devon about 1914 I found the species well-established and spreading rapidly eastwards. Even then it had not crossed the Exe, Haldon being its limit in that direction. In 1921 I happened to witness the first appearance of buzzards in living memory over Woodbury Common, sharing the experience with a local gamekeeper, met by chance during a walk. Four of the beautiful strangers appeared literally out of the blue, cruising, fortunately at a great height, over the new country which they probably regarded as a promised land. It soon became apparent that my companion's reactions towards them were very different from mine. He regarded them with marked disfavour and proceeded to describe how "the likes of they" were treated upon the estate from which he came.

Still for the time being the buzzard continued to multiply at an extraordinary rate. Excepting perhaps the somewhat similar and corresponding increase of the fox, there has been nothing like it in natural history. By comparison the southward drift of the Fulmar petrel was simple, being a natural and unopposed overflow. The buzzard, on the other hand, had no reason for multiplying apart from the decline of intensive game preserving, which was offset in the case of so conspicuous a bird by the ever-increasing number of guns and the swollen army of rabbit-trappers, Under the same circumstances other birds of prey should also have increased at a similar rate, which was not the case. Montagu's harrier, for example, proved unable to regain a footing in country through which the buzzard made rapid progress. Now and again little colonies of harriers spring up, as at Bradworthy and Fernworthy, receive every encouragement and then after a few years disappear for no apparent reason other than lack of tenacity.

This self-restoration of the buzzard, only too short-lived as it seems likely to prove, is not a case of the survival of the fittest. It seems more like the meek inheriting the earth. The bird holds nothing by right of conquest, peaceful infiltration having constituted his tactics during the steady recolonizing process. He has, wrote F. St. Mars, "the appearance of an eagle but the heart of a rabbit," and one usually takes it for granted that a buzzard at strife with warlike neighbours means a buzzard that has been attacked. In conflict he merely takes avoiding action, and this proves one of his trump cards, since he survives, if not to fight another day, at least to evade once more when next a similar necessity arises. When differences occur, however, he can always take care of himself by adopting the simple policy of keeping out of reach, since the air does not contain a pair of wings superior to his own. He is certainly no warrior, leaving the paths of glory to be trodden by his bellicose fellows, the sparrowhawk and the peregrine falcon, yet by that curious, though common mingling of contrasts, he is bolder in actual defence of his young than any other bird of prey. During the breeding season even the pugnacious raven dare not perch in a buzzard's nesting spinney. Admittedly, when man is the intruder, defensive action seldom goes farther than clamorous though hostile protest. Even so, the big wings may sweep very near a climber's head and positive attack is not out of the question.

A few years ago, when accompanying a fisherman on Dartmoor, I left him to cross a ridge between two streams while following another quest of my own. He was barely out of sight when the furious scream-ing of a buzzard arose from the direction he had taken, the great hawk appearing now and again as it swooped low over the sky-line. At the moment I attached little importance to the disturbance. A buzzard's wail is one of the most familiar sounds upon the Dartmoor heights, but as it proved, the incident was most unusual. When rejoining my friend an hour later, he hurried to meet me, bursting with the news that a "kite" had attacked him on the ridge, striking repeatedly at his bare head, and he had only warded it off with difficulty by the use of his rod. Having lived in India, where all hawks are "kites", and being no naturalist, species was immaterial to him. The buzzard, of course, had young parked on the hill-side and the fledglings being incapable of long flights were peculiarly vulnerable, this accounting for the parent's excessive agitation.

The legal protection enjoyed by the buzzard may be discounted as purely incidental in the story of its recovery. In Devonshire at any rate such considerations exist only to be ignored or forgotten. Pending arrangements for an official pigeon shoot, one man, himself a district councillor possessing, one would have thought, some knowledge of law, proposed that the anti-woodpigeon campaign should be extended to include buzzards, the "menace" slogan being then at its height. "We bain't really allowed to kill them," was the remark of another Devonian, a gamekeeper, after which he proceeded to describe structural points of interest noted in birds that he had shot. The only prosecution for shooting a buzzard within my experience was the case of a man who vaunted the feat with great pride in a local newspaper. The bird destroyed was carrying a viper at the time, this being con-sidered the point worthy of publicity.

There was always the danger that the increasing abundance of the buzzard would bring it into disfavour, but certainly nobody anticipated the extraordinary virulence of the campaign that was launched against it. Logically, a beautiful animal, like a flower that is reasonably plentiful, should be more highly appreciated than another that is extremely rare. Its value to the country in general is so much greater, the pleasure and interest that its presence imparts being shared by so many more people. A fine bird that lends character to the landscape and may be seen by anyone who possesses an aesthetic sense is surely more important and worthier of preservation than some passing "rarity" which will probably never be seen again, or some jealously guarded inhabitant of a reserve to which only a few privileged observers have access. Unfortunately the reverse appears to be the case. Greater store was set upon the lost sheep or piece of silver than all which remained, and such is the prevailing attitude towards wild life. The country boy's remark that there were "too many primroses" was typical of a mentality by no means uncommon, while many shooting men regard any bird or beast other than those preserved for the gun as possibly inimical to sport, or at least as something that might as well be killed. A bird of prey, however innocuous, is always suspect, and when the whisper "too many buzzards" first arose, the seed fell upon fruitful soil.

The idea gained ground with miraculous rapidity and for no apparent reason. The buzzard had done nothing abnormal, yet the bird acquired a bad press overnight, as it were. The slogan "too many" became a convention, or fashionable phrase, repeated by people not concerned in any way and quite ignorant of the truth. The idea had caught on, and once afoot it took the customary course of most erroneous notions. The obvious argument that an eminently beautiful creature which harms nothing cannot be too abundant had as much effect as logical contention usually achieves in such circumstances.

The phase would probably have petered out had not the myxomatosis epidemic among rabbits provided the anti-buzzard agitators with a new line of attack. Even as the grey squirrel was renamed the "tree-rat" for propaganda purposes, so the buzzard was dubbed the "rabbit hawk". Since rabbits had been practically exterminated, so ran the argument, buzzards would be obliged to seek other game and might attack anything.

The new campaign, like most of its kind, was cleverly conducted. To counter any sympathy for the grey squirrel, the alien was represented as a destroyer of the popular native species, and upon the same principle, to forestall protest from ornithologists, the theory was circulated that buzzards, deprived of their alleged customary fare, would prey upon "other birds." What "other birds" they were capable of destroying did not transpire, while nobody seemed to realize that myxomatosis affected the buzzard's way of life very little, As a general rule it merely preys upon a few young rabbits during summer. The golden eagle is the only British bird that habitually kills any mammal larger than a rat.

The false trail had been laid, however, and served its purpose only too well.

Soon the buzzard was carrying off ducks and fowls of twice its own weight; attacking babies and boys; menacing women and lorry-drivers, killing dogs and sheep; not to mention many other feats quite beyond its capacity. Indeed, it was putting any fabled exploits of lammergeiers to shame. One achievement was reprinted in the *Field* magazine, under the "Without Comment" headline. Undeterred the disciples of Iago proceeded from strength to strength, and a competition for the most improbable buzzard story could scarcely have produced a richer crop. Eventually imagination, exaggeration, and sheer mendacity combined to manufacture a bird of prey unrivalled in the world's avifauna.

Indeed, never within personal experience has any wild creature been so unjustly villified. Fox, carrion-crow, magpie, blackbacked-gull, and even the grey squirrel were forgotten. The new public enemy was represented as the evil genius of nature's stage, destroyer of all living things from pet Pekinese dogs to woodpigeons. Buzzards were also blamed for a general dearth of young birds, a circumstance really due to a bad hatching season, from the effects of which the buzzard itself suffered as much as any species. This also applied, incidentally, to the buzzards of Lundy, where rabbits were still plentiful.

Among farmers and poultry-keepers, any loss real or imaginary, was attributed to the same cause, rather than to the customary and real predators. At the first glimpse of a big hawk circling high in the blue, as its kind had done harmlessly for half a century, consternation ensued. The farmer reached for his gun and his wife seized the nearest imple-ment that might serve as a bird-scarer. Clamour arose for the exter-mination of this terror from the skies. The Home Secretary was petitioned to remove so pernicious a bird from the protected list, while even the Women's Institutes drafted a resolution to the same effect. Here, however, the movement encountered its first check. The Home Secretary most laudably declined to do anything so unjustified, and although legal "protection" in effect means little, its retention at least saved the bird from officially organized destruction.

Protected or otherwise, a large number of buzzards undoubtedly perished, and many people who had preserved a sense of proportion feared an extermination of the species. They were as much surprised as relieved when the agitation subsided like a pricked bubble. The main reason for this seemed to lie in a verdict pronounced by the agricultural correspondent of a West-country paper. He described the buzzard as a mainly inoffensive species which had been the victim of "unfair and exaggerated publicity". Thereafter no further stories appeared in print and controversy upon the subject suddenly ended.

Although sanity has now been more or less restored, in general effect the campaign reduced the number of buzzards in Devon and Cornwall very considerably. Upon a rough estimate, the status of the species today is much as it was thirty years ago, leaving a great deal of lost ground to be recovered.

A buzzard's circling flight is always spectacular, his broad wings glinting silver in the sunlight as the hill-wind tilts his buoyant body. Watching him there, one sees the only answer to the endless conflict between the aesthetic and the material. Surely those still-winged sweeps and curves, that sublime and wondrous soaring, leave no doubt as to his value to the scene. Were he the only buzzard in Devon, would not fifty ornithologists be watching him at this moment? Surely the glory of his flight is no less wonderful because he happens to be one of a race reduced, indeed by foolish persecution, but still far from uncommon.

Half a century was required for the buzzard to reach the status that he enjoyed before the recent and quite unprovoked attack was launched against him. Should so beautiful a species again become threatened with extinction as a sacrifice to irresponsibility and lawlessness?

2. Birds of the Moor

Although mainly inhabitants of conifer woods, birds of prey have benefited very little as yet from modern afforestation. State forestry is upon the whole a short-term policy. Trees are felled when of marketable size, which means before a sufficient height or solidity has been attained to tempt the larger branch-builders. For that matter, one sees very few nests of any description in the new State forests, indeed the areas might be described as singularly birdless. Scarcely a note is heard, and even the buzzard on its interminable circlings appears to avoid them, and for obvious reason. Nothing of which either buzzard or kestrel is in search, such as small mammals or reptiles, is visible through the dense screen of tree-tops, nor are there any carcases of sheep in the plantations to attract the many carnivorous birds which feed mainly upon carrion all over the open moor. Doubtless, in course of time, sections reserved to make larger timber will acquire a characteristic avifauna, but meanwhile birds of the natural woodland remain true to their habitat. The ground afforested mostly consisted of open moorland or rough intakes devoid of trees, and therefore of the birds which build in them. They have not taken readily to the new facilities. Again, few branch-builders in any case are birds of the moorland. Sparrowhawk, kestrel, and even the ubiquitous magpie seldom nest above the line of cultivation. Such is a more or less general rule to which, however, there is one notable exception. That is, of course, the carrion crow whose nesting habits are both curious and interesting, if not indeed unique.

Upon the lowlands the carrion crow builds high, its nest being normally one of the least accessible. There are no high trees upon Dartmoor, however, for which reason most of the carnivorous birds which visit the hills make their nests in the surrounding woodlands. The carrion crow on the other hand is not primarily a bird of the dense woods. It prefers isolated trees or coppices and being solitary by nature, in general frequents the wilder parts of the country. Upon Dartmoor it finds an ideal home, and failing the lofty trees considered indispensable elsewhere, makes the best of the situation building in the low mountain ashes, dwark oaks, hawthorns, willows and even holly bushes which fringe most of the hill streams. These nests which may be found anywhere upon the hills, often in the most remote areas, are remarkable from a naturalist's point of view, being rarely, if ever, seen elsewhere unless upon outlying parts of Exmoor. They are sometimes so low that one may inspect their contents from ground level and I have seen them in trees—so called—no bigger than gooseberry bushes, the bulky nests, indeed, filling the crowns like cauliflowers among their leaves. Sometimes a slightly larger tree may contain two or three nests, only one, of course, being occupied in the same year. At one time, Blacktor Bere, where the stunted oaks are somewhat taller than on the open hill-sides, almost suggested a miniature rookery, with nests old or new dispersed along the straggling wood.

For some reason no other bird such as a sparrowhawk or kestrel ever seems to take advantage of a crow's abandoned nest even on the fringes of the moor, with the occasional exception of a merlin. Although contrary to the merlin's customary habits, its eggs have been found in the nest of a crow, both on Dartmoor and Exmoor. The buzzard which sometimes builds in hawthorns, both upon the molinia moors of Devonshire and also on Exmoor, does not, as a general rule, choose the humble sites which Dartmoor offers. During recent years I have, indeed, found one or two nests well out on the Forest, both in mountainashes. Each nest, however, had been built upon crotches overhanging a precipitous rock, as an apparent concession to the birds' instinct for height.

Although not primarily a moorland species, the kestrel may be seen more frequently than the sparrowhawk around the fringes of Dartmoor being a bird of wider spaces and in general a hunter of fur rather than feather. Upon the open moor there are mice and voles, also quantities of grasshoppers which figure largely in the kestrel's menu, not to mention the big black slugs, erroneously called "snails" by the country people. There is one slope on the southern shoulder of Cosdon Beacon over which, in early autumn, several kestrels may often be seen at the same time, quartering the ground at a low height and cruising in narrow circles hour after hour.

These interesting little groups are not necessarily family parties, although broods of young kestrels frequently cruise in company, like buzzards or ravens. In these cases it seems to be rather a matter of common purpose or of sharing a good hunting ground, as the party is often increased by two or three harriers during the migration season. Very big the visitors look as they wheel and spread their far wider wings as though in competition with the evolutions of the graceful but minute falcons. This slope, indeed, has some special attraction to birds of prey. It was there, not long ago, but before the number of buzzards had been so regrettably reduced, that I once counted eighteen of the great hawks, behaving in very much the same manner as the kestrels and harriers, but acting more sociably. Although frequently dropping to the ground, they appeared to be as much interested in one another as in any food which they might have been collecting, and spent most of the time in aerial acrobatics as though engaged in some ritual. Indeed, but for the coincidence of place one might have considered the buzzard assembly an entirely social affair. Actually, all the gatherings mentioned may have some gregarious significance for that matter. Possibly this remote and wild hill-side is a recognized *rendezvous* or port of call where birds of a feather, or at any rate birds of a similar character foregather in their own peculiar fashion.

Away in the heart of the moor one seldom sees the kestrel. It breeds nearer cultivation, nesting mainly among the rocks or in disused quarries, Like the buzzard, it avoids the remote tors leaving the "solitary raven" in sole possession of Dartmoor's wildest and most lonely heights. In many respects the story of Devonshire's raven during comparatively recent years has much in common with that of the buzzard, although it is less spectacular. The raven's range is confined mainly to the Dartmoor area, but comparatively speaking there is the same record of quite unaccountable increase, a "peak" of abundance and subsequent decline, although in the raven's case without any organized campaign to reduce its numbers.

For most Westcountry people, the raven's once sinister croak has lost much of its significance. All along the coastline of Devon and Cornwall, on Dartmoor's heights and over the wilder inland districts generally, the impressive sound has now become so familiar that it is taken for granted if noticed at all. Certainly it no longer arouses the superstitious awe which the voice of the "death bird" once aroused. Within living memory, if a raven's shadow drifted across a Devonian or Cornish mine, the circumstance was considered so ominous that no man would work in the pit until a complete inspection of the machinery had been made. One can only assume that ravens were not frequently seen in the days of the mining boom. Had they been as plentiful then as now* an inspection staff for every district would have found full employment. Upon the other hand it might perhaps be contended that the omen has been fulfilled upon a long-term basis, since every mine upon which a raven cast its shadow has by now ceased to function. But that is an after-thought. Now the raven nests in the abandoned shaft or ruinous masonry of the old mine workings, and the course of its flight is watched with less concern than that of a magpie, to which for some unaccountable reason superstition is still attached.

Doubtless the raven acquired its reputation as a bird of ill omen by figuring, as it did, upon the standard of the marauding Danes, and was therefore regarded in Britain since very early times as an emblem of disaster. In more ancient days, however, its character was not represented as necessarily evil. Ravens ministered to the prophet Elijah and one was selected by Noah as the first scout to be dispatched from the Ark, presumably as a bird of character and intelligence. Its failure to return, as did the dove, was typical of its wilder and more independent nature, for a raven seldom returns voluntarily to captivity. Its one idea is to regain its native state. According to old legend, Noah's raven actually found its way to Dartmoor, and was the first of its kind to take an interest in mining. For centuries it was alleged to perch upon the precipitous crag above Chaw Gully, guarding the

* During the last few years the Dartmoor raven population has declined.

mineral treasures which lay below, and uttering a warning croak upon the approach of any intruding prospector.

That characteristic independence was shown by an injured bird which we nursed back to health some years ago. He missed no opportunity to attempt escape, and upon recovering his ability to fly, took wing without a backward glance, let alone any expression of thanks. That particular raven, a grand specimen, was brought in to us by a man who picked him up on the moorside as "one of they Dartmoor birds", which classification aptly defined the status that he has acquired in Devonshire today. Above all others, perhaps, he is the bird of the National Park and certainly one of its most distinctive features, although a pony has been adopted as the park's official emblem. Almost every inland eyrie within the county is situated either upon the moor or its fringes, mostly inside the park area. Few visitors who hear the sonorous croak from the lonely tors realize that the sound is the voice of Dartmoor, the one essentially raven-haunted region in southern England, apart from the seaboard.

As a general rule, the age of a wild creature which never actually comes to hand can only be a matter for conjecture, and this applies particularly to any species that uses some favourite breeding place over a long period of time. "Immemorial" rookeries remain, while human owners of the "stately homes" to which they are attached come and go, but the almost equally ancestral buildings in the tree-tops must also change ownership frequently, although unrecorded, since birds pay no death-duties. The raven of Morwenstowe doubtless still chortles to his hungry mate, but nobody would imagine him to be the identical bird that inspired Stephen Hawker's satirical ballad "A Croon on Hennacliffe". Such is not impossible, the species being an emblem of longevity, but one would probably be more accurate in regarding him as a remote descendant.

The only real raven-tree in Devonshire was an enormous spruce on the banks of the Taw within the National Park, and should certainly have been preserved as a unique ornithological feature. It was sacrificed to "progress", however, about five years ago, and with it went an irreplaceable institution. Ravens used it for more than thirty years, but if the birds which last occupied it were indeed the founders of the eyrie, their habits changed considerably in the course of time. The pair which built the first nest guarded it so assiduously that nobody could approach within a hundred yards of the spot unchallenged, and by this means they publicized the very secret that they wished to guard.

The last tenants were as notably unobtrusive and few people unaware of the nest realized its presence. Apparently the birds had learned that "silence is golden".

A raven's nest in the first season is not appreciably bulkier than that of a carrion crow, except that larger sticks are often used and the wool-lined basin is more ample. A notable difference, again, between the respective nests of raven and rook is that while the rook merely repairs the old structure, a raven builds a new one upon the old foundation. A rook's nest therefore looks much the same even when used for many years, whereas a raven's increases annually, reaching an enormous size after long occupation. The particular nest that I have been describing became as bulky as a well-filled sack, but in this case the spruce, not having attained its full great height, grew even faster. It mounted until the nest, which was originally in the topmost crotch, at last occupied a fork ten feet below the crown, and since nothing but the loftiest site possible satisfies a raven, the birds solved the problem by moving up. So standards rise, even in bird life, but whether this change was due to an elderly housewife's discontent with old-fashioned accommodation, or the more advanced views of a young successor is another matter. All considered, circumstances suggest a transfer of ownership. Most elders have conservative habits, while juniors incline for change. A younger bird, when taking over, would probably start afresh, since few use the abandoned nests of their own or kindred species. Whether old or young, the birds have not deserted the area however. They made a new beginning, mounting moorwards and built in a Scotch pine about half a mile away, this time virtually on the open hill-side. The pine is not nearly as lofty and inaccessible as was the original great spruce, owing to its windswept position; but fortunately, it appears to have escaped notice up to date—possibly on account of its significance. Nobody expected the ravens of the great tree reputation to be content with so inferior an exchange.

The respective nests and eggs of raven and carrion crow are often so alike that even an expert may find distinction difficult. On Dartmoor, however, the site of the nest is a reasonably sure guide in cases of doubt. A nest found on a tor, an old chimney stack, or in an abandoned quarry may safely be attributed to a raven. It seldom, if ever, builds in the hawthorns or dwarf trees and bushes so freely used by crows, which for their part never nest on rocks, or anywhere except among branches. On Dartmoor indeed, almost any rock with a precipitous face will serve for a raven; almost any tree for a crow, but no crow's nest on crag or ruin; no raven's nest in dwarf oak, mountain ash or willow.

3. Moorland Music

Since this chapter only concerns birds with particular Devonshire associations, no mention need be made of those which are equally or more abundant elsewhere. Species eminently characteristic of the county are mostly found, as might be expected in districts essentially Devonian, such as high Dartmoor and the wide molinia wastes of the north where unusual conditions provide an unusual fauna.

Even as the raven is the bird of the National Park, so the curlew is certainly the most outstanding bird of the molinia, occupying, indeed a wider range although its presence is confined to the summer months, or more correctly from early March until late August when the marshes become silent and one realizes that another summer with its wild music is over.

The avian orchestra includes no contributor comparable with the curlew, aptly termed the silver-tongued bird, and there is little wonder that its recorded call was chosen to introduce the radio programme entitled "The Naturalist". Like most great musicians its vocal register is wide, ranging from the inexpressibly soft and melodious to a strident alarm note eminently harsh and menacing. Robber birds have a wholesome respect for the curlew, since the long, curved beak is far from being a mere flute, and the four olive brown eggs, so invitingly laid in the open, are seldom sampled by any feathered marauder. It is satisfactory to record that the curlew has extended its range over Devonshire during the past thirty years, although the molinia country remains its principal stronghold. It shuns high Dartmoor, breeding only along the edges, and might, upon the whole, be described as a bird of the marginal lands or rough pastures. It shows no liking for the heather upon which it rarely alights unless during migration.

Yet curiously enough, the most wonderful curlew concert to which I ever listened was upon a Dartmoor hill-side, actually the slope already described as a favourite hawking ground for the kestrels and harriers. Precisely why the curlews had assembled then and there well away from their customary haunts, was a complete mystery. Whatever the reason, the hill seemed to be brown with them, and as in the case of the buzzards, the proceeding suggested a social gathering. Neither food nor rest seemed to be the object. Numerous birds were on the wing, intermittently rising and falling as one sees them over a tidal estuary, filling the air with cries strangely unfamiliar to the normally silent landscape. I made no note of the precise date, but it was in late July, before the ling had come into full bloom or the last broods of ring-ouzels were fully fledged. It proved to have been a one-day entertainment. On the following morning only the wheatears chattered—a contrast between the sublime and the harsh—and one could scarcely believe that silver tongues had ever made melody over so unlikely an auditorium.

Apart from the curlew, Devonshire cannot claim priority in possessing any feathered musician with the exception of the golden plover. This bird is still perhaps more plentiful upon Dartmoor than anywhere else south of the grouse line during the winter months. In voice, of course, this sturdy little upland plover is only a poor relation of the curlew, yet there is a distinct family likeness in their respective cries, and the first whistle of the golden plover when heard under the harvest moon always brings the call of its more distinguished relative to mind. According to ornithological text-books the golden plover does not reach Dartmoor until late October or November. Actually the first arrivals occur about a month sooner, little flocks resting for a day or two on the hills before passing on, seldom noticed and not officially recorded. These birds obviously form the vanguard of the general movement, being bound for some destination farther south, the main body following later according to schedule.

Even as the curlew's call is greeted as the first note of spring, so the whistle of the golden plover announces that the upland winter is well upon its way. Once the birds arrived in immense flocks like homing starlings, darkening the skyscape as they swept along in orderly flight as though to the tune of countless fifes, sounding clearly and sweetly above the hurtling roar of their wings in impressive accompaniment. The biggest flock that may be seen today, however, is a mere travesty of the former abundance, and the whistle more frequently takes the form of a solo than of one voice among a thousand others. It is a plaintive sound when heard unaccompanied over the wintry landscape. It strikes a tuneful note, however, upon the desolate moor where all other song is hushed and only the sinister voice of raven or crow intimates that any form of life is abroad on the lonely land.

The white-splashed plumage of the golden plover proclaims it a bird of colder latitudes, and while it tolerates the Dartmoor winter, with March the call is "Excelsior" and Devonshire's uplands are abandoned to the ring-ouzel and the wheatear which enter the stage as the plover vacates it. Perhaps the most distinctive voice heard upon the summer heights, although never below the thousand-foot level is that of the ring-ouzel. The bird has practically no song, merely another whistle, but clear, far-sounding and at times persistent. Oddly enough it is seldom identified by the country people, and I once heard an old moorman of lifelong experience attribute it to a sandpiper, although little resemblance between the calls can be traced. Not many years ago every Dartmoor coombe reaching the required altitude could show a pair of ring-ouzels at intervals of perhaps half a mile or so. They ranked high upon the list of birds peculiar to Devonshire, as far as southern England is concerned. The species still occurs but in ever-decreasing numbers, although there is no really apparent reason for the decline.

Certainly a brood is destroyed by fire now and again, as the ring-ouzel is fond of building its blackbird-like nest in deep heather. Obviously as heather fires became more frequent, the greater was the loss of bird life and that, undoubtedly, is one of the reasons for the virtual disappearance of the stonechat from valleys where once its metallic note was the most familiar sound. Upon Dartmoor the nest of the stonechat was almost invariably concealed under heather and even if comparatively few eggs or young were actually burned, the loss of essential habitat or cover always discourages any animals which used it.

In the case of the ring-ouzels' decline, however, fire can only have been a contributory cause, destroying merely the odd brood here and there. The bird breeds twice during a season, usually in places which escape the conflagrations, and of countless nests observed down the years only a negligible minority have come to grief. Everything suggests a natural decrease—one of those unaccountable ebbs in wild bird population, which upon Dartmoor has been by no means confined to the ring-ouzel. The wheatear also has lost ground notably, a circumstance in which once again the curse of fire can have played no part. No flames have ever yet penetrated the nest of a wheatear, placed as it is deep under protecting rocks, usually beyond the reach of a human arm, the jaws of fox, the beak of crow, or of any natural enemy except weasel or viper. Yet the puzzle remains. Most immune from persecution of all moorland birds, with every opportunity to multiply, the wheatear has today become a bird which attracts notice as an individual, rather than as one in a crowd. One misses the harsh

Statue of Charles Kingsley at Bideford

protesting chatter on every side and the twinkle of white from boulder to boulder. Now the tentative note heard or the odd bird seen where once they were everywhere in evidence, only emphasizes the contrast—absence instead of presence.

Wheatears and ring-ouzels being migrants, may recover their status, meanwhile the skylarks and meadow-pipits are always with us. Like the snipe which drums over the lonely bogs, larks of course are not essentially Dartmoor or Devonshire birds. These lowland minstrels, however, are no mean contributors to the music of the hills and when addressed as "bird of the wilderness" the skylark was not altogether misplaced. The earliest note of spring may be sounded in a setting from which spring seems farthest removed. On a bitter March afternoon a year or two ago, I heard the first larks of the season when high upon Dartmoor's northern bastion. From the dark ridge of Kennon Hill, across desolate and dangerous Raybarrow Mire, on an icy wind came the song as though in defiance of the harsh conditions—an assertion of the maxim that life can be very much as one makes it.

Whether the lark strictly belongs to the plains or the hills, and although it is equally at home on meadow grass or heather, I have always associated the bird with Dartmoor. The nest of the skylark was the first that I ever found on the moor. Another was perhaps more notable, having been built upon the windy crest of High Willhayes and must have been the loftiest nest south of the Peak District. Indeed over the high moor on a fine early summer day the lark's song is never silent. As a rule one bird only can be seen, trilling as it mounts but it is scarcely out of sight and sound before another minstrel ascends to carry on the refrain from hill to hill.

The grand concert, however, is reserved for the upland twilight and few human ears ever listen to that wonderful performance. Everyone has heard of the dawn chorus with which ordinary songbirds of the countryside greet the sunrise, but there is no evening equivalent. Thrushes sing as dusk falls but mainly solos. In general there is more twittering than song as the light fades, and most birds, even the warblers, gradually relapse into silence. Far up on the now deserted moorland the story is very different. As the landscape darkens, birds which are not brooding—and that means the vocalists—assemble along some favourite slope, and even as the dawn chorus on the lowlands begins with a few uncertain notes as performers tune up, so upon the wild hill-side one or two birds begin to sing. The music, once started, mounts in a slow crescendo until a volume is reached which must be

A deer-haunted Exmoor coombe

heard to be believed. Since the main performers are skylarks and therefore superb singers, the effect can be imagined. The purple gloom rocks with a melody which no avian music excels. Every bird capable of uttering a note appears to take part, and even an old cock grouse will sometimes roll out an accompaniment like a kettledrum. The chorus mounts to its grand finale, gradually dying away as the stars come out, when presumably the choristers steal back to roost beside their nests and silence settles over the lonely scene. Such is moorland music, of a kind about which little has been written but after once being heard is never forgotten.

Returning to the lowlands, around the more urbanised districts a new note has lately become familiar. This is the rather owl-like *hoo-hoo-hoo* of the collared dove, an eastern species that is extending its range westwards. Budleigh Salterton, for instance, has a considerable colony of them, whilst they have also adopted the leafy outskirts of Okehampton.

If its increase is accelerated, it, too, may eventually develop into a numerical "menace". Meanwhile, this black-collared dove, more slender in figure, and more fawn-coloured than the blue wood-pigeon, may be considered an ornamental addition to our sadly decreasing bird population.

XVII

FROM FEATHER TO FUR

1. Deer and Fox

To many people, even if not particularly interested in sport or natural history, North Devon has a special appeal, being the land of wild red deer. They may not be seen—indeed comparatively few of the countless tourists who visit the region ever set eyes on one. But the knowledge gathered from a guide book that the beautiful animals are there imparts a special glamour to the woods or coombes described as their haunts. Everybody is on the look-out for the glint of antlers on a hill-top or a glimpse of a tawny form stealing across a glade.

Conventionally considered inhabitants of Exmoor and therefore mostly belonging to Somerset, in reality red deer range the greater part of the wooded country north of a line which might roughly be drawn from Dulverton to Tavistock, a few occasionally crossing the Tamar and spreading as far west as Lew Trenchard. Their survival is remarkable, the presence of animals so big and so destructive being quite incompatible, one would think, with modern conditions and particularly with intensive modern agriculture. The position is the more curious since in Devonshire, deer are most abundant in agricultural areas, although about 1780 they were exterminated on wild Dartmoor and the marginal hill country where they could have done comparatively little damage.

Amongst the general public, red deer attract most notice as animals which are hunted, and it was, of course, for the purposes of royal sport that they were originally preserved throughout the country. Stag-hunting ceased to be the recognized and primary sport of kings long ago, and with the sport, for the most part, went the animals which provided it. Few monarchs since Saxon times in person hunted Devonshire stags, however, for which reason it is again curious that the animals should have so long outlived their original use. In the present century they undoubtedly owe their existence to hunting, about which controversy has raged so incessantly that realities, let alone the issues involved, have become completely obscured.

Indeed anyone not engaged in the controversy might genuinely and reasonably wonder what is desired, whether extermination, which would soon be effected, or preservation—at a price. There are the clear alternatives, the choice from the deer's point of view, being whether it is better to live and be hunted or not to live at all. There is one other form in which the price might be paid. Red deer, like swans, might be declared the property of the nation or Crown—taken over by the National Trust as it were. Such a scheme would involve endless complications, however, but more about that later.

For that matter, nothing could be more complicated than the situation as it now stands. Upon the question of stag-hunting, even sporting people are divided. As a general rule, however, the distinctions drawn can only be described as invidious and not always very logical. At a recent discussion I heard a Devonian M.P. denounce deer-hunting, but enthusiastically defend fox-hunting. The fox, so ran the contention, is itself a rapacious animal, and therefore deserves all it gets. Cruelty to any bird that eats an insect could be excused upon similar grounds. Actually it is no more or less cruel to hunt one animal than another. None the less, a disposition to exclude the red deer from legitimate beasts of chase is certainly gaining ground and for obvious reasons.

These might be summarized in one short sentence: it is too big a beast. That covers everything. True, the size of an animal should make no difference in such a connection, but "the heavens themselves blaze forth the death of princes" and a red stag, being the largest of hunted creatures in Britain, gets most of the sympathy and all the publicity. A beautiful stag with his wide gleaming antlers has such an aesthetic appeal. To hunt and kill so ornamental a creature seems nothing short of sacrilege, a relic of barbarism. That a stag, being an eminently pugnacious animal capable of effective self-defence, must actually suffer far less than the infinitely timid hare is a point frequently over-looked. The fate of the one is spectacular; that of the other unnoticed.

The hunting of a stag attracts considerable attention; if dispatched by other means, often far more cruel, few people know anything about it. Deer *can* be killed with ordinary sporting guns and that is the end of a great many—the majority were the truth realized. Indeed, in the red deer country, most of the large shot issued to the Home Guard during the last war was used against invaders of their fields very different from the foreign enemies who did not materialize. With buck-shot, as it is called, a deer can be dropped at twice the distance from which an ordinary cartridge is effective, Nowadays, however, few farmers have got or can get large shot, and fewer still possess a rifle, even were it safe to use one, which is seldom the case. Therefore an ordinary shot-gun, loaded with No. 5 as a rule is used. Some deer fall; more get away wounded, often to suffer a lingering death. That is the other side of the story.

So the controversy rages, as it has raged for the past half-century. Opponents of hunting deplore and demonstrate against its cruelty which nobody can deny. Upon the other hand, not long ago the Secretary of the Devon and Somerset Staghounds publicly protested against the shooting of deer in the Kings Nympton woods to which hounds are denied access. He suggested that the means by which the animals were killed left much to be desired and that carcases sold for venison should be subject to inspection. And here again one assumes that the protests were not lodged without some justification. There have been other reports of deer-snaring and of considerable numbers being destroyed on the Quantocks—also for market.

Of course, as with most controversial subjects, a case can be made for either point of view, backed by incidents or arguments which appear conclusive. The actual position may be summarized quite simply. Red deer owe their survival to the protection afforded by sporting land-owners and farmers. Hunting provides a measure of control and is an institution of long standing, accepted as the *status quo*. Also a fierce light beats upon the activities of the stag-hunter, ensuring that proceedings are conducted as humanely as possible. Upon the other hand, agriculturists not interested in or actually opposed to hunting have no use for the deer, which from a farmer's point of view might as well be herds of hungry mischievous cattle which no ordinary fence can exclude. At the same time, if a stag is too big to be hunted, he is certainly too big to be attacked with weapons only suitable for the destruction of small game. The feeling against deer-hunting is certainly gaining ground, but opposition to date has been ineffectual, reaching no more than nuisance proportions, and no satisfactory alternative is apparent.

Legislation upon the subject has been long deferred, and does not seem to be imminent. The problem mainly concerns Devon and Somerset and therefore arouses little national interest. In any case, apart from the abolition of hunting, which could not be carried on surrepti-tiously, one can think of few measures easy to enforce, particularly in a county such as Devonshire. If the preservation of red deer as a national asset is desired, from a purely humanitarian point of view the answer would undoubtedly be complete protection, with authorized and strictly expert stalking as the means of control. In Sweden where the position might be described as similar, although upon an altogether larger scale, the shooting of elk, even by land-owners, is only allowed under special licence, subject to further definite restrictions. Much the same system, of course, prevails in most countries to control the killing not only of deer, but of all large animals. In Sweden again, a part of the revenue so obtained is used to compensate agriculturists for damage caused by deer depredations.

Devonshire conditions, however, are very different from those in Sweden or any other country with great forests or barrens over which sportsmen can seek big game. In this country special licence could only entitle a man to shoot deer on his own holding of perhaps 100 acres—where he probably shoots one in any case if he can get near it, with gun and cartridges formerly reserved for rabbits. As for State control, it would mean authorized stalkers employed by government or local councils officiating wherever they pleased—pest-controllers upon a big scale whose activities would be anything save popular. State protection with controls would also necessitate a system of compensation, likely to prove very difficult in practice, and the claims for damage would certainly be astronomic. Upon the whole, if stag-hunting is ever abolished as a concession to sentiment and deer are not wanted for their aesthetic or ornamental value, some measures for their compulsory extermination, as in the case of rabbits, will probably provide the answer. Meanwhile, their destruction with unsuitable weapons, or by means of snares and crude traps should certainly be prohibited and a "close season" imposed.

The above remarks, of course, apply to deer of all species. The fallow, although a less spectacular animal, actually deserves as much consideration as the red. Fallow deer are not hunted with hounds in Devonshire. Over the eastern side of the county, however, they have become a problem during recent years, being, needless to say, not indigenous but descendants of animals which originally escaped from parks. Years ago before tenant farmers on big estates received formal permission to shoot red deer from land-owners who wished to divest themselves of responsibility, fallow or "park" deer, as they were then called, had always been the farmer's perquisite. A rifle with which to shoot them was considered necessary, however. That was the position on the Exmoor side in the heart of the stag-hunting country. In south and east Devon, escaped deer and their descendants had little thought bestowed upon them until they multiplied sufficiently to become a nuisance. Their position now is much the same as that of red deer upon a minor scale, and should not be overlooked. They have not as yet penetrated to the country west of the Taw, or that occupied by the red species.

The minute roe, so common in west Dorset, the country to which he was first introduced, has not proved a wide colonizer and to my knowledge has never set timid foot westwards beyond the Otter. Being so inconspicuous—indeed a roe-deer is very rarely seen unless disturbed—his case has aroused little interest or sympathy. Also his presence is not welcome in the newly afforested areas, owing to his propensity for nibbling bark. Hunting people too, regard him with disfavour since he often—though doubtless most unwillingly—acts as a red-herring which few foxhounds and no harrier can resist. In spite, or probably because of, his elusiveness and timidity, he is perhaps of all deer the best able to take care of himself, and even in country where the species is most plentiful very few people are even aware of his presence.

Hare-hunting has decreased considerably in Devonshire, being now almost entirely confined to packs of beagles. Harriers, for the most part, have abandoned their official but less exciting quarry, and assumed the status and function of foxhounds, not so much because hares have decreased—although such is the case—as because foxes have become abundant beyond the wildest dreams of twentieth-century sportsmen.

Yet a curious change has come over Devonshire fox-hunting during the past ten years or so, not indeed by any means confined to this county, but perhaps more noticeable here than elsewhere because the distinction is more marked. This is entirely due to a new habit adopted by the fox. Once mainly a creature of rough wild habitat, the fox has become, like the hare, equally addicted to cultivated lands, with kale as the cover which he appears to prefer above any other, Often nowadays one sees a meet of foxhounds advertised at some place nowhere near coverts of any description and at the moment wonders where any fox could be found in the neighbourhood. Then one remembers kale-fields and all wonder ceases. One day when I was out with the mid-Devon Hounds at Belstone, a fixture which once meant and necessitated a day on the rocky hills where the mountain fox was hunted in characteristic environment. I found that the actual programme was to draw a field of kale near the village. This, of course, proved to be alive with foxes, of which the moor, when eventually reached, seemed to be as notably destitute.

The example illustrates the rule rather than the exception, and no convincing reason for the fox's change of habit has yet been advanced. He certainly eats kale, as post-mortems have proved, but whether from necessity or choice is known only to himself. Again, the fox began to frequent kale long before the rabbit went, so myxomatosis had nothing to do with it. The habit appears to have started with the more general adoption of kale as a crop, and one can only assume that it caught the fox's fancy as providing cover after his own heart, damp and chilly as it might seem when compared with a gorse-brake. That again is his business, and since kale probably harbours innumerable grubs, it may be merely another case of sleeping where he dines.

In all other respects a fox remains a fox and continues to thrive under the new conditions, although not to multiply at quite the same rate as when the abnormal increase began twenty years ago. Possibly the wave of abundance has reached its peak, and a corresponding swing back of the pendulum is not improbable. In the past, epidemics of vulpine mange have proved almost as devastating as myxomatosis among rabbits, or the disease which virtually exterminated the English red squirrel about 1912, and from the consequences of which the species has never recovered its status, in the West Country at any rate. Incidentally, the red squirrel had become as rare as gold in Devonshire a quarter of a century before the grey alien reached the county, although many naturalists, misled by propaganda, seem to be unable or unwilling to recognize the fact.

When my *Devonshire* in the County Books series was published in 1950, the grey squirrel could only be listed as unknown west of Exeter. Since then its steady increase resulted a few years ago in its being declared a pest. Organised shoots reduced its numbers, but latterly there have again been complaints from agriculturists and foresters of damage to crops and young trees. On the other hand, it must in fairness be said that many park-keepers and gardeners tolerate the squirrel, finding its depredations no more serious than those of blackbirds, mice or pigeons.

Newly classified as a menace are mink. Originally escapees from fur farms, like most introduced species, they staged a population explosion now being found on almost every Devonshire river. Trapping has slightly reduced their activities, which game-keepers, poultry farmers and nature preservationists regard very seriously.

Nothing need be said about animals such as badgers and otters, whose position remains unchanged, or, like the ordinary birds of the countryside, have no habits peculiar to Devonshire. Among certain of the smaller furred creatures, however, the new conditions have wrought changes unexpected and scarcely realized.

2. After Myxomatosis

The loss of the rabbit made little apparent difference to the fox, but the stoat, after transferring its attention to rats for a while, seemed to throw in its hand. Everything suggested that it either followed the rabbit to the shadowy hunting grounds, or so completely adapted its way of life to changed conditions that its ancient haunts knew it no more.

Here in mid-Devon, where stoats were so numerous even when spring-trapping was at its height, their absence soon became taken for granted. For some time after the horrors of myxomatosis, which polluted the countryside, I heard of only two stoats. One was lying dead in the middle of a field with nothing to indicate the manner of its end. The other, still very much alive, seemed to have forsaken the empty burrows and taken to a new form of hunting. At any rate he was up a tree, sitting at the end of a lateral bough, along which he had probably chased a squirrel only to find that as a climber he had his limitations.

Unlike the squirrel, he could not whisk from one swaying branch-tip to another with the agility of a nuthatch, and although an accomplished nest-robber during the period of eggs and young birds, the stoat is mainly a creature of the earth—underground for choice—and his part in the natural drama was as the inveterate destroyer of rabbits. Indeed, rabbit meat, or rather blood, was the essence of his existence, his staff of life so to speak. There can be no doubt that the loss of so essential a plank in his economy is the reason for the virtual disappearance of this indefatigable little hunter, once the veritable Satan of the hedgerows, the bugbear of game-preservers and warreners, arch enemy of every living thing less formidable than himself.

According to Surtees, a guest who outstays his welcome can best be dislodged by lowering the standard of entertainment, and the principle applies equally to wild life. A supply of accessible food soon or late attracts the creatures that like it. Remove the food, and the animals seek a living elsewhere. An empty granary, like a rick of threshed straw, harbours no rats.

So when rabbits swarmed, carnivorous animals were also numerous. With the virtual extinction of rabbits for the time being in many areas, the stoats which mainly preyed upon them also went as a natural consequence. But the problem what became of them remains. One could only assume that the stoats must literally have starved, since they would neither migrate nor continue to hunt the countryside unnoticed.

The weasel has been comparatively scarce for many years, although his absence aroused little comment. Indeed, he was not generally missed. Always a mere understudy of the stoat, the two were often confused.

For many years, at my special request, a professional rabbit-trapper kept a list of all other animals which accidentally got into his gins. During a normal season he recorded upon average thirty stoats, but made no mention of weasels, which were presumably included under the same heading. In the West Country all members of the family were grouped under the comprehensive name of "fitchie", formerly reserved for the redoubtable polecat, long since superseded by the stoat upon which his mantle as well as title descended.

This confusion of identity is not unusual in the vernacular. A heron, for example, has always been a "crane", a nightjar a "landrail", while the choughs of old Dartmoor were certainly jackdaws. The nightjar, incidentally, is unknown by its real name among the country people. So also is the weasel, the fierce little creature occasionally found in mole traps and known as a "vairie"—if identified at all. Half a century ago, when middle-aged trappers and keepers remembered the polecat, the stoat was still known as a "stottie", a name I have not heard for many years. When the polecat passed and the weasel became scarce, distinction ceased, all becoming "fitchies" alike, as a bat of any species is merely "a bat".

For the weasel's decline in the first instance one can find no satisfactory reason. On the contrary, all circumstances considered, the reverse might have been expected. He has never been the prey of any wild animal, man being his only enemy, and against the worst that man could do he stood a better chance than his larger relatives. His economy was sound, his needs not being ambitious. Much of the fare despised by the stoat was good enough for him. Obviously he had every advantage, yet seemed to be one of the creatures that fell behind in life's race, where the fittest are not necessarily the winners. Anyhow, without apparent cause, the weasel never became as plentiful as the stoat and decreased rather than otherwise during the peak years when so many other wild animals multiplied.

If however, his gradual decline all down the years, like that of red squirrel, wryneck and chough, can be regarded as mainly natural, the extremity of his present status is probably due to a definite sequence of events. During the autumn which followed the rabbit's departure, carnivorous animals launched a furious onslaught upon mice, rats, and rodent life generally. This, as time went on, caused at least a temporary shortage of rats and mice which brought famine to the stoat. The weasel could still pick up a living as long as snails and similar fare could be collected, but when iron frost in late winter drove every grub underground, his real troubles began.

Wild animals in such a case fade out imperceptibly. Many species of birds have not yet recovered their status since the great frosts of early 1947 and 1963, when they died like flies although leaving little evidence of their passing.

It is a far cry from the sabre-tooth tiger, mentioned in the first chapter, to the little furred folk of the Devonshire fields today. The intervening pages have endeavoured to trace the changes that time has brought, and to picture the present as well as the past. The future baffles speculation. Meanwhile Time is always the present, and its problems suffice.

INDEX

Alfred, 21, 42
Alpington, 48
Amicia, Countess of Devon, 144
Ammicombe, 44
Armada, 33
Ashburton, 121, 124, 130
Athelstan, 21
Avon, River, 45
Axe, River, 50
Axminster, 40–41, 124, 140

Baldwin de Bryonis, 144
Baring Gould, 80, 117, 131, 146, 152, 158
Barnstaple, 33, 55, 121, 124
    Bridge, 54, 124
Beaford, 148
Bedford, Earl of, 37
    Duke of, 56, 147
Bellever, 78
    Bridge, 114
Belstone, 51, 52–3, 107, 183
    Cleave, 51, 79
    Copper mine, 135
Bere Alston, 136
Bere Ferrers, 136
Berry Pomeroy Castle, 147
Bicton, 145
Bideford, 33, 55, 121, 155–6
    Bridge, 54, 55, 124, 140
Bird Watching and Preservation Society, 161
Blackmore, R. D., 137, 157-8
Blacktor Beare, 76-7, 169
Bleak House, 113
Bloody Assizes, 41
Blundell's School, 124
Bonham Carter, V., 157
Book of St. Albans, 57
Bovey, River, 47
    fishing, 58
Bovey Heathfield, 138

Bovey Tracey, 139
Bridges
    Barnstaple, 54, 124
    Bideford, 54, 124, 140
    Exe, 42
    Tamar Suspension, 43, 63
    Sticklepath, 54
Bridle Paths, 60
    Mariner's Way, 61
Bronze Age, 14, 15, 120
Brunel (Isambard), 45
Buckfastleigh, 46, 120, 124
Buckland Abbey, 143
Budleigh Salterton, 50
Burial in Woollen Enactment, 123
Burrator (reservoir), 45, 47, 101
Buzzard, 163 et seq.

Cad, River, 114
Cadover Bridge, 115
Carrion Crow, 169
Cassiterides, 127–8
Castle (camp), 17
Cathedral, Exeter, 28–9
Cattedown, 14
Cattewater, 35, 45
Cattle, 87–8, 108
Caves, 14
Celts, 17, 18, 19
Chagford, 47, 64, 130
Charles I, King, 37, 39, 40
Charles II, King, 40, 74, 77, 123
Chase, Beatrice, 154
Cholwich Stone Row, 114
Civil War, 34, 37–40, 137
Clay, ball, 68
    china, 114–15
Clyst, River, 49
Coleridge, Samuel Taylor, 159
Collared dove, 178
Combe Martin, 136
Commons (Dartmoor), 105 et seq.
Constantine, 20

Cornwall, Duchy of, 103
Corringdon Ball, 15
Cosdon Beacon, 52, 113–14
Cotehele, 56
Countess Wear, 48–9
Courtenays, 27, 30–31, 41, 142
Crediton, 28, 121
Creedy, River, 48–9
Crockern Tor, 128–9, 130–31
Crossing, William, 156
Cuckoo Ball, 15
Curlew, 174

Damnonia, 18–19, 20–21
Danes, 21–2
Dart, River, 45, 46, 74, 76–8
    fishing, 58
    East, 78, 114
Dartington Hall, 88. 146, 148
Dartmeet, 77, 114
Dartmoor,
    afforestation, 78
    antiquities, 15, 114
    barrows, 14
    birds, 169 et seq.
    Bronze Age, 14, 15, 120
    castles (camps), 17
    copses, 76–7
    Dolmens, 15
    hutments, 15–16, 114
    mists, 117
    ponies, 108
    prehistoric man, 15–17
    Prison, 149
    Stannary Parliament, 128 et seq.
    Stannary Towns, 130
    Stone Age, 15
    tin-mining, 16–17, 127 et seq.
    Tors, 44, 69, 78, 101, 113–14,
128–9, 130–31, 139
Dartmoor Commoners' Association,
    105
Dartmoor Preservation Association,
    79
Davis, 32
Dawlish Warren, 49
Dean Prior, 159
Deer, 179 et seq.

Devon, Earl of, 30
Devon and Somerset Staghounds, 50
Devonport, 33–5, 43–4
Dixon, Charles, 161–2
Dolmens, 14–15
Donewold (forest), 74
Drake, Sir Francis, 31–3, 78, 143
Drewsteignton, 15, 138
Drizzlecombe, 114–15
Dunsland House, 147
Dyfnaint, 43

East Budleigh, 45
Edgar the Peaceful, King, 21, 56
Edward the Confessor, 21, 28
Edward the Elder, 21
Edward IV, 26
Eggesford, 79
    House, 147
Elfreda, 21
Elizabeth I, Queen, 30, 31, 32, 42
Elm (South Tawton), 80–81
Elmhirst, Dr. L. K., 148
Emma, Queen, 21
Endsleigh, 56, 147
Erme, River, 45, 76, 78
    Pound, 45, 114
Essex, Earl of, 38
Ethelred, King, 21
Exe River, 22, 23, 42, 46, 48, 162
    fishing, 56
    floods, 48
Exeter, 19 et seq., 34–5, 37–9, 40, 45,
    161
    Railway, 65
    Wool trade, 121
Exmoor, 50, 78, 108, 110, 169
Exmouth, 49

Faggotty Copse, 73, 76
Fairfax, General, 40, 48
Fernworthy, 163–4
    reservoir, 46–7
Fire-raising, 105
Fishing, 55 et seq.
Flete, 146
Forest, royal, 23, 103
    Donewold, 74
Forestry Commission, 77–8

Fox, 179 *et seq.*
Fox-tor, 53, 139
Fremington, 68
Frobisher, 32
Fur Tor, 44

Garvice, Charles, 156
Geraint, 20
Gidleigh, 64
Gilbert, 31
Godwin, 21
Golden Hind, 32
Great Links Tor, 101, 113
Grenville, Sir Richard, 31, 143, 155
Grey Wethers, 114
Grimspound, 114
Gytha, 21

Hamoaze, 34, 43–5
Hare, 173
Harold, King, 21–2
Harveststore, 92
Hatherleigh, 55, 92
    Railway, 68
Hawkins, 32
Haytor, 69, 113–14
Hendy, E. W., 157
Hennock (reservoirs), 45, 47
Henrietta, Princess, 38–9, 40
Henrietta Maria, Queen, 38–9
Henry III, King, 23
Henry VII, King, 26
Henry VIII, King, 26–7, 30, 110, 122
Herrick, Rev. Robert, 157
High Willhayes, 113
Hobbs, Rev. Francis, 157
Holne, 46
Hooker, 156
Hoskins, Dr. W. G., 56, 123, 156
Hound Tor, 113
Huntingdon Warren, 45
Hutments (prehistoric), 15–17

Iberians, 17–19
Ine, King, 21
Isabel, Countess, 23, 48
"Isca", 42
Isca Damnoniorum, 19

James I, 37

James II, 40–41
Jay's Grave, 155
Jeffreys, Judge, 41
Jenkins, Alan, 157
John, King, 106

Kenn Brook, 49
Kent's Cavern, 14
Kestrel, 170
Kingsley, Charles, 155

Lady Paramount, 21–2, 35, 38, 41
Lambert, Dr. Margaret, 157
Lark, 177
Laughtor (Tor), 78
Lee Moor, 138
Leofric, Bishop, 28
Lew House, 146
Lifton, 122
Lopwell Dam, 44
Lundy, 162
Lundy Field Club, 161
Lyd River, 113
Lyme Regis, 40
Lynn River, 50–51

Marchant's Cross, 64
Maristow, 44, 142
Marlborough, Duke of, 41
Marsland Brook, 50, 54
Marsland Mouth, 155
Martin, E. W., 158
Mary, Queen, 30
Maud, Queen, 22
Maurice, Prince, 36, 38
Meeth, 139
Meldon, 53, 138
Merrivale, 114
Merton, 40
Mining,
    clay, ball, 139
    china, 138
    copper, 135
    lead, 137
    lignite, 138
    silver, 137
    tin, 15, 127 *et seq.*
Mink, 184
Monk, General, 40

Monmouth, Duke of, 40–41
    rebellion, 40–41
Montagu's harrier, 164
Moretonhampstead, 76
Morwenstowe, 54, 172

National Park, 99, 102, 112, 174
National Trust, 145
Neolithic man, 14
North Devon Water Board, 52, 90
North Hessary Tor, 101
North Molton, 137
North Wyke, 146

Oak, 74–5, 79
    coppices (Dartmoor), 76
    Meavy, 80
    Pascoe, 80
Oaklands, 147
Okehampton, 83, 148
Okement, River, 55, 74, 101
    West, 51, 53, 76
Otter, River, 49–50
Ottery St. Mary, 159
Oxenham, John, 154

Paleolithic man, 14
Parsons, Hamlyn, 114
Pensylwood, Battle of, 20
Petrockstowe, 68
Phillpotts, Eden, 113, 118, 151
Piles Copse, 76
Pixies, 117, 154
Plover, Golden, 175
Plym, River, 35, 45–6, 114
Plymouth, 23, 29, 33–6, 40, 45
    Railway, 65
Poltimore, 146
Ponies, 108 et seq.
Postbridge, 107
Powderham Castle, 142
Prayer Book Rebellion, 27, 38
Princetown, 77
    Prison, 149

Quarrying, 138

Rabbits, 95–8, 185

Railways,
    Great Western, 45, 66
    Hatherleigh-Halwill, 68
    Haytor, 69
    Moretonhampstead, 66
    Princetown, 66, 67
    Turnchapel, 66
Raleigh, Sir Walter, 31, 37, 49, 145
Rattlebrook, 44, 101, 113
Raven, 171
Ring-ouzel, 175
Roborough, 122
    Down, 111
    lords of, 142
Rodd, Capt. A., 145
Russell, Lord, 27, 41
Ryders Rings, 114

Saint Thomas (parish), 48
Salmon fishing, 56–8
Saltash, ferry, 63
    suspension bridge, 63
    viaduct, 44
Sampford Courtenay, 27–8
Sayer, Lady Sylvia, 79
Scotch pine, 74
Sea-trout fishing, 57–8
Sedgemoor, Battle of, 41
Seymours, 41
Sheep, 85, 105, 108, 120
Shovel (Shuffle) Down, 114
Sid, River, 50
Sitka spruce, 77, 102
Slapton Ley, 162
Somerset, Lord, 27
Sound, Plymouth, 33, 34
South Hams, 84, 87–8
South Tawton, 79
    Church Tree, 80
    copper mine, 135
Spinsters' Rock, 15
Stamford, Lord, 38
Stannary Parliament, 128 et seq.
    towns, 130
Staple Tors, 113
Stephen, King, 22
Stevenstone (House), 148
Sticklepath, 54, 140

Stoat, 186
Stoke, Gabriel, 80
Stone Age, 15, 120
Stover, 146
Sutton, 35,
     Pool, 45
Swincombe, 53
Sweyn, 22

Tamar, River, 34, 43–4, 48, 54, 69
     fishing, 56
Tavistock, 44, 56, 76, 130, 138
     copper-mining, 136
Tavy, River, 34, 43–4, 46, 69, 74, 78
     fishing, 56
Taw, River, 46, 51–5, 74, 78–9, 90
     fishing, 56, 58
Taw Marsh, 51–3
Teign, River, 45–7, 74, 78–9
     fishing, 58
     South, 46
Teignmouth, 47, 139
Thornton, Rev., 158
Tin-mining, 16, 127 *et seq.*
Tinners' Hall, 131
Tiverton, 48, 121, 140
Topsham, 49
Torbay, 47
Torquay, 46
Torridge, River, 54–5, 156
Torrington, 40, 55
Totnes, 46, 148
Trevena, John, 154

Two Bridges, 76, 130
Tyrwhitt, Sir Thomas, 69

Vanguard, 34
Vespasian, 20
Vixen Tor, 113

Walkham, River, 44, 74
Walton, Izaak, 57
Warbeck, Perkin, 26
Ware, E. H., 161
Wars of the Roses, 23, 35
Warwick, Earl of, 38
Watern Oak, 114
Weasel, 186
Westcote, 64
William the Conqueror, King, 21–3,
     144
William III, King, 41–2
William IV, King, 54
Wistman's Wood, 76–7
Woodbury, 74
     Common, 102, 159, 163
Wool, 120 *et seq.*
Worth, R. Hansford, 156–7

Yarty, River, 49
Yealm, River, 45
Yeo, River, 50
Yes Tor, 113
Yew, 80
Young Farmers' Clubs, 89